LAKEWAY:

A HILL COUNTRY COMMUNITY

BY LEWIS H. CARLSON

Life without memory is no life at all. . . . Our memory is our coherence, our reason, our feeling, even our action. Without it we are nothing.

LUIS BUÑEL

This book is dedicated to the spirit and accomplishments of the countless volunteers who have turned Lakeway into a marvelously unique community and to the memory of Byron Varner, who did so much to create a sense of history among its residents.

ISBN 10: 1-59152-088-6
ISBN 13: 978-1-59152-088-7

Published by the City of Lakeway

For more information or to order extra copies of this book, contact the City of Lakeway.

sweetgrassbooks
a division of Farcountry Press

Produced by Sweetgrass Books
PO Box 5630, Helena, MT 59604; (800) 821-3874;
www.sweetgrassbooks.com.

Printed in the United States.

15 14 13 12 11 1 2 3 4 5 6 7

CONTENTS

ACKNOWLEDGMENTS		iv
INTRODUCTION		v
PART I	**BEFORE THERE WAS A LAKEWAY**	
Chapter 1	Prehistory	3
Chapter 2	Native People of the Hill Country	5
Chapter 3	American Migrations into the Hill Country	13
Chapter 4	*Hin Nach Texas* - Johann Heinrich Lohmann and the German Impact on the Hill Country	35
Chapter 5	A River Runs Through It: The Colorado, Mansfield Dam, and Lake Travis	49
PART II	**LAKEWAY: FROM RESORT AND VACATION SPA TO DIVERSE HILL COUNTRY COMMUNITY**	
Chapter 6	Three Wise Men from the East and a Goat Farm	61
Chapter 7	Lakeway's Formative Organizations	71
Chapter 8	A Community and Government of Volunteers	75
Chapter 9	The Lakeway Ecumenical Church	81
Chapter 10	Lake Travis Independent School District	85
PART III	**THE ESSENCE OF LAKEWAY**	
Chapter 11	Lakeway Painters and Photographers	93
Chapter 12	Greenbelts, Canyonlands, and Friends of the Parks	107
Chapter 13	The Battle over City Park	121
Chapter 14	The Lakeway Activity Center	133
Chapter 15	The Fourth of July: A Community Celebration	137
Chapter 16	Heritage Park	143
Chapter 17	Children in the Garden of Eden	151
PART IV	**WHAT DOES THE FUTURE HOLD?**	
Chapter 18	As the Houses Grew Larger, the People Became Smaller: The Battle over Expansion and Development	159
Chapter 19	Visionaries: Then and Now	165
PART V	**TIME LINES**	
	A Brief Travis County Time Line	176
	Lakeway Time Line	177
APPENDIX		
	Map of Lakeway's Annexation History	207
	Lakeway's Vision and Mission Statements, 2002	208
	Lakeway Governance: Mayors, Commissioners, Aldermen, and Councilmembers	208
	Lakeway Civic Corporation's Outstanding Citizen of the Year Award Winners	209
	Lakeway Civic Corporation's Annual Meritorious Service Award Winners	209
	Photo Credits	209

ACKNOWLEDGMENTS

Among the countless Lakeway residents who have contributed to this book, I am especially grateful to Cole Rowland and Steve Swan, both former mayors of Lakeway, and to current mayor David DeOme, all of whom enthusiastically supported this project. Steve Swan provided additional guidance after he became chairman of the Lakeway Heritage Commission in 2010. Thanks also go to the director of the Department of Parks and Recreation, Andra Dearing, for her endless patience when faced with my ofttimes arcane queries. Peggy Point was chair of the Heritage Commission in 2007, when she recruited me to do this book, and I thank her for her confidence and her keen editorial eye. Peggy's successor, Caroline Ryals, helped me in myriad ways, but none greater than opening doors that I hesitated to enter alone. Three meaningful examples were persuading Johnnie Fields to paint the cover for this book, introducing me to Linda Wells, whose paintings are found in Chapters 11 and 15, and tracing down some long-missing local Indian artifacts.

Willis Bodine, Jim Ferrill, Mary Stewart Hicks, Bill Maul, and Peggy Maul Smithers, all of whom are direct descendants of German immigrant John Henry Lohmann, provided exceptional photographs and valuable information on the Lohmann family, which is generally recognized as being the first group of white settlers to homestead the area that one day became Lakeway.

Retired Colonel Arthur Stewart, who still resides in Lakeway, provided the Heritage Center with copious notes on the Stewart family, which also owned considerable land along the Colorado River before the Mansfield Dam flooded the area and created Lake Travis.

Lower Colorado River Authority corporate archivist Dixie Owen Wells located and made available the photographs of the Colorado River and the Mansfield Dam that appear in Chapter 5.

City archivist Mike Boston not only has Lakeway's important documents at the tip of his fingers but also knows where several skeletons reside. In this we share a morbid curiosity.

Elaine Perkins, who has written a marvelously detailed history of western Travis County, was always willing to share her knowledge and photographs of a time before there was a Lakeway.

Thanks as well to Peg and Marv Hein, Mickey Wright, Bernie Redding, Fred Hazen, and the other members of Friends of the Parks for introducing me to Lakeway's magnificent trails and parks and for the photos of their handiwork that I have included in this book.

Dallas Gorman, Bill Hawkins, and Cal Rice generously opened up their award-winning photographic collections. Bill Hawkins also enhanced the marginal quality of some of the older photographs that appear in this book.

Paul Meyertons and Cindy Hufford of B2B Copies provided invaluable assistance in enhancing and reproducing old photographs and maps.

Finally, I am humbly grateful to Gary Lee, Ed Marcin, Tom and Sharon Rogers, and David Roos, who most mornings walk their dogs in City Park alongside my Bruno. On more than one occasion, they reminded me of the task at hand by politely asking, "Hey, when is that damn book of yours finally going to be finished?" Wife Simone and canine Bruno often posed the same question. Well, after four long years, it finally is.

INTRODUCTION

John Steinbeck once wrote, "Like most passionate nations, Texas has its own private history based on, but not limited by, facts." Cynical? To be sure, but I agree that traditional histories of Texas begin with its heroes, and particularly those who died at the Alamo. At the very least, such creations emerged long after the fact. The real history of Texas begins with the people who first settled the region and their direct descendants.

***

On April 23, 2005, Byron Varner sent an e-mail to Lakeway archivist Mike Boston explaining the importance of local history: "When I first decided to write *Lakeway: The First 25 Years,"* wrote Varner, who died less than a year and a half later, "some people took a negative view of the idea. 'We are practically a brand-new community. There's no history to write about,' was the general feeling most naysayers expressed, as if we were the only humans whoever occupied the territory."

I must confess that I too had my doubts when Peggy Point asked if I might be interested in writing a history of Lakeway. I thought to myself, "How can I write a history of a community that is nineteen years younger than I am? That's not history; that's current events."

I was wrong. The geological history of the region that now includes Lakeway goes back millions of years, and Homo sapiens have been treading these surroundings for at least 10,000 years; however, these earlier inhabitants were not as freshly scrubbed or as nattily attired as our current Lakeway residents.

The challenge of writing the history of a community is one of selection. Does one pursue the "one-damn-fact-after-another" philosophy or simply tread lightly over the highlights? There is, of course, no simple or correct answer to this dilemma. Texas sage Jim Hightower suggests the only thing to be found in the middle of the road is a yellow streak or a dead armadillo. Jim is right. History does include peaks and valleys, although I have relegated the latter mostly to the time lines that appear in Part V of the book.

Critics have also accused historians of not seeing the mature forest because of their preoccupation with its elaborate root system. I also plead guilty to this transgression. The five chapters of Part I examine the antecedents of the general area that would one day become Lakeway. Chapter 1 takes us back millions of years to those creepy, crawly creatures that bear no resemblance to any current Texas organisms, not even those found on Austin's Sixth Street. I am also not referring to Indians, as Columbus so mistakenly labeled them, although Native Americans do appear in Chapter 2. Chapters 3 and 4 deal with the lives of the earliest white settlers in our area. Chapter 5 covers life along the Colorado River and the building and impact of Mansfield Dam, which, some two decades before the beginning of Lakeway, flooded the Colorado River and created Lake Travis.

The five chapters of Part II introduce the reader to the establishment of Lakeway and its formative institutions, the success of which would be maintained by an army of remarkably competent volunteers.

Part III focuses on what I call the essence of Lakeway, as portrayed through paintings and photographs by local artists. Also included are the spirited public battles over the Hamilton Greenbelt, City Park, and the Activity Center, which I consider the crown jewels of the community, as well as the noncontroversial Fourth of July celebrations and the Lakeway Heritage Center and Park.

Part IV briefly speculates on Lakeway's future, and Part V provides a chronological record of the development of Lakeway and its environs. This time line is arguably overly long and excessively detailed, but every community deserves its personal diary. It is also my preemptive defense against those who might target the sins of omission in the previous chapters. What appears missing from the main text will hopefully be found in the time line. This is especially true of many of the fine organizations and clubs that so enrich our community, as well as the golf courses that are such an integral part of the Lakeway scene. Many of the controversies that imprint any community's history are also found in considerable detail in the time line. In this regard I am grateful to the sagacious advice of Allan Hitchcock: "Don't try to explain the Lakeway MUD," implored Allan, a long-time member of its board of directors. Well, I do touch on the MUD briefly in Chapter 8, but I have remanded most of its battles with residents and city officials to the time line.

Lakeway: A Hill Country Community is neither a continuation nor an elaboration on Byron Varner's *Lakeway: The First 25 Years,* which did such an admirable job of covering the first quarter of a century of Lakeway's existence. *Lakeway: A Hill Country Community* must stand on its own merits. It is, of course, impossible to give adequate recognition to all the individuals responsible for making Lakeway into such a unique community, other than to quote Byron Varner: "Perhaps no other community of its size anywhere can boast of the volunteerism and citizen activism with which Lakeway has been blessed." Hence, what is positive and worthwhile in this book reflects the superlative quality of the community and its citizens. Omissions and errors are the exclusive domain of the author.

Wendy Severance, "Lakeway"

PART I

BEFORE THERE WAS A LAKEWAY

There was no Lakeway before 1963, but there had long been human and other exotic creatures traversing the area that one day would be called the Hill Country.

Lewis H. Carlson

CHAPTER ONE

PREHISTORY

LEANNE WAS NOT A VERY ATTRACTIVE DAUGHTER OF the Hill Country, at least by today's standards, but we must realize that she was more than 10,000 years old when University of Texas archeologists discovered her remains in 1982 about fifteen miles north of Lakeway near the town of Leander.[1] She traversed a terrain that in its natural state would be recognizable today, although not its people or animals. Leanne's ancestors were first thought to be part of the Clovis migration from North Asia that traversed the Bering Strait land bridge. More recently, a number of archeologists believe our earliest settlers may have come from South or East Asia or even Ice Age Europe, traveling to our hemisphere via some kind of raft or animal-skin kayak. In any case, there were continuous migrations to North America before and after Leanne, and archeologists have found considerable evidence of these earliest residents of Central Texas, including campsites containing crude tools and weapons made of bone and flint. They have also discovered the remains of beasts such as mastodons

1. Needless to say, no one can reproduce Leanne or her contemporaries' appearance with absolute certitude. Nevertheless, after her discovery, forensic specialists and artists at Dow Corning created a photographic reproduction of Leanne that can be seen on the website Texasbeyondhistory.net. Sandi Boston writes of her painting: "I felt my best attack would be from written descriptions. What I found was she would have slight Mongoloid features, with single eyelids, tilt to eyes and wide nostrils with no bridge to her nose. She also likely suffered from tooth decay and had missing teeth in front. From there, I assumed she would have dark hair with brown eyes."

and early species of horses, camels, elephants, and bison, all of which no longer exist. Travis County contained several prime archeological sites; unfortunately, most of these have been lost either to development or man-made lakes and reservoirs.

The origins of our region actually began long before these earliest immigrants arrived in the Hill Country. Geologist Charles Woodruff, who wrote his doctoral dissertation on the Lake Travis area, traces 600 million years of geological change, evidenced by the more than 500,000 fossil varieties embedded in the limestone and dolomite rock cliffs and canyons that border the Lower Colorado River and its various tributaries. According to Woodruff, "These rocks and fossils are a window into the past."

Some 200 million years ago, the original "Lake Travis" was a very large, shallow sea, replete with sandy beaches, oyster reefs, great tidal pools, and a wide variety of creepy, crawly creatures, including dinosaurs. To the west and north of this sea were rugged hills and bluffs that had once been part of the massive Llanorian or Ouschita Mountains that stretched from the present northern border of Texas to San Antonio and westward to El Paso. There is also evidence of volcanic activity. Over time these mountains eroded and sank beneath widening seas, buried under the enormous multi-layered deposits that today allow us to discover our prehistory.

Eventually, these seas too would recede, to be gradually replaced by the rugged hills, rivers, and lakes we so admire today. Among the many fascinating reminders of this early era are the fossilized reminders of twenty-one different types of dinosaurs that lived in Texas between 65 and 225 million years ago. The imprint of one of these enormous creatures was discovered at low water along the Lakeway shore of Lake Travis. This same limestone, of course, forms the exterior of countless Lakeway homes.

In 1997, Pleurocoelus officially became the state dinosaur of Texas. It lived approximately 100 million years ago, grew to between thirty and sixty feet, and weighed more than ten tons. Another Texas dinosaur was the Iguanodon, which had teeth like an iguana and five-fingered front feet, reached thirty feet in length, and weighed as much as five tons. Despite the preachments of various unscientific voices, including Fred Flintstone, the dinosaurs died off approximately 65 million years before human beings appeared on earth. Today, these magnificent creatures live on via museum facsimiles, lurid movies, and artistic re-creations.

Lakeway artist Sandi Boston re-creates the dinosaur Pleurocoelus, which looked a bit like a large reptilian giraffe. The dinosaur on the right is an Iguanodon, meaning "iguana tooth." He was a vegetarian whose remains were also found in Central Texas.

CHAPTER TWO

NATIVE PEOPLE OF THE HILL COUNTRY

I believe these people see and hear better, and have keener senses than any other in the world. They are great in hunger, thirst, and cold, as if they were made for the endurance of these more than other men, by habit and nature.

SPANISH EXPLORER CABEZA DE VACA
ON TEXAS INDIANS, 1528

There shall be a firm and lasting peace forever [between whites and Indians].

SAM HOUSTON,
FIRST PRESIDENT OF THE REPUBLIC OF TEXAS, 1836–1838

The white man and the red man cannot dwell in harmony together.

MIRABEAU LAMAR,
SECOND PRESIDENT OF THE REPUBLIC OF TEXAS, 1838–1841

IN THE 1980s, UNIVERSITY OF TEXAS ARCHEOLOGY student and Lakeway resident Scott Brosowske roamed the area looking for Indian artifacts. Because many of the sites archeologists and anthropologists had explored in the 1930s were now impounded by Lake Travis, Brosowske turned his attention to the banks of Rough Hollow Creek and Hurst Creek. He discovered considerable evidence of human activity dating back at least 10,000 years, when wooly mammoths, mastodons, and an ancient species of buffalo dominated the area, along with Homo sapiens who predated modern Indians.

At one time, Indians frequented this cave below Star Street. The fence and deck, of course, came much later and were the work of Lakeway settlers.

More recent stratifications of limestone produced tiny flint arrowheads, which led him to conclude that the bow and arrow probably did not appear in Central Texas until about 700 A.D., by which time the giant creatures who had earlier roamed the area no longer existed.

Other Lakeway residents have also found ample evidence of the Indians who occupied the area. Tim Henderson discovered a small cave along Marina Cove below Star Street that appeared to be an ancient cliff dwelling. According to Lakeway historian Byron Varner, the Lakeway Company thought the cave might make a good beer garden, which happily did not happen. Varner further explained, "Indians occupied the area from the present Inn site along Lakeway Drive to Comet Street and along both sides of Comet. A clump of trees in the front yard at 304 Lakeway Drive is a well-defined Indian mound." Varner also targeted another cave dwelling behind 603 Robin Dale Drive and pointed out that "most of the houses on Edgewater Cove are built atop large Indian mounds."

***

Most anthropologists believe that the ancestors of native peoples of North and South America originally walked across a long-vanished land bridge from Asia; in fact, recent DNA studies suggest that a single Siberian group, crossing some 10,000 to 12,000 years ago into what is now Alaska, possessed the genetic link to most native groups found in the Americas.

Precisely how and when these original "immigrants" dispersed southward is not clear, but archeologists and physical anthropologists, who labeled them and their immediate progeny Paleo-Indians or Paleo-Americans, have found remnants of their primitive tools and weapons in Central Texas. They were hunters and gatherers who formed small, highly mobile groups that moved from place to place in pursuit of food. With handheld lances or throwing spears tipped with stone or flint, they hunted for long-extinct and very different species of elephants, horses, camels, and bison. They also dined on smaller creatures, fish, and a variety of flora. Eventually, the advent of agriculture, the domestication of animals, and improved metal tools led to more complex societies.

Over the millennia, these earliest Americans evolved into countless tribes or clans known collectively as "Indians." Of course, none of these groups called themselves Indians. No, that name was the work of a fifteenth-century Italian explorer named Christopher Columbus, who made one of the worst geographical guesses in recorded history. Native Americans also take issue with any European declaration of New World discoveries. As one copper-hued observer put it, "How does one discover a land where there are already people living?"

The precise nomenclature for these early tribes or clans is equally obscure, as early Spanish and French explorers reproduced names phonetically in their own languages. Nevertheless, white Americans historically lumped them together as Indians, and seldom in very complimentary ways.

Nineteenth-century Texans accepted the prevailing view of most white Americans, immortalized in Hartley Alexander's 1902 poem, "The Only Good Indian Is a Dead Indian." Theodore Roosevelt was scarcely more temperate when in 1889 he declared, "I don't go so far as to think that the only good Indians are the dead Indians, but I believe nine out of every ten are, and I shouldn't inquire too closely into the case of the tenth. The most vicious cowboy has more moral principle than the average Indian."

U.S. Army Colonel Richard I. Dodge was also sure that a sense of right and wrong was absent from the Indians he fought against on the Texas frontier:

> Where all are such magnificent thieves, it is difficult to decide which of the Plains tribes deserves the palm for stealing. The Indians themselves give it to the Comanche. . . . For crawling into a camp, cutting hobbles and lariat ropes, and getting off undiscovered with the animals, they are unsurpassed and unsurpassable."[1]

1. Colonel Richard I. Dodge, *Our Wild Indians,* 1883; quoted in W. W. Newcomb, Jr., *The Indians of Texas: From Prehistoric to Modern Times* (Austin: University of Texas Press, 1961), 155.

Only slightly less judgmental were those nationalist historians, politicians, and clergy who drummed up images of the noble but doomed savage who stood in the path of what they labeled manifest destiny. It was an unfair battle for the greatly outnumbered and outgunned Indians, but in reality it was disease and the loss of the buffalo that killed more Indians than the white man's bullets. According to anthropologist John C. Ewers, between 1528 and 1895, as many as 95 percent of Texas Indians died from diseases, mostly smallpox and cholera.

***

The nomadic tribes of Lipan Apaches and Tonkawas established themselves in the fourteenth century in what would become Travis County, with Kiowas and Comanches moving into the area in the late seventeenth and early eighteenth centuries, in part to be closer to the Spanish horses they so dearly loved. All moved freely up and down the Colorado River. Some of the earlier tribes farmed and others set up trading centers for bartering with each other and with the Europeans after their arrival in the sixteenth century.

The Lipan Apaches lived in small villages that later made them particularly vulnerable to marauding Comanches and Kiowas. The Tonkawas, who believed they originated from a hole in the ground after being uncovered by an eagle or a wolf, were timid hunters and gatherers. As part of a boundary commission sent by the Mexican government in 1827, José María Sánchez visited and later wrote a rather whimsical description of Tonkawa domestic life:

> In the center of each Tonkawa hut is located the fireplace around which lie the male Indians in complete inaction, while the women are in constant motion either curing the meat of the game, or tanning the skins, or preparing the food, which consists chiefly of roast meat, or perhaps making arms for their indolent husbands.[2]

Tonkawa and Comanche Indians

Photos courtesy of the Dolph Briscoe Center for American History, University of Texas, Austin

2. José María Sánchez, "Travels in Texas," *Southwestern Historical Quarterly,* April 1926.

During the 1980–81 construction of Jack Nicklaus' Hills of Lakeway Golf Course, hundreds of Indian artifacts were uncovered. At one time, a representative sampling appeared on the wall of the Hills Country Club, but these disappeared. Fortunately, Jessie Griffith, who had worked in planning and development for both Bob Alpert's Lakeway Company and its successor, Ross Perot, Jr.'s Hillwood Company, was able to save the above sampling. First row, left: scraping blade, 6500 B.C.–5500 B.C.; first row, middle: flake modified on one end to a small point for use as an engraver; first row, right: pedernales blade, 1460 B.C.–650 B.C. Second row, left: blade, 300 B.C.–200 B.C.; second row, right: barbed blade. Third row, left: blade, 300 B.C.–200 A.D.; third row, middle: a typical tool that functioned as a knife or possible spear point; third row, right: blade, 2600 B.C.–2000 B.C. Fourth row, left and right: arrowheads.

The Tonkawas, like the Lipan Apaches, were caught between the Spanish and Mexicans moving up from the south, the French from the southeast, the Kiowas and Comanches from the north and west, and white Americans from the east.

The Tonkawas did give Texas the word *pedernales*, meaning "flint," evidence of which abounds in the Lakeway area; in fact, according to Byron Varner, the Abe and Jeanne Hutto ranch on Flintrock Road contained "a veritable flint factory," as did the site for the Hills Country Club.

***

The nomadic Comanches became the scourge of both Indians and white settlers. According to historian W. W. Newcomb, "The Comanches were the principal and most stubborn adversaries the Texans had . . . . They raided . . . and killed or captured men, women, and children, carried off what they could, and burned the rest."[3] The Comanches also fought against Spaniards, Mexicans, and other Indians. They tied their existence to the buffalo, and when the buffalo began

3. W. W. Newcomb, Jr., *The Indians of Texas: From Prehistoric to Modern Times* (Austin: University of Texas Press, 1961), 155.

Comanche brave - Photo courtesy of the Dolph Brisco Center for American History, University of Texas, Austin

to disappear, so did their nomadic way of life, although disease, the Texas Rangers, and the U.S. Army hastened their demise.

Stories of marauding, scalping Indians were common in Central Texas, but none received more publicity than J. W. Wilbarger's 1889 *Indian Depredations in Texas* and its description of his brother, who in 1833 survived being scalped just east of Austin:

> Josiah fell apparently dead, but though unable to move or speak, did not lose consciousness. He knew when the Indians came around him—when they stripped him naked and tore the scalp from his head. He says that though paralyzed and unable to move, he knew what was being done, and that when his scalp was torn from his skull it created no pain from which he could flinch, but sounded like distant thunder.

Wilbarger chronicled every Indian "depredation," real or imagined, that anyone passed on to him. Although his treatment of marauding Indians was decidedly one-sided, the danger to isolated families on the frontier was real, as Lakeway resident Peg Hein relates in her account of her great-grandparents homesteading in the San Saba area in the 1850s:

> There were numerous stories of mothers taking their children into the fields to hide from Indians, of children being stolen by Indians, or settlers being brutally scalped and killed by Indians. One

day, Esther saw a lone Indian sneaking towards the cabin. She hid behind the door with her heavy iron skillet in her hands, and when the Indian opened the door, hit him over the head with all her strength. The Indian was knocked unconscious, and she took the children and ran to the field to get David. When they returned the Indian was gone. At least six men were killed by Indians in the surrounding area before 1860 and several more later. Dogs became necessary to warn and guard families.[4]

Bee Cave resident Emmett Cade told of his mother "going to bed with the hogs" when Indians were reported in the area because Indians disliked the taste of pork and believed that pigs, unlike cattle, could not be herded.[5]

The rugged terrain of western Travis County made an ideal sanctuary for marauding Indians to launch their raids on Austin and nearby settlers. They were primarily interested in stealing horses, but they remained a threat to isolated settlers. Years after the fact, Alma Buchanan Babb described what happened to her great-grandfather, John Henry Lohmann, shortly after he built his new home along the banks of the Colorado River in what would one day become Lakeway:

> He was about 70 when he personally undertook the building of his new home, a large two-story, of native stone.... Indians lurked from time to time in the cedar brakes - Apaches Lipanes, or Comanches. Once his stout walking stick, aimed like a gun, was enough to scare off a party of them. And his stepson was killed by Indians about 10 miles from home, some said. Others said it was bushwhackers who accused the boy, not yet 18, of running away [from his Civil War obligations], and shot him.[6]

There had been an estimated 30,000 to 40,000 Comanches in Texas in the late eighteenth century. That number had been reduced to less than 1,500 by 1875, when they and the Kiowas surrendered at Fort Sill. The Comanches, like most Texas Indians, were decimated by disease. Anthropologist John C. Ewers chronicles thirty major epidemics, particularly smallpox and cholera, but also measles and mumps, that by 1890 had wiped out all but a handful of Texas Indians. The Comanches alone lost an estimated half their population to smallpox and cholera epidemics in 1848 and 1849. Also taking its toll was poverty and malnutrition, particularly after the buffalo were wiped out. The U.S. Army and the Texas Rangers, however, delivered the final blows.

The Texas Rangers had been reorganized into two groups in 1874, one for controlling bandits along the Rio Grande and the other for eradicating hostile Indians. The final conquest of the Comanches and Kiowas took place in the Red River campaigns of 1874–75, after which the few survivors were pushed onto reservations in Oklahoma.

Of the vanquished Comanches, Larry McMurtry, who wrote *Comanche Moon*, penned a haunting epitaph:

> They were deadly, merciless killers, but they were also the last free Indians on the southern plains. When the last of them had been killed, or their freedom taken from them, their power broken, the plains . . . would be a different place. It would be a safer place, of course, but a flavor would have been taken out of it—the flavor of wildness.

Unfortunately, precious few Indians have told their own stories, and even fewer have written them down for posterity. During the Great Depression, the New Deal's Work Progress Administration (WPA) did sponsor a series of

4. Peg Hein, *Frontier Life on Cherokee Creek: A Pioneer Family in San Saba County,* unpublished manuscript.
5. Interview with Emmett Cade, February 23, 1992, Elaine Perkins, *A Hill Country Paradise? Western Travis County and Its Earliest Settlers,* unpublished manuscript.
6. Alma Buchanan Babb, "After the Captain Reached the River," unpublished Lohmann family memoir.

Western Travis County's Hamilton Pool and its enchanting surroundings had great spiritual significance for many Native Americans.

oral histories with surviving Indians from Texas and Oklahoma who had been herded onto local reservations. The following example from an old Comanche warrior suggests that the "Holly-wooden" Indian, first made popular by the dime novels and perpetuated in our broader popular culture and even in early textbooks, greatly distorted the lives of this continent's earliest indigenous human beings.

> The older Indians taught the younger ones to live a true life. Be true to the Great Spirit, which was the man above the sun. I was taught to always be kind to those that aid you and never take anything that doesn't belong to you. If a task is done, we owe it to the Great Spirit for enabling us to do the task. Always be kind to father and mother. Never make fun of any older person, for we some day may be old and make the same mistakes as they make. . . . This is the truth, and the way the Great Spirit meant for us to live. We must love our God.[7]

Except for their cooking utensils, flint tools, arrowheads, and parched bones, little remains of the Indians who inhabited Texas for several thousand years. Locally, there are private collections of arrowheads and tools, numerous burial mounds, and a few cave dwellings carved into the ridges overlooking the old river bottom. Then, too, older settlers told stories of hearing Indian chants on quiet, moonlit nights along Hurst Creek. There is also the question of the naming of the Union's twenty-eighth state, although that story too is a bit murky. Was it lifted from the Tejas Indians or did it come from the Caddo Indian word *tesha*, meaning, ironically, "friend"?

7. John Wa-Ka-Quah, quoted in David La Vere, *Life among the Texas Indians: The WPA Narratives* (College Station: Texas A&M Press, 1998), 215.

CHAPTER THREE

AMERICAN MIGRATIONS INTO THE HILL COUNTRY

This is strong country. Not only does it produce fearless soldiers and people with great courage, but the grass that grows in the rock has a lot of minerals in it and the cattle that eat this grass are more valuable. . . . There is always sun here. We don't have dreariness. We don't have those dull gray skies when you look up. Here you have birds singing, flowers growing, girls smiling.

President Lyndon Baines Johnson

The good folks of the Hill Country worked hard for everything they had. The frontier life demanded that each be thrifty, capable, and self-sufficient. You had what you won from the soil. Sometimes it was sufficient, and then you shared with your family or your neighbors . . . , who through circumstances, were less fortunate than you. "It is more precious to give than to receive," was not merely mouthed but practiced in the Hill Country.

Thomas F. Gunn, author of *Good Folks*

Why men would take their families out in such danger, I can't understand.

Nineteenth-century Hill Country housewife

The topography of Travis County could not have been more diverse when the county was first organized in 1840.[1] To the east and south lay prairie land on which one could raise cattle, cotton, and other crops; to the west and northwest lay the hill country or "mountains," as they were then called, more suited for sheep, goats, and cedar shakers, although early settlers in western Travis County did try to raise their own food and even some cotton. Cutting through the heart of the county was the Balcones Escarpment, giving rise to lovely little creeks with such colorful names as Barton, Bear, Shoal, Boggy, Walnut, and Onion, which flowed into Texas's longest river, the Colorado. Lining the creek bottoms were cypress, cottonwood, and sycamore, while on the higher ground grew live oaks, hackberry, chinaberry, and elm, although cedar would eventually come to dominate the landscape. Bluebonnets, winecups, redbud, Indian blankets, and Indian paintbrush exploded in vibrant spring colors. Buffalo still roamed its western regions, as did many other wild creatures.

***

They wrote GTT (Gone to Texas) on their gates and headed for the promised land and what they hoped would be paradise. Historian Cary Clayton estimates that between 1820 and 1860, as many as 600,000 Anglo-Americans migrated to Texas, most from the central and southern states. The earliest among these settlers sought the downstream flatlands along major Texas rivers before they flowed into the Gulf of Mexico. Later settlers had to seek sites farther upstream that were not so easily cultivated. In the case of the Colorado River, those migrating above Austin encountered the formidable landscape of western Travis County. They had heard the stories of a land teeming with wild game, a wonderful strain of wild cotton,[2] and lush vegetation that would fatten their livestock. Nature, however, played a cruel joke on them. After holding out promises of tantalizing riches, it suddenly snatched them away until only the strongest could survive. Lyndon Baines Johnson biographer Robert Caro vividly described this enticing landscape that lured so many settlers:

1. Initially, Travis County covered approximately 40,000 square miles. Today it is just under 1,000 square miles.
2. Although cotton is now cultivated worldwide, virtually all of it developed from indigenous American strains.

> And the streams these men discovered were full of fish. The hills were full of game. There were, to their experienced eyes, all the sign of bear, and you didn't need sign to know about the deer—they were so numerous that when riders crested a hill, a whole herd might leap away in the valley below, white tails flashing. There were other white tails, too: rabbits in abundance. And as the men sat on their horses, staring, flocks of wild turkeys strutted in silhouette along the ridges. Honeybees buzzed in the glades, and honey hung in the trees for the taking. Wild mustang grapes, plump and purple, hung down for making wine.[3]

Then there was the knee-high grass that seemed to stretch as far as the eye could see. Surely, they thought, the soil beneath the grass must be deep and rich, but in truth it had taken hundreds of years to mature in the shallow, crumbled limestone that nourished it. Once it was gone, either because of overgrazing or nutrient-destroying crops, it did not come back; instead, brush, cedar, and uncovered rocks emerged to dominate the Hill Country. So overwhelming became the cedar that by the beginning of the twentieth century a single cedar brake northwest of Austin covered 500 square miles and was continuing to spread. Cedar could be used for posts, building materials, charcoal, and shingles, but its rapid growth was at the expense of tillable farmland.

Moisture triggered another crucible. As Caro put it, "The Hill Country was a trap baited with water."[4] Some years it was plentiful; in fact, so much so that it washed the thin veneer of topsoil down raging creeks and rivers to be lost forever. Even worse were the prolonged dry periods when nothing would grow, livestock had to be slaughtered, and families went without. Drought was truly the great destroyer of dreams in the Hill Country, as described by Thomas Gunn, whose family in the late nineteenth century settled in Fitzhugh just south of Bee Cave:

> Streams stopped flowing. Water holes grew stagnant. Every blade of grass had long since dried up. The suffering stock, grown scrawny, listlessly straggled over the sun burned hills and grizzled valleys foraging for food and water. . . . Springs that had formerly gushed forth, became only damp spots between the worn rocks and dead ferns. Our crops, planted so hopefully in the spring, wilted and died after sprouting.
>
> Drought and famine take a heavy toll in human misery. Insecurity and hardship breed broken hearts and homes. Many of our good folks, seeking greener pastures, went job-hunting in the cities or into business, and many were unprepared for so drastic a change in their simple lives.[5]

Then came the winter winds that swept down from the north. Cold and unrelenting, they too blew away the precious topsoil. For the women left alone with their children while husbands were gone, often on long cattle drives, such winds contributed to a desperation and loneliness that made insanity all too common.

Even when nature was relatively beneficent, there were other dangers on this untamed frontier. Until they were subdued and successfully pushed out of Central Texas in the 1870s by the Texas Rangers and the U.S. Army, marauding Comanches constantly put the settlers at risk. For these fierce nomads, the white settlers were interlopers, whose horses, livestock, and even families were fair game. According to folklore, something called a Comanche Moon could incite them to destroy farms, kidnap women and children, and scalp their victims, although arguably not to the degree exploited by popular legend, dime novels, and lurid Hollywood films. Nevertheless, the threat of violence and death was constant on the frontier, and the courageous

3. Robert A. Caro, *The Path to Power: The Years of Lyndon Johnson* (New York: Random House, 1981), 9.
4. Ibid., 12.
5. Thomas F. Gunn, *Good Folks* (Denver: Big Mountain Press, 1964), 44.

and determined people who survived became the backbone of the Hill Country.

***

Lakeway resident Peg Hein has written about the lives of her great-grandparents, who were typical of the hardy and determined Midwesterners who migrated to Central Texas in the nineteenth century.[6] In 1851, David and Esther Matsler left Illinois and floated down the Mississippi to New Orleans, from where they took another boat to Port Lavaca, Texas. Next came fifteen days by horse and wagon to Round Rock. Two years later, hail and high winds destroyed their crops and new house and pushed them farther west until they settled on aptly named Cherokee Creek in what would become San Saba County.

Esther and David built a cabin in 1854, about the same time the existing Wunneberger cabin was built in Lakeway. She did her cooking over a fire outdoors or, during bad weather, in a skillet in the fireplace. She followed wild bees to their hives and scooped out the honey. She harvested berries and pecans along the creek bottom and cultivated a small garden that produced beans and onions. David hunted deer and turkeys, and Esther made jerky by cutting the meat into thin strips and hanging it outside to dry. David also cleared the land for corn and sweet potatoes. They shared their land with rattlesnakes, bears, wolves, panthers, hordes of grasshoppers, and "visiting" Comanches. There were no nearby doctors, so Esther cared for her family using plants and herbs, which she probably learned from friendly Indians.

Despite these hardships, within two years Esther, David, and their neighbors started a school. In 1855, the Texas legislature allotted $1.50 per year for each child, and the teacher augmented her salary with food and other gifts from the parents. There were no desks, and the children wrote their lessons on slates because paper was too expensive. Their only study materials were readers, simple arithmetic books, and a Bible.

Esther raised fourteen children of her own, three children of a daughter who died, numerous other grandchildren, and a partially blind younger brother. When Esther died at age ninety-three, daughter Teck said, "I never saw my mother

The house where David and Esther Matsler raised most of their children.

6. Peg Hein, *Frontier Life on Cherokee Creek.*

sit in her rocking chair unless she had a child, a mending basket or a Bible on her lap."

***

When Arkansas-born Wiley Hudson and his wife, Catherine, filed an affidavit for presumption of land in 1854, they were certainly among the first whites to settle on the bend in the Colorado River that bears their name. Local historian Carole McIntosh Sikes describes what the 4,000 acres that made up Hudson Bend might have looked like when Wiley and Catherine arrived:

> Imagine hills covered with tall, thick pasture grass rather than choked with cedar trees. The land along the river was fertile and the soil deep enough to sustain cotton and corn. There were tall cypress and pecan trees along the banks of the river. The simple timber and log homes of the settlers, built at the end of dirt wagon trails, were high above the river to protect against the all-too-frequent floods.[7]

According to the 1860 census, there were then four families living in the Hudson Bend area, including Wiley and Catherine and their eight children, along with Wiley's father, James. Their primary crop was corn, which they took across the river to be ground at Anderson Mill. Several of their children and grandchildren married into such prominent area families as the Williams, Toungats, Haydons, Sylvesters, and Stewarts, who eventually owned considerable land in what would become Lakeway.

After the Mansfield Dam began operating in 1941 and created Lake Travis, there were no more floods, but Hudson Bend lost approximately half of its 4,000 acres along with its cemetery, which had to be moved to the Teck Cemetery on RR 620.

Benjamin K. Stewart and his wife, Sarah, first traveled from Tennessee to the Burnet area, but about 1870 they purchased 1,500 acres near the

The children of Wiley and Catherine Hudson. From left to right: Henry Gregg Hudson, Harriett Hudson Haydon, Basheba "Bash" Hudson Gilcrease, Ann Hudson Toungat, Joseph Alexander Hudson, and Emeline Hudson Williams.

7. Carole McIntosh Sikes, "Recounting Hudson Bend's Founding," *Lake Travis View,* February 26, 1998.

mouth of Hurst Creek on Vineyard Bay. According to fifth-generation Betty Ann Stewart Hanson, the Stewarts were called the River People by old-timers, most of whom had purchased their land on higher ground:

> If there had been a recent hard rain and the river was going to rise, they would say, 'the river is going to roll' and get to higher ground . . . .
>
> When the dam was built and the water started to rise, all the graves on Graveyard Point had to be dug up and moved to our cousin's land on R.R. 620 called Teck Cemetery. My Dad told us about the corpses that were exhumed. One body had real long straight hair, assumed to be a man because women always plaited their hair. Before the bodies were moved to the Teck cemetery, this land had a school on it. . . .
>
> All the kids in the area came to school by walking, riding a horse, or by horse and buggy. Their lunch was a biscuit with syrup poured on it. . . .
>
> One of the favorite family stories that we loved as children was the tale of Ol' Blue, who was the biggest catfish ever seen in Lake Travis. He kept eluding every hook and had lots of secret hiding places. To this day, Ol' Blue has never been caught; hence, one of the streets in that area is named Blue Cat.
>
> The A. L. Stewart property has seen many changes over the years due to floods, droughts, and severe storms that have affected the geography of this area. My dad was a true helping hand in the lake area. He allowed the property owners who were escaping the floods to put their belongings in our Rock Cabin many times. He also was instrumental in helping Joe and Rosie Arriago in achieving their dream of owning Rosie's Tamale House, which originally opened on the corner of RR 620 and Highway 71, where the Springhill Restaurant now sits.
>
> [In the early 1960s], our father, A. L. Stewart, told us that someone bought some of Mr. Hutto's property and was going to build beautiful home sites on the lake. Thus, the beginnings of Lakeway and the beautiful place that has evolved. My brother, Col. Arthur L. Stewart, and his wife Helene are still living in Lakeway near Hurst Creek Road and the view from the upstairs balcony oversees the original Stewart home site.[8]

In the early 1930s, Ernest C. Stewart purchased the old Teck Store in the community of Teck, so named because his grandfather, Leonard Eck, had been informed that he needed at least four letters in his name if he wanted to open a post office. More than a half century later, Ernest's brother Truman recorded his memories of the store and life during the Great Depression of the 1930s:

> We had a cotton gin behind the store and a little corral for people's horses. Folks would bring in some freshly caught catfish, a dozen eggs, or a pork ham to the store for trading. Fish was then 10 cents a pound. . . .
>
> We had one teacher for grade primer through the eighth grade, and everybody learned together. The only school supplies we needed were a cedar pencil and a writing tablet. All our books were furnished.
>
> Unlike the school, there were two churches to choose from, a Baptist and a Methodist, and there were always debates as to which one was better, and which one was the church to go to if you wanted to get into heaven.
>
> It's hard to describe the depression years of the 1930s. You hear about 500 or 600 people getting laid off at Lockheed

8. Betty Ann Stewart Hanson, "My Memories," unpublished and undated, Lakeway Heritage Center Archives.

The Teck School

now. Well, you had that many people out of work every day back then. Every house in the area had two or three families living in it. People got any job they could, like bailing hay for 75 cents a day. Still, life was a lot better then because you didn't have to worry about money–because you didn't have any.[9]

Both of these photos were taken in front of the Teck Store; the photo on the left was taken after Ernest Stewart purchased the store. The musicians in the photo on the right were called The Deaf Band.

9. Truman Stewart was eighty-four years old when interviewed on May 14, 1986, by Mike Burton of the *Lake Travis View.*

Bird K. Stewart (1846–1923), the son of Benjamin K. Stewart (1805–1872) and Sarah Stewart (1811–1899), moved to western Travis County about 1870. Bird was the father of Albert Kendrick Stewart (1872–1944), who is portrayed on the right.

Albert Kendrick Stewart (1872–1944), wife Annie Lucinda Collier Stewart (1874–1952) and seven of their eight children, one of whom is Arthur L. Stewart, Sr. (1905–1975). His son, Arthur Stewart, Jr. (1932–), is a retired U.S. Marine colonel who still lives in Lakeway. The other children in this photo are Lillie Naomi Stewart (1893–?), James Irvin Stewart (1895–1964), Ernest C. Stewart, Sr. (1898–1973), who purchased the Teck Store, Emmett Noah Stewart (1900–1975), Truman Albert Stewart (1902–?), and William F. Stewart (1907–1931). Ivan Milton Stewart (1911–?) was not yet born.

***

Located several miles south of Hudson's Bend and the Teck community was Bee Cave, which was also first settled in the last half of the nineteenth century. The origin of the name, which sometimes appears as Bee Caves, is uncertain. One story has bees building hives that looked like a cave in the gabled end of Carl Beck's store, but another version suggests the community was named after the bees that inhabited the limestone caves along Bee Creek, Barton Creek, and Little Barton Creek. Stamped postcards from the early years of the twentieth century contain postmarks for both Bee Cave and Bee Caves.

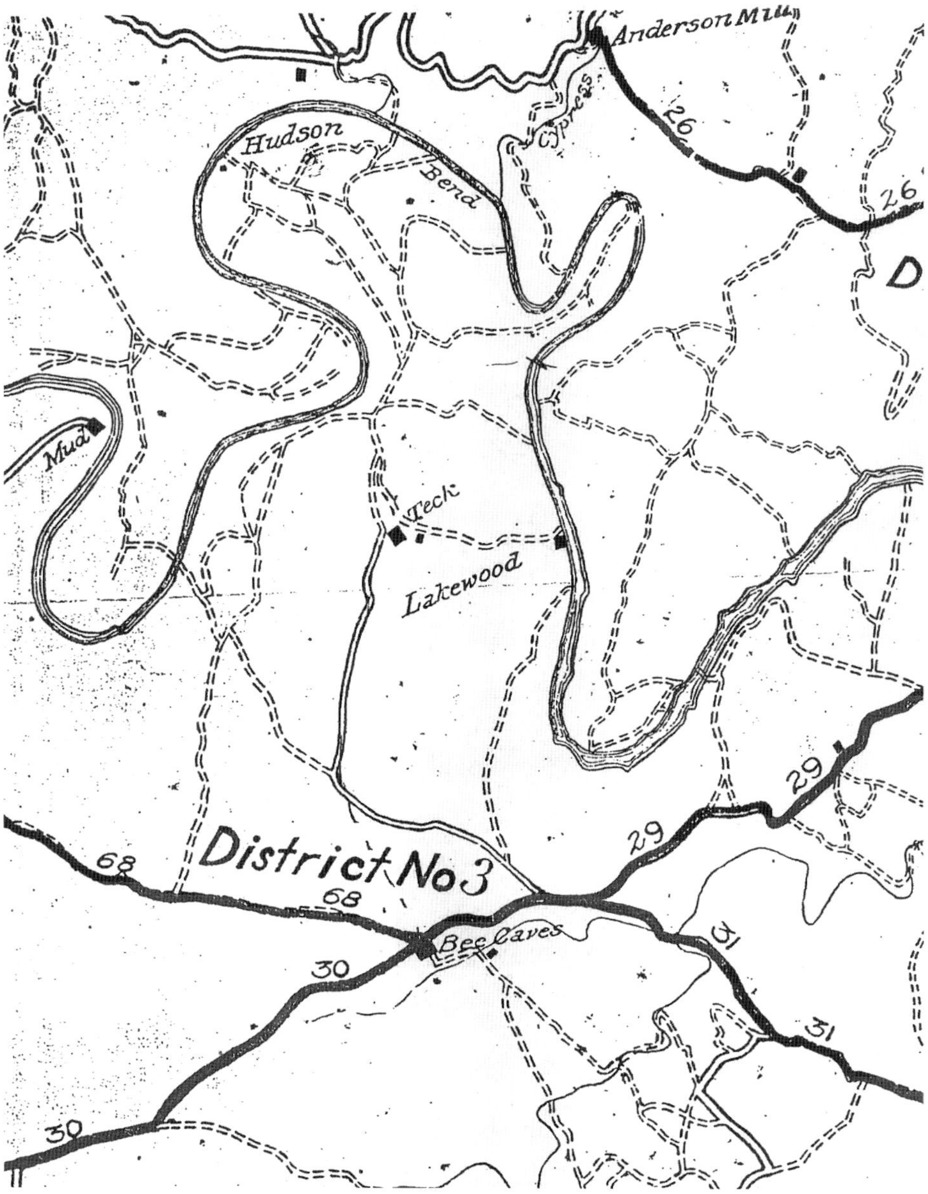

This map of Hudson Bend, Teck, and Bee Cave in the 1890s included the name Lakewood, about which little is known.

According to Thomas Gunn, the early settlers in the Bee Cave area had to be self-sufficient, although this was not easy when farming under such adverse conditions:

> It was a dry-farming area, requiring long hours of toil every day except Sunday to wrest from the land even the simplest necessities of life. Crops were cotton, corn, milo-maize, small quantities of oats and wheat. The land was tilled behind a horse-drawn, single-row plow. Everything was done by hand, including the sowing of seed, weeding with a hoe, picking of cotton, corn, and whatever crops that might have ripened, but only if there was sufficient rain. Most farmers had a few chickens, some pigs, and one or two milk cows. No refrigerators or ice meant packing meat in salt or lard and putting it down in barrels, or it went to the smokehouse for curing.[10]

According to Bee Cave historian Elaine Perkins, "Beans were the staple in every family. They were easy to grow and store, they could be dried and kept in airtight containers, and they could be used to make many different dishes."[11] Families also smoked both domestic and wild animals, including deer, turkey, rabbit, squirrel, and an occasional armadillo.

The settlers had to be especially resourceful when it came to health care. Doctors were scarce and distances were great, so the old axiom "patient heal thyself" often applied to the frontier. According to Perkins, home remedies, often learned from friendly Indians, treated a wide range of maladies:

> There was no better remedy for rheumatism than pokeroot and whiskey. Probably, the more whiskey, the better the remedy. Colic was treated with a mixture of paregoric, Jamaican ginger, spirits of camphor, carbonate soda, water and whiskey. For cramps, a cloth was moistened with spirits of turpentine and laid over the place where the pain was felt. If the pain moved, so did the cloth. Corns on toes were wet several times a day with hartshorn, which was derived from deer antlers. . . . For a weak back, two table-

The Dietrich Bohls family smokehouse

10. Gunn, *Good Folks,* 21.
11. Perkins Manuscript.

spoons of finely powdered rosin, four tablespoons of white sugar, whites of two eggs, and one quart of whiskey. This remedy was also excellent for colds, weak lungs, irritating coughs, and anything else that ailed you.[12]

Cynics might argue that whiskey alone might have accomplished the same results, and many of the settlers did make homebrew from wild grapes, domestic fruit, and homegrown corn. So serious did members of the Bee Cave Lodge become about their white lightening that in 1908 they sent a letter to Washington, D.C., protesting a proposal to make the capital dry, lest it set an unwanted precedent for the states. Washington, of course, paid no attention, and turned the entire country dry in 1921 after the ratification of the Eighteenth Amendment. This left the residents of western Travis County high and dry before they too became resourceful bootleggers, just like thirsty Americans across the land.

A colorful local character named Roy Brown enjoyed chewing tobacco, expectorating into a plastic cup, and talking about other notorious masticators during the good ole days of Prohibition:

Jim Puryear was a Baptist preacher who always had a wad of tobacco in his mouth when he preached. But he never did spit. He must've swallowed that juice. He rode horseback to different communities to preach, and was known almost as much for his feisty sermons as for his tobacco habits. Mary Milam had a taste for tobacco too. I can still remember clouds of smoke from the porch every evening as she smoked her corncob pipe.

There used to be a moonshine still at every spring in this county—and there's a lot of springs hereabouts. I remember cutting brush and finding five stills in one day. Once I ran across a 600-gallon, all-copper still. Most people sold their white lightning for a living, and some of them got rich at it.[13]

Despite all attempts at self-sufficiency, there were times when folks had to go to Austin for necessary supplies. This was no simple task in the early years of the twentieth century. The dirt roads were little more than ruts, and the mule- or horse-driven, wooden-wheeled wagons made the twenty-mile trip painfully slow and exhausting. Thomas Gunn, whose home village of Fitzhugh was named after General Robert E. Lee's son Fitzhugh, who had reportedly killed an Indian on that site in 1856, remembers the return trip from Austin when he was five or six years old. Their route roughly followed the Old Fredericksburg Road through Oak Hill and on west to Cedar Valley where it intersected Fitzhugh Road, midway between Austin and Dripping Springs:

The road home was a weary one, rough and rutted, full of chuck holes. By the time we had reached Oak Hill it was time to rest a while. The old storekeeper hailed my father as we crossed a pretty stream which ran high enough for the mules to slosh around, and Papa allowed them to halt amid stream so they could have their fill of this fresh mountain water, and of course while this was going on, our wooden wagon wheels were soaking up lots of it. When you hear the saying, "tight as a wagon wheel," you can bet that's pretty tight. The wood swells up against the iron bands and makes the wheels like new until they dry out again. . . .

It wasn't too long after this that I crawled back in the wagon, and was soon fast asleep on my pallet, oblivious to the wagon's creaks and groans and constant lurch. Some time later I woke to find the wagon standing still, and looking out, I saw Papa was tying the mules to the hitching rack at the Cedar Valley

12. Ibid.

13. Interview with Roy Brown, *Homestead Herald,* June 9, 1978, and reprinted in the *Lake Travis View,* April 25, 1991.

Post Office and General Store. All of us were happy to get out and stretch and be heartily greeted by Doshia Moore, as if we were members of her own family. Doshia was storekeeper, postmistress, and owner of the whole town of Cedar Valley. The town was the store, windmill, water tank, watering trough, house, and tool sheds, and what was most welcome sight of all to travelers, the fine, well-appointed three-holer out back! Families our size just worked out perfectly. But most of our Hill Country people had much larger families and their unfortunate broods had patiently to wait their turn in order of seniority, or in order of urgency of the situation as was more often the case. . . .

[Inside] there was the Bulletin Board that told about all the "bad Men" that were "wanted" and the rewards that were offered for their capture "dead or alive." A more appetizing sight for a child was the row of glass jars that were filled with mixed candies, jawbreakers, licorice sticks, and the era's favorite, horehound drops. There was the sauerkraut barrel and the barrels of vinegar, pickles, crackers, molasses, and over to one side, the kerosene or coal oil barrel. [There was also] cough syrup, Vaseline, cold remedies, patent medicines for kidney trouble, foot remedies, corn cures, worm medicine for the stock, and, of course, the indispensable Asaphoetida that was sewn into a little bag, then hung around your neck and patted down inside your underwear. Even today, I can still smell the stinky stuff. Folks said it was something we got from the Indians' medicine men. If so, you can give it back to the Indians. . . .

This typical general store, of course, was a social center, too, where friends and distant neighbors met and exchanged scraps of information, and now and then a bit of local gossip.[14]

As early as 1870, Bee Cave had a postmaster but no home mail service. Mail had to be picked up at the nearest post office or general store. By the end of World War I, this had changed and rural mail delivery extended to the far western regions of Travis County. The aforementioned Cedar Valley Community Post Office and Store's rural mail carrier was Miss Lizzie Nolan, who began delivering the mail in 1918. On August 10, 1947, the *Austin-American Statesman* published a feature on this remarkable lady, who had just completed twenty-nine years of service:

> Nearing 60 years of age, but still energetic, Miss Lizzie started her mail carrying career during the "horse and buggy" days. Roads over the hills around Cedar Valley were merely cow trails in those days. Often after a rain when the "branches" (creeks to city-bred folks) were running high, Miss Lizzie would unharness the horse from the mail buggy and ride the horse into the water to see if it was safe to cross with the rig.
>
> With the coming of the Automobile Age, Miss Lizzie replaced her horse and buggy with a Model "T" Ford.
>
> "I cranked that car for five years—sometimes I would be stuck on some out-of-the-way road and crank and cry and crank trying to get it started," she recalled. "It always started sooner or later."
>
> Self-starters brought a welcome relief to Miss Lizzie's daily 46-mile mail route. . . . Her friends and people on her route would help pull her car out of the mud or other tight fixes or change a tire. Said Miss Lizzie of her favorite people, "It is the people I meet along my route that makes my job such an enjoyable one."

14. Gunn, *Good Folks,* 13–16.

Above: Bee Cave Yellow Schoolhouse, circa 1920s. Below: Mark and Virgil Spillman and Lena Wolber ride an early Bee Cave "school bus."

A later-model Bee Cave school bus

Early on, the settlers set up schools for their children. Sometimes classes were held in the open or in homes. John Henry Lohmann even hired a private tutor for his children. More common, however, were the small schoolhouses that dotted western Travis County. Many had colorful names, such as Lone Ives, Rocky Creek, Haynie Flat, Cat Hollow, Pleasant Grove, Mud, and the Yellow Bee Cave Schoolhouse.

Two nineteenth-century schools in the Lakeway area were at Hirsh Creek and Hudson Bend, although in 1890 they consolidated to form the Teck School, close to the present corner of Debba Road and RR 620. These early schools had few amenities, as Thomas Gunn makes clear when describing the Fitzhugh School he attended as a youngster:

> Inside, homemade benches and plank-topped desks faced the blackboard and the teacher's table. In the back of the room was a cast iron wood-burning stove with a stovepipe going out to the side between the two windows. Also in the back was a partition with wooden pegs on it; one side was for the girls and the other, for the boys, a place to hang their coats and stow their lunches. Near the door were two wooden water buckets with a dipper for each. For a long while the teacher and the girls had enjoyed the luxury of a multiple-equipped outhouse—a four passenger job, but the boys still used the familiar brush thicket just over the hill. Sometimes the distance seemed very great, and sometimes, particularly when there was a "norther" blowing, this errand was accomplished "on the double."
>
> Under a spreading oak there was a hitching rail for many of the pupils and, occasionally, the teacher would ride horseback or come in a buggy.[15]

15. Gunn, *Good Folks,* 37–38.

Students who were seldom absent or late received a special certificate at the end of the school year, such as the one below from Bee Cave in 1933:

These early schoolhouses had no electricity, plumbing, or running water. The boys fetched drinking water, which often included floating flies and crickets, from nearby streams in a bucket. Elaine Perkins tells of mischievous boys throwing rocks when the girls used the outhouse and placing the scent sack of a skunk behind the blackboard, which the teacher then punctured when she wrote on the board. Boys had to leave their firearms outside upon arriving at school. A few of these schools even had athletic teams, such as the 1933 Bee Cave baseball team pictured below, which included the sons of several prominent families.

Classes were often interrupted for harvests, and the schools of western Travis County seldom

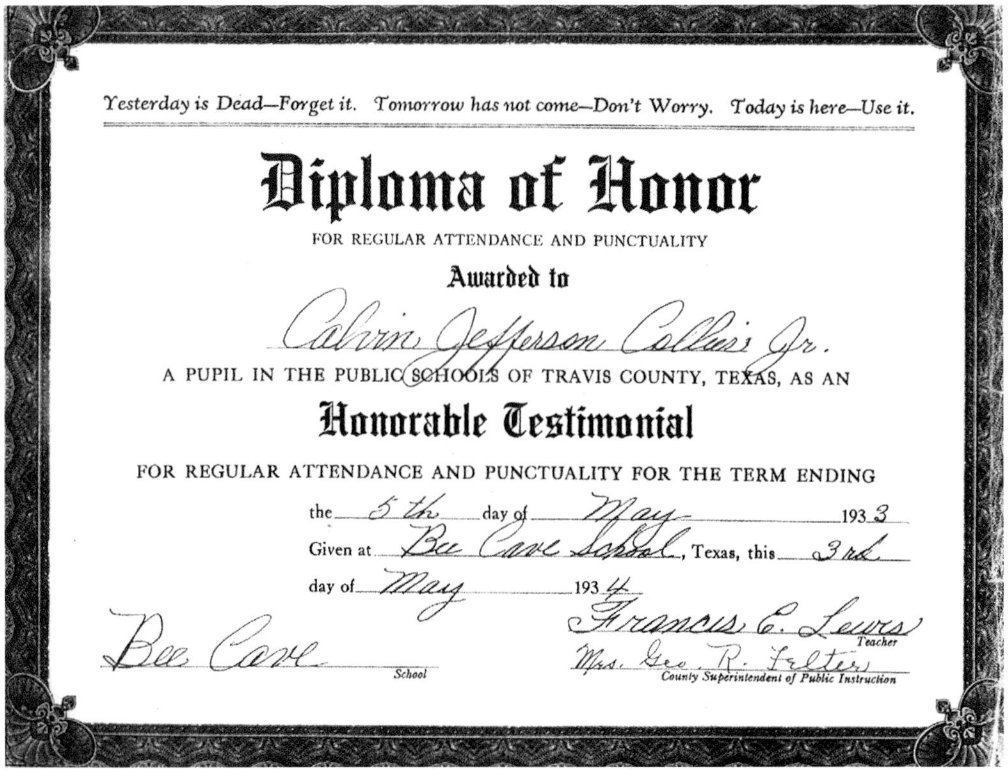

Yesterday is Dead—Forget it. Tomorrow has not come—Don't Worry. Today is here—Use it.

Diploma of Honor

FOR REGULAR ATTENDANCE AND PUNCTUALITY

Awarded to

Calvin Jefferson Collier Jr.

A PUPIL IN THE PUBLIC SCHOOLS OF TRAVIS COUNTY, TEXAS, AS AN

Honorable Testimonial

FOR REGULAR ATTENDANCE AND PUNCTUALITY FOR THE TERM ENDING

the 5th day of May 1933

Given at Bee Cave School, Texas, this 3rd

day of May 1934

Bee Cave School

Francis C. Lewis Teacher

Mrs. Geo. R. Felter County Superintendent of Public Instruction

Left to right: Calvin Collier, Wilford Maul, Oscar Hughes, Leonard Grumbles, Edgar Dohls, Everett Dohls, George Roberts, Raymond Brown, and Beauford Maul

went past the eighth grade. If a student wanted to complete high school, special arrangements had to be made to live and study in Austin.

These early settlers also built churches. Baptists predominated, although other denominations certainly existed, including Presbyterians, Lutherans, and the Church of Christ. Attending church was a social as well as a spiritual affair. Parishioners often picnicked between morning and afternoon services. Revival services also attracted people from near and far, especially during hard times, when participants prayed for rain or for sons who were off fighting America's wars. Revivals were often held under a brush arbor built for the occasion and could last anywhere from a few days to a couple of weeks. There was lots of praying and singing, along with box suppers for which the men could bid, thereby hoping to win the hearts of the ladies responsible. Resolutions were occasionally passed against such sins as mixed bathing, Sunday baseball, radio and movies, foul language, and drunkenness.

Without question, Hill Country folks were deadly serious about their religion, but they did not neglect having fun of a less spiritual nature. They loved to socialize, dance, and listen to music, often provided by local fiddlers. Sometimes they picnicked after a hard day's work, but there were also impromptu parties in people's homes, as well as scheduled dances in such places as the Bee Cave Dance Hall, the Sons of Herman Hall, and Sander's Hall, all of which were in or near Bee Cave. There was always plenty of food and alcohol, which was usually handcrafted. Elaine Perkins writes that "many a night an inebriated merrymaker would be dumped onto the back of his rig and the horse turned loose to find its own way home."[16]

Settlers' homes were often simple log cabins of the dog-run or dog-trot variety. The latter were common in the last half of the nineteenth century and consisted of two separate buildings covered by a single roof. The passageway between the two structures provided shade and allowed breezes to pass through on hot, sweltering days.

This early dog-run structure had no windows, and the logs were probably chinked with sticks and clay.

16. Perkins Manuscript.

The Ella Heffington Perkins House, above, goes back to the 1880s, although it was rebuilt and moved to its present location on Hamilton Pool Road around the turn of the century. The exterior table and chairs were obviously added later. The interior telephone goes back to the 1930s.

Deer were obviously larger in western Travis County some seventy years ago when this photo was taken. The successful hunters represented several well-known area families. From left to right: Ernest Brown, Henry Hudson, Jessie Gunn, Roy Brown, A. D. Eberhart, Will Brown, and Ernest Stewart.

***

Although most of the earliest settlers of western Travis County attempted to support themselves through farming, there were also the so-called cedar choppers, who cut down cedar trees for posts, building materials, railroad ties, and shingles. Some were also known for running moonshine and selling furs. One source estimates that as many as five million acres of cedar were cleared in Texas between 1900 and the 1940s.[17]

Once the bark was stripped off, the cedar's oils acted as a natural pesticide and preserving agent. The cedar choppers also processed and sold charcoal. They would cut the cedar into short logs, which they burned in a pit covered with dirt to keep out the air. After smoldering for several days, the resultant charcoal could be sold, especially in Austin, for heating and cooking. One cedar chopper loudly announced his arrival at market with this doggerel verse:

> My hands is black,
> My face is black,
> And I sell my coal
> Two bits a sack.
> Chah-coal![18]

According to local historian John Renford Taylor, "The cedar choppers worked very hard and played very much harder, turning their primitive, back country way of life into a proud culture as strong and unique as that of the Louisiana Cajuns."[19]

Certainly one of the most colorful cedar choppers to roam the woods of western Travis County was Alfred "Buck" Simpson, who also happened to be one of America's most highly decorated

17. Barbara Langham, "A Man's Got a Right to His Own Mind: Hill Country Cedar Choppers," *Texas Highways,* February 1985.
18. Ibid.
19. John Renford Taylor, "Discovering All There Is about the Lakeway Area," *Lake Travis View,* April 25, 1991.

World War I veterans. He grew up in Eanes (later absorbed by West Lake Hills), but headed west to "the mountains" for a week at a time to make charcoal. Buck never learned to read or write; in fact, he got into so many fights in school that the headmaster pointedly suggested he discontinue his formal education. Buck's brother had a slightly different explanation for their school exodus: "We went to Pleasant Valley School for three months and got in fights three times a day until we quit school." A few years later, Buck was part of America's Expeditionary Force, sent to Europe to help England and France defeat Germany in World War I. On October 12, 1918, Buck wiped out a German machine gun nest and held a German company at bay until reenforcements came up. His captain later wrote his family, "I told him to run, but he told me, 'Hell, I come from Texas, and I don't run from nobody.'" According to one account, only Sergeant Alvin York received more World War I medals than did Buck Simpson. When Buck died in 1969, at age seventy-three, a slightly hyperbolic Austin journalist wrote, "Buck Simpson was America's most decorated soldier of World War I. Buck grew up in the cedar hills around Austin. He could shoot a flying bird with a 22. He could whip his weight in wildcats. He didn't take too kindly to education or to the ways of the city. He was more at home in the hills."[20]

Buck Simpson

***

Gwendolyn Wunneberger is of a more recent vintage than most of the early settlers of western Travis County; in fact, she is still alive. Now in her early eighties, she is as feisty as ever. She recently announced to several Lakeway residents, "I am determined to fight to the death the Yankees and Californians who have come to destroy our history." (Author's note: When I first met her, she took one look at me and said, "You're not from here, right?" I responded that I was not. She then asked, "You're a Yankee, aren't ya?" When I allowed that this was also correct, she said, "I could tell by that frown on your face!")

Gwen's Grandfather Stubbs ran a grocery store in Austin, but he swapped it for a small ranch northwest of Dripping Springs on Fitzhugh Road because he no longer thought Austin a fit place to raise children. His new land produced cotton and corn, as well as Gwen, who was born there on February 6, 1930. After marrying World War II and Korean War navy veteran Joe Wunneberger, Gwen and Joe purchased forty-four acres on RR 620 in 1963, the same year the Lakeway Inn opened. She and Joe raised some cattle, geese, ducks, and chickens, but mostly goats and sheep, many of which were miniature in size. As late as 2008, she still had a llama and lots of dogs, which she insists she trains "with a small flyswatter."

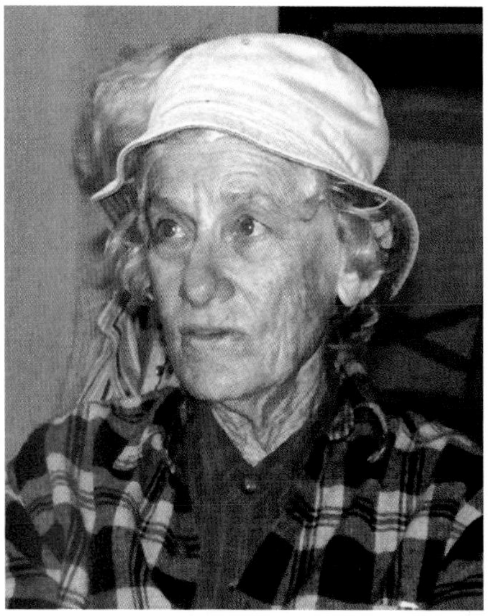

Gwendolyn Wunneberger

The two loves of Gwen's life are hunting and music, both of which she still enjoys. She shot her first deer when she was only eight, and as an adult she has hunted elk, antelope, and bear in Montana and Wyoming; moose, caribou, mountain goats, and grizzlies in Canada; and assorted big game in Africa. At age seventy-eight, she shot two

20. *Alfred "Buck" Simpson Scrapbook,* Lakeway Heritage Center.

marauding alligators, each of which exceeded ten feet. The first music she remembers consisted of religious songs played on Sunday by her daddy on the fiddle and her momma on the piano. When her brother returned from the Korean War in 1953, they started a family band called the 620 Ranch Hands. Her brother played the fiddle, her mother was still on the piano, and Gwen played guitar and sang. Other members were R. P. Sconci, David Bryant, and Calvin Buckhorn. The band was still playing in 1996, when it performed at Lakeway's annual Fourth of July celebration. Gwen's mother was then ninety-nine, and the youngest member of the band was seventy-one. Says Gwen, "People have no idea what they've missed if they don't have music in their lives."

According to her reckoning, Gwen has played in "about twenty-five movies," including *Big Dolly and the Texas Wheel, Heartbreak Hotel,* and *Red-Headed Stranger.* Her horses, goats, sheep, and even a goose have also appeared in several Hollywood films.

Gwen has lived in four log cabins in her life, but the most important one is on her Lakeway property. She says it was built in 1852, with its lean-to additions added later. Its cedar logs came from the small creek that still runs through the land. Without question, because of its age and its original construction, it is the most historically important building in Lakeway.

Gwen and Joe recently sold their property, and the fate of their cabin remains uncertain. In the best of all worlds it would become a treasured landmark to remind future generations how folks once lived long before there ever was a Lakeway.

***

In 1955, Abraham Lincoln "Abe" Hutto and his brother Nevil purchased 2,600 acres in what would eventually become part of Lakeway. Abe's land was on both sides of Flint Rock Road and Nevil's was farther to the north. Abe, who was born in 1925 near Del Rio, fought and earned a Purple Heart in World War II while fighting with the U.S. Marines in the South Pacific. He later worked in the oil business, but he became better known as a bronc rider and roper during his forty-year rodeo career in Texas and Oklahoma. He also did some semi-serious guitar-picking and singing. Abe and his wife, Jeanne, raised Angora goats, sheep, and a few cattle on their Flint Rock Road ranch, where their prize herding dog, Sam, became almost as famous as his master.

One of Abe's closest friends was legendary Texas writer J. Frank Dobie, who inscribed a book he gave Abe, "To my partner in several crimes, including sheep raising." Abe summed up his life by saying, "I'd rather have one last grain of luck than a whole rice paddy full of brains."

Abe died in 2004. He was seventy-nine and had never been sick a day in his life. In an interview in 2008, his widow Jeanne recalled what the area looked like when they purchased their land in 1955:

When we first looked at our land, people asked us, "Why do you want to buy land out there? There's nothing out there but cedar choppers and bootleggers." The only way onto the property was an old cedar chopper's road approximately where Flint Rock Road is today. There was also no electricity.

Abraham Lincoln "Abe" Hutto

RR 620 was then two lanes and much of Highway 71 was still a dirt road. There was no bridge over the Pedernales River. If you wanted to go to Marble Falls, you had to take a ferry across the Pedernales or you had to drive down to Johnson City. When we drove to Austin, we took 71. As far as I remember, 2244 had not yet been built. There was the Old Bee Cave Road that went to Oak Hill which at the time was nothing but a big beer joint.

Tommy Johnson ran his Trading Post where Jim Bob's Barbeque now is on Highway 71.[21] Tommy was a wonderful fellow. He got burned out twice, but the entire community helped him rebuild. He was a good old Texas boy and very generous. There was also Wallace's filling station on the other side of 71, where the Spring Hill restaurant now is. Mr. Wallace sold gas, cold drinks, and bait. There was precious little on 620. For any kind of serious shopping, we had to go to Austin.

John Henry Lohman's granddaughter Anna Reinke owned the land just to the northeast of us. She lived in her trolley car where Lohman's Spur and Flint Rock Road now meet. The county delivered water to her cistern, and Tommy Johnson delivered her groceries. After we moved in, Abe would go down and chop wood for her. When she needed anything else, she would put up a red flag and Abe would help her. She was so afraid that our property would be cut off from 620 that she deeded us a small

The Hutto Ranch overlooking Lake Travis

21. The Johnson family had a long history of running the Trading Post in the Bee Cave area. Over the years, it burned down several times but was always rebuilt. When the Huttos bought their property in 1955, the Trading Post included a gas station, a store, and a café, which Tommy's wife ran. Tommy also had a bulldozer he used for various construction and excavating work, including laying out some of Lakeway's earliest roads. In 1991, the Trading Post building became Jim Bob's Barbeque, which closed in 2008.

parcel of her land so we would always have access.[22]

Most of the land we owned is now part of Flint Rock Falls or The Hills of Lakeway.[23]

***

Those who settled western Travis County were a courageous and determined lot, made doubly so because of the rugged terrain and the capricious whims of Mother Nature. How challenging, even frightening, must have been the first impressions of those accustomed to the more hospitable environs of the South or Midwest from which they came. Lakeway's current Parks and Recreation Department director, Andra Dearing, was only eight years old when her family moved from Illinois to the Pace Bend area in 1976 yet her description of the terrain was little different than settlers might have encountered 100 years earlier:

> Western Travis County was very different from the cornfields of Illinois where I was born. I remember thinking that the Hill Country resembled something more like mountains than hills. And everything seemed "out to getcha." By that I mean, there were cactus, red wasps, scorpions, poisonous snakes, centipedes, fire ants, and no running through the grass barefoot because of stickers or sand burrs, not to mention the stifling heat of summer. I also remember the trees looked more like shrubs than actual trees, very tiny in comparison to Illinois trees. Then there were the rocks—rocks and more rocks, everywhere!

***

Lakeway would eventually be carved out of lands situated between the Teck community to the north and Bee Cave on the south, both of which had existed for more than 100 years before the beginning of Lakeway in 1963. At the time, cultured Austinites might still have considered the western end of Travis County to be a remote wilderness, inhabited by hardscrabble folks barely eking out a living, but in truth, these rugged souls typified the hardworking, determined people who made America into a great nation, and whose progeny can still be found in the area, even in sophisticated Austin.

22. For a copy of Anna Reinke's will, see Chapter 4.
23. Interview with Steve Swan and Lew Carlson, January 17, 2008.

CHAPTER FOUR

HIN NACH TEXAS - JOHANN HEINRICH LOHMANN AND THE GERMAN IMPACT ON THE HILL COUNTRY

The beautiful blue of the skies, the clear atmosphere so peculiar to this country, the sun and its powerful rays, charmed me, [as did] the great uncultivated, uninhabited land, tempting tropical fruits, Indians and wild animals, too, to break the monotony of existence, and above all else, golden freedom.

EMMA MURCK ALTGELT, WHO EMIGRATED TO TEXAS IN 1854.
HER GREAT-GRANDSON, ERNEST ALTGELT, IS A LAKEWAY RESIDENT.

Nowhere does the German race prosper better than in the Republic of Texas, where are untied all of the advantages of the tropics with the comforts of the temperate zones.

VEREIN ZUM SCHUTZE DEUTSCHER EINWANDERER IN TEXAS
(SOCIETY FOR THE PROTECTION OF GERMAN IMMIGRANTS IN TEXAS)

OFFERING GENEROUS LAND GRANTS, THE NEW Republic of Texas encouraged both domestic and foreign immigration to help populate its vast empty spaces. Among the foreigners taking advantage of this opportunity, by far the largest numbers were Germans. By 1860, there were more German-born residents in San Antonio than American born. Immigration societies often controlled large tracts of land and frequently aided the immigrants. Typical was the *Adelsverein,* an aristocratic society formed in the early 1840s to aid Germans heading for Texas. Many came to farm, but there were also educators, clergymen, musicians, writers, architects, and skilled artisans, some of whose stone buildings still stand. Without question, they raised the quality of life in Texas, and some of their names can still be found on Lakeway street signs and gravestones.

The first German colony in Texas was the Industry Settlement, established in 1831 some eighty-five miles southeast of Austin. Later immigrants made their way west toward Austin, settling in such places as Oldenburg, New Ulm, Weimar, Freisburg, Waelder, Uhland, and Niederwald. The more famous settlements, such as New Braunfels and Fredericksburg, resulted from a second wave of immigrants who settled to the south and west of Austin.

Not all was milk and honey for these new residents, at least not according to one early German traveler in Texas:

> The vice of drunkenness has reached the highest level here, and the number of those selling alcoholic beverages is beyond all belief. In no other country is more alcohol being consumed in relation to the population than here. Anyone who enters an establishment where alcoholic beverages are sold is welcomed with a glass in his hand. It would be in bad taste if one refused. Since one often has company, it frequently happens that man ceases to be human and sinks to the level of an animal.

Considerably more salutary were the German musical contributions to the culture of the new republic. In 1845, a well-known, albeit controversial, German poet and lyricist by the name of August Henrick Hoffman von Fallersleben composed a song for his friend Adolph Fuchs, a Lutheran minister who had recently migrated to Texas, where he eventually settled near Marble Falls. The first song of a volume titled *Texanische Lieder (Texas Songs)* was called "Der Stern von

Texas," this more than a half century before Long Horn fans first sang "The Eyes of Texas."

> Der Stern von Texas
> Hin nach Texas! Hin nach Texas!
> Wo der Stern im blauen Felde führt
> Jedes Herz für Recht and Freiheit
> Und für Wahrheit froh entzündet
> Dahin sehnt mein Herz sich ganz.
>
> The Star of Texas
> Onward to Texas; onward to Texas
> Where the star on its blue field leads
> Every heart for right and freedom
> And for truth that burns so brightly
> That's where my heart will forever be.

Von Fallersleben, who never made it to Texas, is better known for another song he wrote in 1841, "Das Lied des Deutschen" ("The Song of the Germans"), the first stanza of which begins, "Deutschland, Deutschland über alles, über alles in die Welt" ("Germany, Germany over everything, over everything in the world"). Following its notoriety during the Hitler years, "Das Lied des Deutschen" was banned in 1945, along with the Third Reich.

***

Some 30,000 Germans arrived in the ports of Galveston and New Orleans between 1842 and 1845, including several who would rise to prominence in western Travis County. Among them was Johann Heinrich Lohmann, who was born in 1786 in the village of Hildesheim, just southeast of Hannover.[1] Like many of his countrymen, his dissatisfaction with political, social, and military conditions motivated Lohmann to leave his homeland. He had fought in the Prussian army during its brief alliance with Napoleon, but later fought against France and was wounded in the Battle of Leipzig in 1814 and again in the Battle of Waterloo the following year. According to grandson Frederick Lohmann, a saber wound in his grandfather's leg left a scar that allowed the family to identify his body in 1936 when it was removed from the family graveyard because of the rising waters of Lake Travis and re-interred in White Rock Cemetery in Bee Cave.[2]

No longer willing to be cannon fodder for the capricious whims of German princes and kings, Johann Heinrich Lohmann set sail for America in 1842, where years later his name was anglicized to John Henry Lohmann.[3] There would be no regrets. As he later told his son Albert, "Germany is a hot bed of contention and strife. As long as there is a Germany, there will always be wars, and none of my children should ever go back."

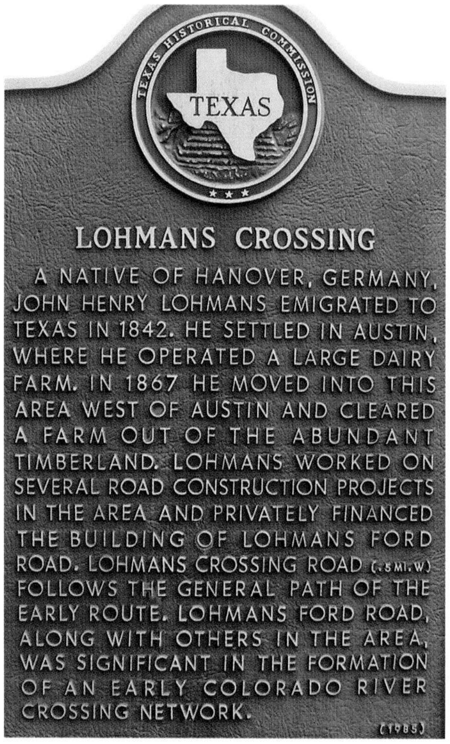

Texas Historical Marker in Lakeway's Ladin Lane. John Henry's descendants preferred the original spelling of the Lohmann name rather than the single "n."

After landing in Galveston aboard the *Neptune*, Lohmann, his wife, Antoinette Sophia, and their four children traveled by a small steamer up the bayou to Houston, which daughter Christine Lohmann Thackera later described as having "fierce mud, making it a most desirable place to leave as soon as possible." The family did leave the next day for Travis County, "traveling in two wagons, each pulled by four yoke of oxen, in weather that was cold and rainy and through mud which made the

1. His tombstone lists Lohmann's birth as 1799, but Travis County records his birth as 1786.
2. Another version has John Henry Lohmann's skeleton being identified because of a scar on his skull incurred in his battles against Napoleon. Willis Bodine e-mail, January 21, 2011.
3. Great-great-grandson Jim Ferril believes that Henry Lohmann first landed alone in Mexico about 1840. He then walked north into Texas and later returned to Germany and brought his wife, Antoinette Sophia, and their four children to Texas, landing in Galveston in 1842. E-mail sent to Lakeway archivist Mike Boston, April 11, 2008. Ferril's e-mail also contained considerable additional material on the early Lohmann family.

journey most disagreeable and fatiguing."[4]

When the family arrived at Hornsby Bend, just east of the Austin Colony, it was evening and they were afraid to continue their journey to Austin because, as Christine put it, "Indians were liable to get their scalp before they could reach their goal." Nevertheless, the family soon continued on to Austin, which one contemporary described as "largely uninhabited with streets filled with grass and weeds, the abode of bats, lizards, and stray cattle." There were also approximately thirty small dwellings and a very primitive, albeit temporary, capitol building.

In 1845, Lohmann opened Austin's first dairy farm about two and one-half miles northeast of what is now the University of Texas campus.[6] He used an oxcart to deliver the milk of his eleven cows to the few dwellings that then made up Austin. That same year, tragedy struck when first wife Antoinette Sophia died. Needing a mother for his four children, Lohmann allowed his friend, Judge Reuben Hornsby, to introduce him to Rosine Caroline Charlotte Weichler-Weber, a German-born widow with a young son. It was a quick courtship. According to one account, they married the day they formally met. Chief Justice Stephen Cumming conducted the ceremony while standing in his oxcart on the grounds where the first permanent capitol building would be completed in 1853.

During the next fifteen years, John and Rosine added nine children of their own. They also prospered financially. The 1850 census valued their property and possessions at $1,800. Ten years later their worth had grown to $2,650.

As was true of many German immigrants, Lohmann did not support slavery or Texas joining the Confederacy, although by some reports he was not a Unionist. His experiences in his homeland had left him abhorring all wars. After twice narrowly escaping being lynched during the early months of the Civil War for "being a Union man," Lohmann homesteaded two pieces of land near where Hurst Creek flowed into the Colorado River. It was the early 1860s, and the Lohmanns were thought to be the first whites to settle in the immediate area, although an Abe Anderson purchased nearby land a few months later.[7]

Marauding Indians were then as common as they were unwelcome in western Travis County.

Sketch of Austin, 1840[5]

4. Christine, who was born in 1837, was John Henry Lohmann's third child by his first wife. She described the family's early history in an interview published in *The Semi-Weekly Farm News*, January 23, 1914. Christine, who married Jacob H. Thackara, died in Galveston, Texas, in 1919. Her older brother Theodore, who was born in 1834, also died in Galveston, but in the infamous flood of 1900.

5. Artist unknown. See Mary Clarke Whatley, *David Burnet* (Austin: The Pemberton Press, 1969), 227.

6. Some sources mistakenly have Lohmann's dairy farm located on what became the University of Texas campus. Great-great-grandson Willis Bodine, who lived on the Lohmann homestead in the 1940s and 1950s, corrected this error. E-mail to the author, January 19, 2011.

7. The story of Lohmann's near lynching in Austin comes from Frank Brown's *Annals of Travis County and the City of Austin*, published in 1901. A very different version has Lohmann being jailed and nearly hanged after being falsely accused of giving aid to the notorious Willys gang. The latter account comes from the aforementioned Jim Ferril (op. cit., note 3). Ferril also believes that Lohmann's alleged Union sympathies might have been involved in the Willys account.

Years later, Christine described her sister's near abduction:

> Father, my brother and I had gone to the creek near the house to gather pecans. She remained at the house. We heard her screaming and brother, who was in a tree, looked and saw an Indian putting her on a horse. We all dashed for the house, and the Indian saw father with gun in hand approaching so rapidly that he became frightened and dropped her as he ran away. Men in those days always carried their guns when they left the premises.[8]

With a fast-growing family that now totaled fourteen, Lohmann built a large two-story stone house near the Colorado River, with massive cedar timbers to support the floors. He used smaller cedar boards for the floors and to frame the doors and windows. He also added five smaller buildings for the tenant farmers who helped him clear and work the land.

In addition to the wild grapes, pecans, fish, and game that were readily found near the river, the family raised vegetables, corn, and cotton, which Rosine spun into yarn for the children's clothing. They also made their own shoes from the tanned hides of domestic and wild animals. In addition, they harvested wild herbs for medicines, kept beehives, and produced soap from lye and candles from animal fats.

John Henry Lohmann was a great believer in education, so much so that he paid Karl Frederick Paul Reinke to teach his children. Karl apparently did such a good job that daughter Emaline married him.

Lohmann also built and maintained Lohman's Crossing Road, which contributed to the growth of the area that would one day become Lakeway. According to Lohmann's great-granddaughter Alma Buchan Babb, "This crossing could sometimes be jumped, but was up to a horse's belly when the waters were high."[9]

In her own way, Rosine Lohmann was just as remarkable as her husband. In addition to raising a family that included fourteen children, her son Albert reported that she had psychic powers. These visions led her to predict forthcoming deaths of family members and even neighbors. She also believed that the power of prayer could

John Henry Lohmann, Jr., born in 1859, and his wife, Lucy Johnson, are in the middle. Their children, from left to right, are Claude, Adolph, Corine, Vera or Burrie E.(?), and Louis. The individual on the far right is unidentified.

8. Ibid.
9. Alma Buchan Babb, *After the Captain Reached the River* (unpublished family memoir, n.d.).

Lohmann's Ford Road allowed travelers to "ford" the Colorado River and reach Anderson Mill and other settlements on the other side. After the county built a low-water bridge in 1934, it became known as Lohman's Crossing Road. The bridge and crossing disappeared when Mansfield Dam created Lake Travis, although Lohman's Crossing is today one of Lakeway's main thoroughfares.

end droughts, and Albert later recalled at least one occurrence when such was the case.

John Henry and Rosine's daughter Emaline "Emma" Lohmann Reinke Maul, who was born in 1852, had her own extraordinary story to tell, particularly after first husband Karl Reinke was murdered in 1882 in what the *Austin Statesman* called "The Assassination at Flint Rock."

Karl was the postmaster and owner of the Flint Rock Store. The perpetrator was Julius Steeb, although his name has also been spelled Steep or Stebbs in public records. The *Austin Statesman* described Steeb as a German with "thick heavy lips who spoke broken English." Steeb allegedly shot Reinke because of "an old grudge about a sewing machine." Singer sewing machines had certainly been prized possessions since their introduction in 1851, but it seems highly unlikely they were worthy of murder. There had to be more to the story than the meager facts in the newspaper, and, indeed, there was.

Years later, Emma, who after the murder married Charles Ernest Maul, told daughter Anna her version of her father's murder, which Anna dutifully recorded:

> My mother and dad had a little grocery store and post office named Flint Rock. In election years the election was held at Flint Rock, and since it was always an all day affair, they had a keg of beer for refreshments, and on one such occasion Mrs. Straile's (correct spelling was Strahle) first husband got drunk and on his way home his wagon turned over while going down Hurst Creek Hill and he was badly injured and died from the effects of it. Then his wife married Mr. Julius Steep. Mrs. Steep always hated my father over the drinkenness and death of Straile and there were always unkind words exchanged between the two. Mrs. Steep hissed her husband on until he came over to Mamma's house and asked for Reinke and Mamma told him that he and Mr. Exner were back of the big hill cutting cedar logs and pulling them out of the hollers by horse, and Mr. Steep sneaked up without Reinke or Exner seeing him and shot daddy twice, once above the knee and the other into his chest. Daddy died instantly without really knowing what had happened. Then Mr. Exner came and told Mamma that Reinke was killed but that he didn't know who did it, and Mamma said it

This large headstone on Ladin Lane belongs to A. C. Strahle, whose accidental death on Hurst Creek Hill set off "the Assassination at Flint Rock." There is, however, considerable evidence that the body is actually buried some forty feet to the northwest, along with his infant son.

must have been Mr. Steep, for he had come to the house and Mamma had told him where he could find him. My daddy was very high tempered and Mrs. Steep was a spitfire and that is the way it all happened. Mr. Steep was soon caught by a sheriff, given a trial, and sentenced for 30 years in the penitentiary, and after he served 15, he received a pardon; in the meantime his wife had died and he married again and had moved to Galveston and there the Flood of 1900 got him.

Left: Emaline "Emma" Lohmann married Charles Ernest Maul after the murder of her husband, Karl Reinke. The two children above are Emma Ida Maul, born in 1885, and Walter M. Maul, born in 1887. The photo was likely taken in 1890. Right: Emma at her Austin home on Avenue C, shortly before her death in 1927.

Emma Lohmann Reinke Maul's daughter Anna was certainly one of the most colorful of John Henry Lohmann's descendants. In addition to being the driving force behind Austin's Baha'i congregation,[10] she cleared a fourteen-acre piece of land on Maul Hill in the late 1930s, which was located to the northwest of the current corner of Flint Rock Road and Lohman's Spur. For twenty-five years she kept a diary describing the preparation of her land, which she called "the Rockies," and where she would eventually live in a transplanted Austin trolley car. The sample pages below are from her original, unedited diary, which is now on display in the Lakeway Heritage Center:

Anna Reinke

On Dec. 30, 1938 - Derril Gene Maul (age 9 years) and I began to burn stumps on the ground on which I expect to build a home in the future, and the following day, while we were on the same job again, Norma Lallier (age 15 years) and Roselle Maul (age 13) rode up on horse and mule back, and we ask them to go back to the Fred Maul home to get us some cake and coffee, and when it was brought we warmed the coffee on the stump coals, and sat down on the ground and enjoyed our little New Years Eve party.

January 6, 1939 - I went home with Edgar Bohls and spent the night with Bettie Bohls. The next day Edgar Bohls, Beuford Maul, Derril Gene Maul, Roselle Maul and I worked again on the plot of ground cutting down trees, piling brush against the stumps and carrying rocks by hand to bridge gulies, but on account of rain we got to work only a few hours that day, although had our little tea party again, serving cake, crackers, candy and coffee.

July 16, 1939 - In July the week beginning the 16th Mr. & Mrs. G.W. Glass and two small children came to Austin to get me to select a place for a well, which Mr. Glass & son Duck drilled that week at a depth of 147 feet and finding plenty water. The cost of well was $100.00.

December 28, 1939 - Ten more fruit trees were planted by Beuford Maul, Roselle Maul, Dirrel Gene Maul and Anna Reinke. And just as we got through it began to snow for about half a day. This ends the years work on the Rockies in 1939. Every thing was paid for out of my savings of one years dress making in 1939.

April 10, 1940 - An old street car for which I paid 30 dollars and 17 dollars & fifty cents for moving it to the Rockies.

January 23, 1941 - I spend two days at the street car, screened the east and west windows by myself, as workmen were scarce on account of flue and the Marshall Ford Dam work.

October 31, 1942 - I moved from 4410 Ave. C Austin Texas to the Rockies to live in my Street Car. And renamed the place Flint Rock, which was the name of this place 70 years ago when my father had a Post Office half a mile from here by the name of Flint Rock.

Grand-niece Patty Maul Smithers said of her Aunt Anna, "The one thing I remember most was her kindness and non-judgmental attitude. She had an aura of peace and tranquility about her. She practiced a religion called Baha'i [and] lived her life by its doctrine. Today, when I go into

10. Founded in nineteenth-century Persia, the Baha'i faith embraced the spiritual unity of all mankind. According to John Henry Lohmann's great-great-granddaughter, Mary Stewart Hicks, Anna embraced Baha'i after a visit to her sister Charlotte Reinke Fosselman in Washington, D.C. Letter to the author, November 15, 2010.

her streetcar, which is my art studio, a feeling of peace and serenity always comes over me. I know she is there with me."

Anna Reinke lived in her Austin city trolley car from 1942 until shortly before her death in 1971. The trolley was then moved to the front of an antiques store across from the White Rock Cemetery on Highway 71, before ending up in New Braunfels as Patty Smithers's art studio.

When Anna became older and needed help, she would hang a red flag outside her trolley car and neighbors Jeanne and Abe Hutto would come to her aid. The Huttos became such good friends with Anna that she included them in her hand-drawn will, which now resides in the Lakeway Heritage Center.

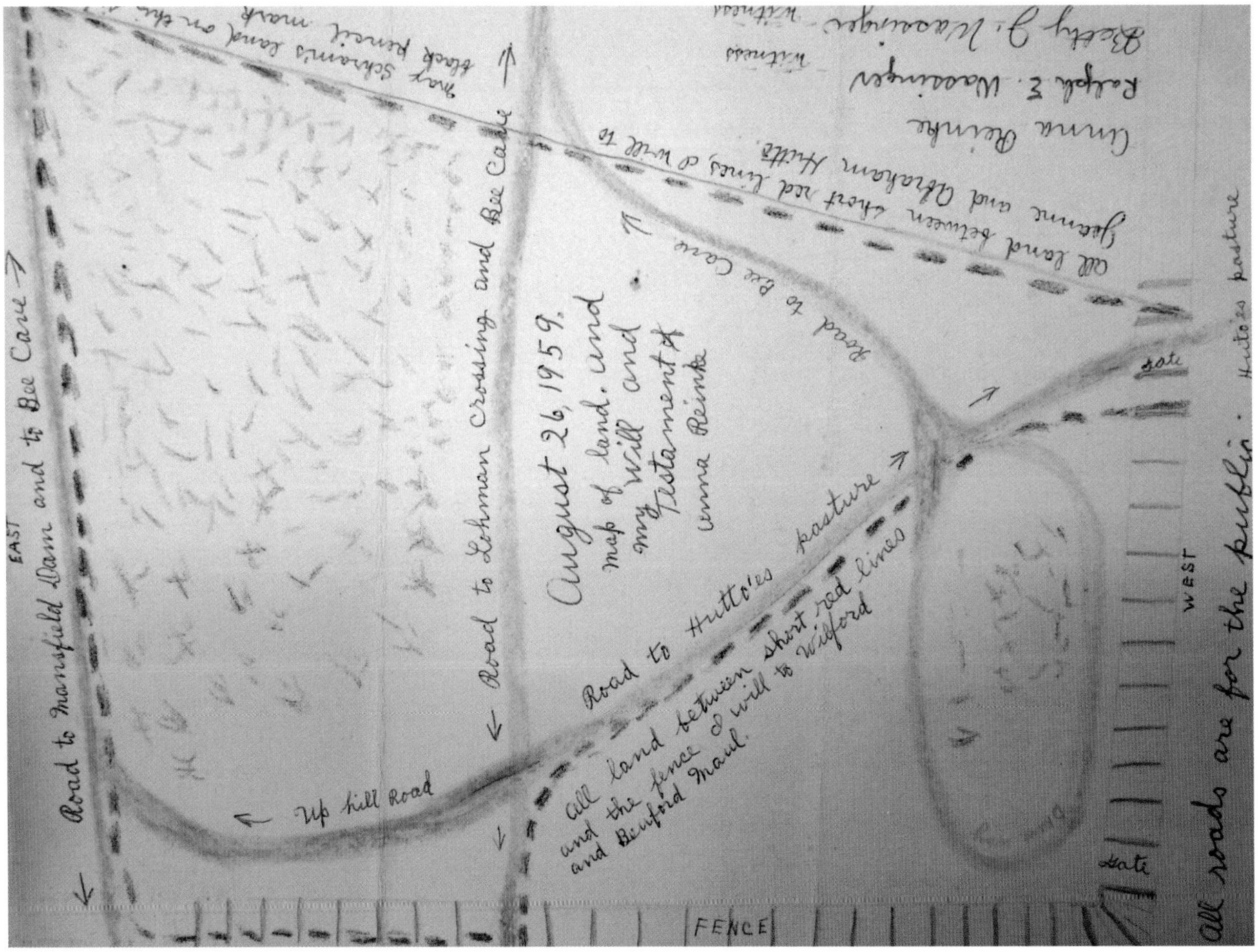

Charlie and Ellen Sylvester Lohmann

John Henry Lohmann, who died in 1872, launched an impressive family of thirteen children, at least fifty grandchildren, and more than 115 great-grandchildren. His second wife, Rosine, died in 1891. Her son from her first marriage, Charles Weber, whom John Henry adopted, was killed in 1864 near what is now Hamilton Pool. Accounts differ as to whether the perpetrators were marauding Indians or bounty-seeking "bushwhackers" looking for Union sympathizers. The descendants of John and Rosine would eventually marry into such locally prominent German-American families as Nelle, Meier, Freirich, Neuenschwander, Reinke, Maul, Thiele, Sylvester, and Wolf. According to great-great-grandson Jim Ferril, their "progeny have been ministers, cattle barons, engineers, policemen, plumbers, doctors, nurses, authors, [and] virtually any occupation you can imagine." They also scattered far and wide; for example, grandson George Lohmann, who left home at age sixteen, became one of Paraguay's largest landowners. Closer to home, grandson Charles "Charlie" Lohmann became a well-known fiddler before his death in Austin in 1956.

In 1936, in anticipation of the completion of

Family records found in the Austin Historical Society list the year of John Henry Lohmann's birth as 1786 rather than 1799 as stated above on his tombstone in the White Rock Cemetery. Rosine Weber Lohmann's name on her tombstone reflects an Americanized spelling of her first name.

the Marshall Ford Dam (now Mansfield Dam) that created Lake Travis, the Lohmann home and outbuildings were dismantled and the family graves were moved either to the White Rock Cemetery near the corner of Highway 71 and Hamilton Pool Road or to the Maul Cemetery in the Yaupon Creek Subdivision on Lohman's Spur.

The night before the bodies of John Henry and Rosine Lohmann were moved to the White Rock Cemetery, Charlotte "Lottie" Lohmann Colley had an eerie dream about her grandfather. She saw a tall man with a wispy goatee, dressed in black, wearing a derby hat, and standing next to an ancient black hearse. When she related the dream to her father, Albert Sidney Lohmann, he told her it was a perfect description of her grandfather and the hearse that transported him when he died.

***

When Leonard T. Eck left his native Germany is unclear, but we do know he owned two stores in Austin, the first of which opened around 1870. According to a contemporary newspaper advertisement, Eck sold his merchandise for "fully 15 to 20 per cent less than current prices in New York City."

For reasons unknown, Leonard Eck subsequently moved twenty miles to the west and opened a general store near the present corner of RR 620 and Debba Road. When Eck petitioned to add a post office in 1900, authorities informed him its name must have at least four letters. Eck thus became Teck. Leonard operated the Teck Post Office until 1919, when it reverted to the Cedar Valley Post Office. It reopened in 1925, and two years later Annie L. Stewart took over until it closed for good in 1929. Leonard Eck also helped establish a one-room school on what is now Kollmeyer Road.

Notice the postmark and address of the postcard on the next page.

SPECIAL
BARGAINS

We have the pleasure to announce a new departure–the purchase and selection of our stock in order to enable us to quote lower prices than others who buy on long time and ask big prices in these days of panic and hard times.

Our Agent has instructions to watch every sale and every failure: to look after every house on the verge of bankruptcy and ruin, and with cash in hand to buy the lump or the lot. Not by favor, but by merit alone, will we maintain and increase our unrivaled reputation.

We deal in good goods and not trash, and believe masses will patronize that house that sells the best goods for the least money. Hence we throw out among the masses these matchless goods and matchless prices, to check the insane and criminal practice of wasting money for the paltry consideration of a little credit.

Respectively submitted to the Cash Trade only, by

L. ECK

101 E. Pecan St. AUSTIN

Congress Avenue., South Austin

New York Office 466 & 468 Broadway

***

Dietrich Bohls and a man named Rhomuller may well have been the first permanent residents of Bee Cave. Bohls was born in Oldenburg, Germany, in 1797 and landed in Texas in 1842, the same year as John Henry Lohmann. He worked his way up the Colorado River before eventually homesteading along the upper reaches of Barton Creek. Rhomuller, who was referred to as "the Swede," possessed unusual masonry and building skills. Perhaps his masonry has lasted for more than 150 years because Swedish masons were then using pigs' blood and horsehair to strengthen their lime, sand, and water mixture. Rhomuller constructed several cabins for Bohls, some of which have been restored. Rhomuller also built a home for the Freitag family on RR 620 near Highway 71. The Galleria Mall and the H.E.B. Store now cover much of the Bohls's properties, as well as those of Edward and Henry Spillmann, who were also German immigrants.

***

Bee Cave's most successful early entrepreneur was certainly Carl Beck, who emigrated from Germany when he was sixteen. He opened a store in 1873 near the current corner of Highway 71 and Hamilton Pool Road, which became a focal point for commerce and news. It also hosted social affairs, including serious poker games that sometimes ended violently. The Beck Store sold food, dry goods, kerosene, harnesses, building supplies, and his own cigars, which were rolled by five employees on the front porch.

Several of these original Bohls cabins built in the mid-nineteenth century have been restored in Bee Cave at the entrance of Spanish Oaks on Highway 71.

Beck also raised cattle and crops and operated a gristmill and a cotton gin. According to one source, bees swarming in the gabled end of his store created the appearance of a cave, thereby giving the community its name. According to local lore, Beck also fought in the Battle of Pack Saddle Mountain in 1871, which allegedly was the last major encounter against area Indians. In 1877, Beck began a thirty-eight-year stint as postmaster. He eventually sold his store to his daughter Helen and her husband, Carl Lallier.

Carl and Louise Otten Beck

***

The story of Henry and Dora Reimers began in 1871 outside a village in Holstein, which was Germany's northernmost province. He was a shepherd and she a dairy maid. They fell in love and dreamed of going to America. But how could they fulfill such a dream when his pay was the equivalent of $40 a year and hers considerably less? Dora was also so sickly that Henry was warned, "You'd better not marry that girl because she's going to die, and you'll be left alone." But love conquers all, and the young couple married and saved, until in 1882 they were able to book passage to America. Henry's marriage to the sickly Dora would last almost seventy years and produce nine children.

Henry and Dora traveled by train from New York to Austin and then Burnet, from where they continued by covered wagon to Shovel Mountain, where they began herding sheep for twenty-five dollars a month. They also purchased their first cow. Three years later they moved to Cypress Mill, some fifteen miles southwest of Bee Cave, where they bought their own 100-acre property and leased additional land from the state for four cents an acre. They also purchased a team of horses and a wagon. Their son Bernhard began driving loads of mutton and wool to Austin when he was only twelve. He would begin in the evening, drive all night, market the meat and wool in Austin the next morning, bank the money, and then drive the thirty miles home. The Reimers became so successful that by 1900 they owned 3,000 acres, including land surrounding Hamilton Pool, which Bernhard later managed as part of his Pedernales River Ranch. Bernhard, who never attended formal school, served on the local school board for fifty years. He also became a land appraiser for the federal government, and for more than fifty years served as caretaker for Hamilton Pool, the most pristine and scenic spot in western Travis County. Another Reimers descendant, James Andre Patton, became an early postmaster in Oak Hill, and in 1964 a more recent descendant, James M. White, opened one of Austin's best known drinking and music establishments, the Broken Spoke. Arguably, the most enduring legacy of the Reimers family occurred in November 2005, when Milton and Joy Reimers sold more than 2,400 acres of their pristine property on Hamilton Pool Road, including three miles of continuous frontage along the Pedernales River, to Travis County. Now known as Travis County's Milton Reimers Ranch Park, it features rock climbing, eighteen miles of mountain biking and walking trails, and fishing in the Pedernales.

***

Without question, the hard-working German immigrants contributed greatly to the development of western Travis County. Many were progressive thinkers who opposed slavery and established literary and music societies. They also began schools and were extremely successful business entrepreneurs. For good reason, Lohman, Maul, Beck, Bohls, Freitag, Haas, Otten, Reimers, Spillman, and Sylvester remain revered names in the Hill Country.

CHAPTER FIVE

A RIVER RUNS THROUGH IT: THE COLORADO, MANSFIELD DAM, AND LAKE TRAVIS

We came to the river, which is sheltered on either side by luxuriant pecan trees, ash trees, poplars, elms, willows, and wild grapes, much higher and larger than those of Castile. The river has sand banks all along its margin, showing the high water mark, and it is three-quarters of a mile wide. Its water is the best we have found.

Spanish priest Isidro Felix Espinosa, who explored the Colorado River in 1709

Not until well into the 20th century, with the creation of the Lower Colorado River Authority, did the Colorado really measure up to the expectations of men and women who first settled along its banks in the 1820s. The chain of lakes in the Texas Hill Country created by LCRA's dams eliminated the problem of catastrophic flooding, provided electrical power, enhanced recreational possibilities and contributed to a quality of life which continues to lure newcomers to the river's sprawling basin.

Mike Cox, *Frontier River*, 1997

This land was nothin' until they put that water over there [Lake Travis]. A man'd get a purty good crop started, then a big rise in the river'd wash it all away.

Bill Johnson, old-time Bee Cave resident

Colorado River at full flow. Courtesy of the Lower Colorado River Authority Corporate Archives.

EARLY CIVILIZATIONS OFTEN DEVELOPED ALONG THE banks of rivers, and Texas was no exception. Among its 11,000 named streams, thirteen are major rivers, including the Colorado, which is the longest in Texas. It is also the longest river in the United States contained within a single state. The Spanish dubbed it the Colorado, meaning red, although they surely were thinking of another river, for there is nothing red about the Colorado. Nor were the Spanish referring to the more famous Colorado River to the west that runs through the Grand Canyon. Perhaps an early cartographer confused the Colorado with the Brazos, which has a crimson appearance and red clay banks. Renowned nineteenth-century landscape architect Frederick Law Olmsted was greatly impressed by its "placid surface and transparent depths." He also accurately described the Colorado as being "blue-green in color."[1] Beginning in Sulphur Springs Draw in Dawson County, the Colorado flows 600 miles to the southeast before emptying into the Gulf of Mexico near Matagorda Bay. Along its meandering course, it drains a watershed of some 40,000 square miles, and, according to its biographer, Mike Cox, it historically served a wide variety of human beings:

> Long before the first European explorers saw the river, it served as a food, water, and timber source for native cultures. Later, the river provided the same essentials for settlers of European descent. They built their cabins and heated them with timber from the river's valley, they drank from the river, bathed in it, cooked with it, caught and ate its fish, hunted and cooked the game along its banks, grew their crops in its rich alluvial soil and when the river was high enough, floated their cotton downstream to market.[2]

***

In 1528, Spanish explorer Alvar Nuñez de Vaca landed close to where the city of Galveston became a reality three centuries later. During the next several years, he explored his way west, including the lower Colorado River, before turning south toward Mexico City in 1536. In two published accounts, he described the vegetation, animals, and Indians he encountered. He also gave the Indians phonetic Spanish names, which the tribes might have survived, but not the European diseases, against which they had no natural immunity.

In 1629 and again in 1632, Spanish explorer Father Juan de Salas reached the upper Colorado, followed by other Spanish expeditions in mid-century, all of which referred to the upper Colorado as the Nueces. In 1690, Alonso De León set up a mission on the Colorado near La Grange, some fifty miles downstream from present-day Austin. A contemporary cartographer named Siguenze mistakenly called it the San Marcos River, which was not corrected until the mid-eighteenth century. One of the early explorers described the river by La Grange as being "made beautiful by trees, especially pecans [but the woods] were covered with ticks, red bugs, and other vermin."[3]

In 1709, Father Isidro Felix Espinosa led a small expedition farther upstream to where Onion Creek flows into the Colorado on the south side of present-day Austin. Father Espinosa, who hoped to convert the local Indians, described an idyllic scene:

> The vines are very large and the bunches are larger and the grapes thicker [than in Spain], the skin being tougher, but the fruit is sweet and palatable. Mulberry trees are found everywhere along the arroyos and rivers. Their fruit is very sweet and the leaves large, as large as those of trees planted in orchards. The

1. Frederick Law Olmsted, *A Journey Through Texas* (Austin: University of Texas Press, 1986), 129. The book was originally published in 1857.
2. Mike Cox, "Introductory Essay," *Frontier River: Exploration and Settlement of the Colorado River* (Austin: Lower Colorado River Authority, 1997), iii.
3. *Frontier River*, 24.

> nuts are so abundant that throughout the land the natives gather them, using them for food the greater part of the year. . . .
>
> The variety of birds of various colors and sweet song is great. The deer are so numerous that they resemble flocks of goats and are met at every step. The buffalo is a singular beast among the wild life of this country. . . . Its flesh is like that of the cows of Castile although better in taste and lightness. It constitutes the most common food of the nations that live in the neighborhood of the Tejas Indians. There are flocks of wild turkeys which are found at every step. There are bears, lions, tigers [probably cougars or mountain lions], foxes, and a great variety of other wild animals. Fish are so plentiful that there is not a creek, river, or pond where mullets, haddock, bagre, sea brim or buffalo fish, mobarra, and every other species known are not found.[4]

Espinosa and his men also discovered hemp growing in abundance, but they were unable to locate the Tejas Indians for whom they planned to set up a mission. The Indians, of course, were not as interested in Christianity as they were in trading for Spanish horses.

The Spanish were not the only Europeans exploring Texas and the Colorado River. In 1685, the peripatetic Frenchman René-Robert Cavelier, Sieur de La Salle, along with 200 men, landed near the mouth of the Colorado, but most of his party were wiped out by disease and Indians. La Salle, who had also explored extensively in the upper Midwest and lower Canada, made a final excursion to Texas in 1687 to chart its rivers, before being murdered that same year by his own men. La Salle's explorations also forced Spain to step up its claims to the Southwest and later led to the United States' unsuccessful claim that Texas should be part of its 1803 Louisiana Purchase.

In 1714 and 1717, another party of Frenchmen, under the leadership of Louis Juchereau de St. Denis, explored Central Texas, ostensibly to work with and set up missions for the Indians. In addition to trading tobacco, liquor, and firearms, these early French explorers introduced dogs, chickens, goats, and pigs, some of which may have come from Haiti. They also triggered an angry response by the Spanish, who claimed what they called Northern New Spain as their own.

The French's failure to compete successfully with the Spanish, in part because of their inability to entice their countrymen to settle in the Southwest, eventually forced them to give up their Texas explorations and claims. Nevertheless, France would be the first foreign country to recognize the Republic of Texas after it successfully broke away from Mexico in 1836, and its embassy still stands in Austin, although it is now a museum.

Nineteenth-century engraving of
Rene-Robert Cavelier, Sieur de La Salle

By the early 1800s, Spain had numerous outposts on the Colorado, San Marcos, and Guadalupe Rivers. But when Spain also was unable to encourage her citizens to settle in Northern New Spain, it opened these lands to Americans, hoping they would be able to control the Indians. Among these early American settlers were Moses Austin and his son Stephen.

Moses envisioned a great seaport where the Colorado flowed into the Gulf of Mexico, which he planned

4. *Frontier River,* 27–28.

to call Austina. Stephen, however, launched his Little Colony on the Colorado near present-day Bastrop. He also claimed another parcel of land upstream, about which he wrote, "It takes in some rough mountain land and wild scenery. . . . I intend to keep this place permanently and make a mountain retreat and large sheep farm of it."[5] That did not happen, although part of this land would later bear his name as the capital of Texas. Clearly, during Austin's lifetime the rugged terrain and the presence of hostile Indians stood in the way of developing the Colorado River above Austin.

John and Mary Crownover Rabb, who had first arrived in Texas in 1823, were among the earliest Americans to settle along the Colorado River below Austin. Years later, Mary told her daughter about their first home in language as humble and disjointed as the cabin itself:

> Your Pa and him bilt a hous in a weeak. Tha [they] made a chimny to it and the door Shetter [shutter] was made of thick Slabs split out of thick peases of timber and the way we facend the door tha bored a hole in one of the logs incide close to the door shetter and then we had a large pin or peg and that was drove in hard and fast of nights and then the Indians could not get in. We had aerthing [earthen] floor in ouer house and then I was in my first Texas hous.[6]

An editor cleaned up Mary Babb's language when he later quoted her as saying, "Texas in the 1820s was a heaven for men and dogs, but a hell for women and oxen."[7]

Mexico declared its independence from Spain in 1821, and Texas did likewise from Mexico on March 2, 1836. In October 1837, the first congress of the new Republic of Texas appointed a committee to find a suitable site for its capital. The following year newly elected President Mirabeau B. Lamar convinced the committee to select the tiny community of Waterloo, where four families had settled near the mouth of Shoal Creek. In the meantime, anxious settlers rushed in to purchase the newly platted lots, including George W. Bonnell, who proudly proclaimed, "Like the ancient city of Rome, Austin is built upon seven hills, and it is impossible to conceive a more beautiful and lovely situation." One of those seven hills appropriately became Mount Bonnell, and on April 13, 1839, Waterloo was officially renamed Austin.

Given the importance of rivers in Texas history, it is not surprising that Austin's first surveyor, Edwin Waller, recommended that the streets be named after the state's principal rivers, beginning with the Sabine River in the south of Texas and the Red River on the north.[8] He also suggested that the main thoroughfare leading up to the capitol building be called Colorado Avenue, although it later became Congress Avenue.

News of available land in the emerging Republic of Texas attracted hordes of land speculators who exploited the situation with glowing accounts of new towns and properties along the Colorado River. Recently established stagecoach and mail services also bolstered sales. One of most colorful and aggressive land merchants was Jacob de Cordova, a Spanish-Jamaican Jew who was raised in a family of printers and spoke five languages. He settled in Texas in 1839 and became a state representative from Houston in the second Texas legislature in 1847. After a single two-year term in the legislature, he began advertising the proprietary rights for the sale of thousands of acres of land in Texas. He also traveled to major cities on both sides of the Atlantic, urging people to settle in Texas. In addition, he published *The Texas Immigrant and Traveler's Guide Book* in 1856 and began two newspapers,

5. *Frontier River,* 74.

6. Ibid., 43.

7. Ibid.

8. Unlike the rivers after which they have been named, the Austin streets named after the major rivers of Texas run north and south, beginning on the western edge of the city with the Rio Grande and moving eastward with the Nueces, San Antonio, Guadalupe, Lavaca, Colorado, Brazos, San Jacinto, Trinity, Neches, Red, and Sabine. A downtown Austin creek was named after surveyor Edwin Waller.

including the *Southwestern American* in Austin, both of which carried ads for land in Central Texas and beyond. He promised his customers that although "Texas is not a paradise; it is a country where the poor man can easily obtain land."

Jacob de Cordova
Austin land speculator

Settlers were now ready to purchase land along the Colorado upstream from Austin, but the rugged terrain and the Comanches continued to present problems. The new government responded by launching several expeditions to wipe out the Indians as far as the confluence of the Colorado and San Saba Rivers. As president of the republic and a later U.S. senator and governor of Texas, Sam Houston, who had earlier been adopted by Cherokees and even had a Cherokee wife, preferred to makes treaties with the Indians, as had the French, Spanish, and Germans. Unfortunately, subsequent leaders, such as Mirabeau Lamar, and anxious settlers demanded more aggressive action, and by the last quarter of the nineteenth century, the few remaining Indians posed little threat.

***

Before the series of dams were built on the upper Colorado, devastating floods periodically raised havoc with settlements and farms along its banks. In 1869, for example, floodwaters reached the steps of the capitol building. Austin took the initiative in the last years of the nineteenth century to harness the Colorado River, because it also wanted a dependable source of electrical power for its various economic enterprises. In 1889, mayor-elect John P. McDonald called for a city-financed dam across the Colorado, for which he and his supporters commissioned an engraving of the dam they hoped would soon be built. An amateur versifier also threw his support to the project:

First a beautiful lake it will form
Whose waters will not be tossed by storm
Hotels, clubs, amusements of every kind
Along its beautiful banks you will find
It will furnish electric lights as well as power
Which will be utilized each day and hour

The most important mission of all
when done
Manufacturers by score to Austin will come
Setting the wheels of industry in motion
Advertising Austin from ocean to ocean.[9]

A more skeptical Austinite was William Sydney Porter, who wrote about the dam in his satirical weekly journal, *The Rolling Stone*. Porter, of course, would become much better known after he began writing short stories under his pen name of O. Henry:

> And wise men of the town of Austin . . . rose up and said, "Behold, let us build a great dam, the like unto which has not yet been seen." And verily then shall come manufacturers out of the land of the pumpkin and the wooden nutmeg and they shall build factories, and we shall gather of their boodle, even shall we wink at the factory girls in the evening.[10]

After four years of construction, the finished dam generated power to Austin's thirty-one light towers, streetcars, and factories. It also formed Lake McDonald, named for the mayor, which provided myriad recreational activities. Unfortunately, the dam collapsed on April 7, 1900, when floodwaters cascaded eleven feet over its top, leaving Austin without water, power, or lights.

The rebuilding of the dam was a long, frustrating process. Repairs were finally nearing completion in 1915, when a storm-lashed Colorado River once again rose up and destroyed the dam, leaving its financial backers bankrupt. When the ensuing years saw additional flooding that cost Austin and other communities along the river millions of dollars, angry voices demanded a more permanent form of flood control. Central Texans, however, would have to wait more than twenty years before the federal government stepped in and financed a series of dams that would not only control flooding but would for the first time bring rural electrification to the Hill Country.

***

In 1934, the Texas legislature created the Lower Colorado River Authority (LCRA) as a nonprofit, public entity to provide reliable, low-cost utility and public services, including electricity, flood management, water and wastewater utilities, and public parks.

Austinite Alvin J. Wirtz, who was then undersecretary of the U.S. Department of the Interior, sought funding for the LCRA, for which he later became a lawyer and lobbyist. Wirtz initially pushed for a series of dams intended only to control flooding, as only such dams were then acceptable to the U.S. Bureau of Reclamation. Wirtz's long-term agenda, however, included dams that could also generate electricity for the still dark Texas Hill Country. Burnet's James P. "Buck" Buchanan, after whom one of the upstream dams would be named, was chairman of the U.S. House Appropriations Committee, but before he acquired all the funding, he suffered a fatal heart attack in February 1937. His replacement, a former Hill Country teacher named Lyndon B. Johnson, stepped in and successfully shepherded the projects through Rep. Joseph Jefferson Mansfield's River and Harbors Committee. In gratitude, the Marshall Ford Dam was renamed the Mansfield Dam in 1941.

Eventually, the LCRA operated the six hydroelectric dams along the Colorado River that created the Highland Lakes: Buchanan Dam (Lake Buchanan), Inks Dam (Inks Lake), Wirtz Dam (Lake LBJ), Max Starcke Dam (Lake Marble Falls), Mansfield Dam (Lake Travis), and Tom Miller Dam (Lake Austin). The Buchanan and Inks Dams led to the formation of the Pedernales Electric Cooperative, which today serves much of Lakeway.

By far the largest and most important, at least for future Lakeway residents, was the eighteen-story, 7,089 foot-long Mansfield Dam. Its construction was an enormous and sometimes dangerous undertaking that took four years to complete:

9. Reprinted in David C. Humphrey, *Austin: An Illustrated History* (Northridge, CA: Windsor Publications, Inc., 1985), 128.
10. Ibid., 150.

The workers built a camp, including a hospital, on a rise east of the dam where they lived. The workers earned 40-55 cents an hour, which was good pay at a time when the country was still pulling itself out of a depression.

An eleven-mile railroad line was laid to the east bank to deliver cement and other materials. Concrete mixing vats were erected on the east side of the river, as were towers on both banks to support the twenty-ton cables along which ran buckets carrying the 1,864,000 cubic yards of concrete needed to build the dam.

One of these concrete buckets caused the gruesome death of a Bee Cave resident. Asa Leonard Grumbles' job was to probe the poured wet concrete to release the air bubbles. For some reason, Asa did not get out of the work area as a bucket of cement was being poured. Eight yards of concrete buried him, and there was no way to rescue him or retrieve his body.[11]

With 900 men working three shifts a day for four years, the power plant began producing electricity on January 27, 1941, at a final cost of $29,620,000. The waters behind the dam created Lake Travis, which, with 279 miles of shoreline, is the largest of the Highland Lakes. The combined shoreline of all the Highland Lakes is 842 miles. Lake Travis can store as much as twenty billion gallons of floodwater. In addition, the lake provides magnificent recreational possibilities for anglers, boaters, and campers. It also made Lakeway a reality. Unfortunately, the Mansfield Dam and Lake Travis also adversely affected many families whose homesteads were now submerged under the rising waters of the lake.

Fred and Allie Arnold, along with the six or seven other families living on Thurman Bend, were typical of those displaced by Lake Travis. Theirs was a tightly knit community, most of whose residents could trace their forebears back several generations. As daughter Ozelle Arnold remembers, "The people in the hamlet were so close they knew each other's barefoot tracks."

Excavation for the Mansfield Dam began in 1937. Photo courtesy of Lower Colorado River Authority Corporate Archives.

11. Perkins Manuscript. See also "Lake and Country Living," *Lake Travis View,* December 23, 1999.

Above: Redirecting the Colorado River. Below: construction shot, December 15, 1938. Photos courtesy of Lower Colorado River Authority Corporate Archives.

Asa Leonard Grumbles was killed when a bucket similar to this, filled with concrete, accidently buried him.

When the Mansfield Dam officially opened in 1943, it featured a two-lane road across its top. When this proved inadequate, a four-lane bridge was constructed just below the dam, opening in December 1994. Photos courtesy of Lower Colorado River Authority Corporate Archives.

Now their homes were being destroyed, along with the beautiful pecan trees from which the Arnolds made their living. For the Arnolds and their neighbors, the dam did not just flood Thurman Bend, it destroyed a way of life. As Allie watched the waters of Lake Travis engulf her home, she wrote a poem that years later was published in the *Austin American-Statesman:*

Good-bye Old Home, Good-bye

The time has come when at last we must bid
  Old Home good-bye.
For Uncle Sam has come along and built a
  dam so high,
That our Old Home we have, must well
  beneath deep waters lie.
And many things we cherish so, will only in
  memory lie.
Such as the land where golden grain has
  grown so bountiful,
And watermelons on the vines as thick as
  they could be,
And the pecan trees Oh! How great the limbs
Would tower and spread its branches full of
  nuts up toward the deep blue sky.
But Oh Alas! They're all cut down and into
  ashes go
And not one trace of them are found
Where hundreds once did grow.
But we can only sigh and say,
Old Home Good-bye,
          Good-bye![12]

12. *Austin American-Statesman,* July 4, 1991.

PART II

LAKEWAY: FROM RESORT AND VACATION SPA TO DIVERSE HILL COUNTRY COMMUNITY

Lakeway's environment is both natural and man-made. Eons of geological changes created its limestone hills; Twentieth Century politics created its marvelous body of water; a few men of vision created a residential development within these surroundings; and its citizens created a rare form of volunteer government.

BYRON D. VARNER, *LAKEWAY: THE FIRST 25 YEARS*

CHAPTER SIX

THREE WISE MEN FROM THE EAST AND A GOAT FARM

No one from Austin would want to buy land out in Lakeway because they wouldn't be able to go home for lunch.

AUSTIN REALTOR, CIRCA 1963

No doubt our wildest dreams have come true. If given a chance, I would do it all over again, starting tomorrow!

G. FLINT SAWTELLE, CO-FOUNDER OF LAKEWAY

Intersection of RR 620 and Lohman's Ford Road as it looked in 1962

THE DATE WAS JULY 13, 1963. THE OCCASION WAS the official opening of the Lakeway Inn and Marina. Among the honored guests were Lady Bird Johnson and Texas Governor John Connally. Not invited was a herd of goats that arrived from a neighboring ranch to graze on the newly sodded grass. The event received little coverage by Austin's media, which considered Lakeway too distant for a sensible commute. The *Highland Outdoor Times,* however, published a special edition, praising the Lakeway Land Company's impressive venture as "a dream come true for the Lake Travis area [which was] woefully lagging in accommodations to match the beauty of the surroundings." Attorney General Waggoner Carr announced, "With projects such as Lakeway to provide guidelines, it is a strong step toward the development of excellent tourist attractions in every area of the State." By 2011, Lakeway had become a city of 14,000 inhabitants, with a total property value of $2.4 billion, while retaining the natural beauty that had first attracted the three wise men from Houston.

***

Flint Sawtelle was a graduate of Lehigh University, a petroleum engineer, and the former president of the Toklan Oil Company of Tulsa. John Crooker, Jr., a graduate of Rice and the University of Texas, was a Houston lawyer with considerable experience in his family's hotel business. Lee Blocker, a graduate of Rice and Columbia, brought a strong financial background to the partnership. All were familiar with the Austin area, especially after they purchased Austin's Commodore Perry Hotel in 1959 for their Gulfmont Hotel Company. They saw no reason why Texas should not have a resort to rival the likes of Hilton Head and Pebble Beach. A rancher named Jack Josey owned several thousand acres of attractive ranch land overlooking Lake Travis. He also served with Sawtelle on the board of directors of Houston's Port City State Bank. One day Josey half-jokingly suggested to Sawtelle that he might want to build a hotel on his land. The rest, as they say, is history.

***

On a hot July day in 1962, Crooker, Sawtelle, and Blocker drove west from Austin to the end of Lohman's Ford Road. Standing on a cliff, where four years later Crooker would build his home at 801 Sailfish, they looked down at a peninsula jutting out into Lake Travis that seemed perfect for a hotel and perhaps even a resort community with attractive homesites. Sawtelle later said of that

Flint Sawtelle took this 1962 aerial photo of where he and his partners planned to build their resort.

A postcard rendition of the Commodore Perry Hotel where in 1962 Sawtelle, Crooker, and Blocker designed their new resort property. They called it Lakeway because, as Sawtelle later explained, "We had given the name Fairway to our hotel in McAllen because it was next to a golf course, so we thought that since this land was next to a lake we would call it Lakeway."

G. Flint Sawtelle

Lee Blocker

moment, "When we saw that expanse of water and the point of land just across the inlet, oh my, we were just about sold right then and there." Crooker was so inspired by the view that he reached for the pad of paper that always accompanied him and sketched the first plans for what would become the Lakeway Inn, including the location of the lobby, restaurant, kitchen, and the building that would house the original sixty rental units.

Sawtelle, Crooker, and Blocker agreed that summer of 1962 to purchase from Jack Josey the first 880 acres of what would eventually become 3,700 acres. When Josey agreed to a sixty-day option on the land, the partners moved into the Governor's Suite in the Commodore Perry Hotel to develop their plans. As Sawtelle later described the scene, "We laid a strip of plywood between a couple of sawhorses and got to work."

Sawtelle, Crooker, and Blocker organized the Lakeway Land Company as a separate entity from their Gulfmont Management Company, although the latter would operate the Lakeway Inn after its completion. They also added seven additional partners: George Sawtelle, Wayne Ankenman, Ben Boshton, Andy Kivlin, Frank Denius, W. A. "Tex" Moncrief, and landowner Jack Josey. The general boundaries of their planned community were the former Teck community to the north and Bee Cave to the south. Lake Travis lay to the west and northwest and RR 620 to the east.

Jack Josey's 3,700 acres on the north side was the largest single land purchase, although to the southeast the Lakeway Land Company added 2,600 acres from Nevil and Abe Hutto and 641 acres from Jack Schramm. Interspersed were numerous other small properties, including some owned by the Stewart family. The resultant map looked like a giant jigsaw puzzle. Not part of the Lakeway Land Company's holdings were a couple of churches and gas stations, the Johnson store, and a few other small businesses, all of which did not amount to much. Nevertheless, the founders of Lakeway were optimistic when they opened their two-room, primitive sales office and erected a billboard on the corner of Lakeway Drive and Sailfish. Andy Kivlin's wife, Sylvion, became the first salesperson. It took her two months before she made her first sale. The buyers were Louise and Irene Hamilton, who paid just over $4,000 for a lot at 303 Comet Cove.

When construction of the Lakeway Inn actually began, there was still no electrical power

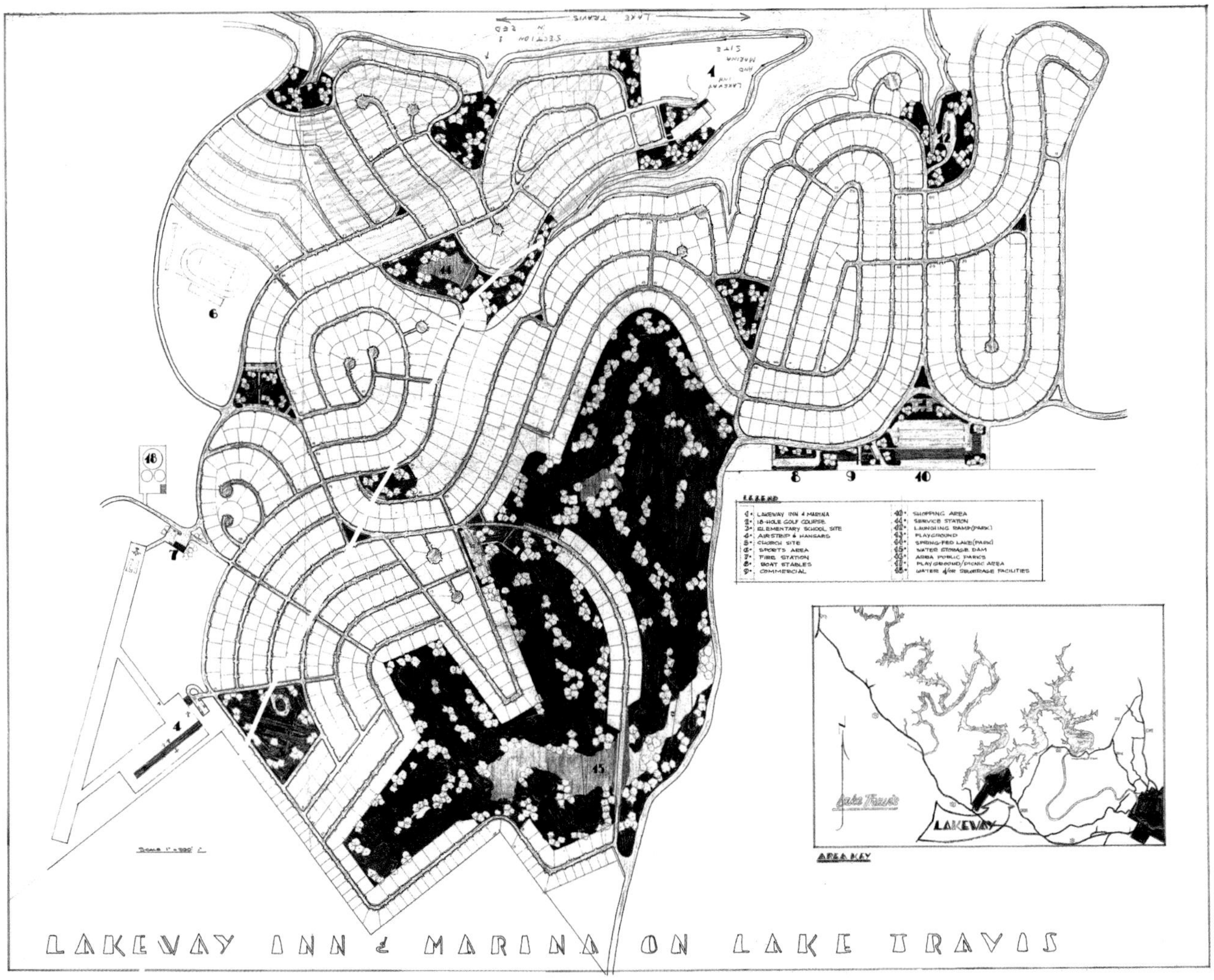

Lakeway did not develop precisely as the founders envisioned in this 1962 map, but what they planned is certainly recognizable today.

and the nearest phone was at Johnson's Trading Post several miles away on Highway 71. To rectify the problem, Sawtelle invited representatives of the Southwest Bell and the Lower Colorado River Authority to a gourmet lunch on the inn's recently poured second deck. Shortly thereafter Lakeway got its first telephone, located at what is now Lohman's Crossing and Lakeway Boulevard. Electrical power soon followed.

The project designer was Merle Simpson. Andy Kivlin formed the Lakeway Construction Company and supervised all building projects, including the laying out and paving of six miles of roads for future homes.

Surrounding the main building of the inn, which was built of native stone and rough-sawn cedar, were fifty "spacious villas," with balconies overlooking Lake Travis. According to an enthusiastic September 1, 1963, review in the *Dallas Times Herald,* "Lakeway is destined to become internationally famous as a luxury resort." Drawing a distinction between the Bubbas and their betters, the reviewer added, "Something new has been added to the Highland Lakes playground, designed to appeal to those who prefer a carpet of nylon rather than grass, the sound of piped music rather than crickets, and butter-broiled lobster tails rather than fried catfish."

The Lakeway Inn featured fifty rooms, a small marina, a tennis court, a swimming pool, a stable of riding horses, and moonlight dining—all proudly promoted in lavish photographic brochures.

Another planned amenity was the Lakeway Yacht and Country Club, which was meant "to provide facilities for social intercourse among its members as well as providing facilities for swimming and other athletic activities," including a planned golf course. Actually, in 1963 there were no yachts or even a putting green, but as a private club it could sell alcohol.

The Lakeway Land Company began selling lots for private homes in May 1963. Because Austin families thought Lakeway too far of a commute, the company initially did much better with Houston buyers, who considered Lakeway a perfect site for vacation homes. Word spread, and before long people from near and far, including foreign countries, were attracted to Lakeway.

The architects of this new community were justifiably proud of their accomplishments. They were, however, occasionally threatened by the capricious whims of Mother Nature, especially

Lakeway's first land office and billboard

when the extremes of drought and flooding affected the beauty and usefulness of Lake Travis and the newly opened Lakeway Marina.

The inn had just opened for business when its owners hired a Frenchman named Pierre Caselli to manage the inn and become its first chef. The date was July 14, 1963, which was Bastille Day in France. The date was also symbolic, as Pierre and his wife, Billie, gave birth to son Christopher, the first newborn resident of Lakeway.

Over the years, the Lakeway Inn has gone through numerous renovations and expansions, as well as several changes of management. It has also become one of Texas's most attractive conference centers. Unfortunately, the inn and the residents of Lakeway have not always enjoyed a harmonious relationship. This was certainly not the case initially.

Early promotional postcard of the Lakeway Inn

Lakeway Inn, 2010

Early promotion for Lakeway

The extremes of Lake Travis: Lakeway Marina at 615 feet in June 1978 and at 707 feet on December 29, 1992

CHAPTER SEVEN

LAKEWAY'S FORMATIVE ORGANIZATIONS

Someone once said, there is no true living without belonging, no belonging without involvement, and no involvement without commitment.

LAKEWAY RESIDENT J. RILEY HASTINGS

LAKEWAY FOUNDING FATHERS FLINT SAWTELLE, John Crooker, Jr., and Lee Blocker created several organizations to help reassure those planning to build homes in their planned community that they were making a wise investment.

The **Lakeway Yacht Club** had no yachts, but it did allow its members to slake their thirst in a state that still prohibited open bars. It welcomed its first members on June 6, 1963, a full month before the Lakeway Inn officially opened its doors. No prospective buyer was allowed to purchase a homesite until approved for membership, although Civil Rights legislation in the 1980s ended this restriction. A 1973 amendment changed the name to the **Lakeway Yacht and Country Club (LYCC)**. An additional amendment in December 1982 allowed anyone of legal age to gain membership if the individual rented a house or condominium or was a resident of the "Lakeway developed community," meaning areas subsequently developed by the Lakeway Company and its successors.

Over the years, the LYCC has organized many social events, especially dances and parties, as well as sponsoring and conducting numerous golf tournaments.

***

Of more lasting significance was the **Architectural Control Committee,** which guaranteed that Lakeway would be a community of quality homes and neighborhoods. More specifically, it enforced deed restrictions, including "land use, type of structure, signs, nuisance factors, use of firearms, trash disposal, storage of boats and materials, pets, drainage, off-street parking, developments, easements, and types of building materials." It was reorganized in 1975 as the **Architectural Control Board**, which also provided indemnification against lawsuits directed at its members. The Lakeway Village Council formally took over its duties in 1989, although for several years both the board and the council had been responsible for enforcing architectural restrictions. A few citizens have argued that such restrictions interfere with the free and independent spirit that Texans so love, but most residents agree that protecting everyone's property values supercedes the right of an individual to raise chickens and llamas, cultivate gardens, or park house trailers, non-functioning autos, bathtub grottoes, and various other peculiarities of personal taste on front lawns.

***

Without question, the **Lakeway Civic Corporation (LCC)** has done more than any other organization to guarantee the beauty, uniqueness, and functionality of Lakeway. Local historian Doris Besperka once described the LCC as "the anchor which holds our community together." Formed as a nonprofit corporation and trust fund on September 29, 1965, the LCC's objective was "to promote the special welfare of the community and of its property owners and residents [and] to acquire and maintain property and funds for charitable community services and recreational facilities." Additionally, it pledged to support "wholly or in part, arts and beautification enhancements, parks and recreational improvements, and other civic projects for the betterment of the city of

Lakeway property owners and residents."

The LCC was originally administered by a five-person board of trustees, with three members elected by the membership and two appointed by the Lakeway Land Company. The first board included Lee Blocker, Andy Kivlin, and G. Flint Sawtelle, all associated with the Lakeway Land Company, and residents Lloyd Jones (president) and H. A. West. Today's six-member board is elected by Lakeway property owners for three-year terms. There are no initiation fees or dues to belong to the LCC, only that one own a Lakeway residential lot.

To fund its projects, the LCC took 10 percent of the purchase price or $200, whichever was less, from each lot sold and put these monies into the Lakeway Property Maintenance Trust Fund, which it established in 1966. The founding developers also made an initial contribution of $50,000 to cover properties sold before the establishment of the LCC. The trust fund designates that the LCC can receive the net income from the trust on a quarterly basis, to be used exclusively for community charitable, civic, and recreational purposes. The LCC's charter also allows it to own property and use the trust fund income to maintain and beautify that property. This became particularly important in 1974 when the Lakeway Company deeded several parks to the LCC, including Dragon Park, Lakeway Drive Park, Porpoise Park, Rebel Park, and Sailfish Park. In 1987, the LCC donated these parklands to the City of Lakeway. It did much the same thing after Jack and Myrtle Hamilton donated $44,000 to the LCC in 1989 for the purchase of 85 acres of pristine parkland, which was renamed the Hamilton Greenbelt when it too was donated to the city.

As of 2011, the Lakeway Property Maintenance Trust Fund had grown to more than $1,200,000. The only additional LCC revenue comes from advertising income in its annual Lakeway Residents Directory.

Among the LCC's earliest funded projects were a community telephone directory, a resident's newsletter, and a volunteer fire department, which the community realized it desperately needed after an August 1967 fire came perilously close to destroying Lakeway. At the time, there was no local fire fighting equipment or 911 to call for help. Only the quick work of a man named Brooks, who used his bulldozing equipment to build several fire walls, saved the community. Hoping to avert even worse disasters in the future, the LCC formed a committee that in

Lakeway's Volunteer Fire Department's first truck. In 1983, the Hudson Bend Volunteer Fire Department extended its territory to Lakeway. Two years later it became the Travis County Rural Fire District. In 2007, it evolved into Travis County Emergency Services District #6, which now covers more than 200 square miles.

1968 approved a volunteer fire department. It also provided operating expenses and lent the VFD $4,000 to purchase its first truck, which was delivered in January 1969. The volunteers manning the truck were, as fire chief Al Saenger described them, "nearsighted, partially lame, and sometimes overweight." Nevertheless, when the siren sounded, they responded, including Harry Stevenson, who had to hold on with one hand while his other tightly gripped his cane. In July 1983, the LCC recognized Al Saenger as its first Outstanding Citizen of the Year, an award that would become a greatly respected annual tradition. Beginning in 1988, the LCC also presented annual awards to citizens for meritorious service.

In 1969, the LCC organized volunteers to provide dusk-to-dawn, four-man security patrols, paid for by a $2.50 contribution from homeowners. The LCC continued to marshal this program until a village police department became tax supported after its formation in 1974.

In 1971, the LCC sponsored a study committee to evaluate Lakeway becoming something more than a corporate-owned resort community. As a result, Lakeway was incorporated as a village in 1974.

Over the years, the LCC has given back to the community more than $1,270,000. It has helped fund the care and maintenance of Lakeway parks and trails, as well as various landscaping and beautification projects. It also contributed financially to the Lakeway Swim Center, the Activity Center, the Lake Travis Youth Foundation, the Lake Travis Community Library, the Service League, the new City Hall, the Lakeway Garden Club, Friends of the Parks, Fourth of July celebrations, and countless other worthwhile community organizations and causes.

Inspired by Lakeway's twenty-fifth anniversary in 1988, the LCC sponsored a committee to create a historical society. That same year, the LCC funded Byron Varner's *Lakeway: The First 25 Years*. In 1994, it donated $10,000 to the Lakeway Historical Society toward building a permanent home, which eventually became the Lakeway Heritage Center.

On February 15, 1997, the LCC created the Lakeway Community Foundation, a tax-free, nonprofit organization that accepts funds in trust for any civic purpose specified by the donors. The first gift under this umbrella was Jack and Myrtle Hamilton's donation of $260,000 to the LCC to be used for the operation and maintenance of Hamilton Greenbelts I and II.

***

The Lakeway Recreational Association (LRA) was formed in 1975 because of deteriorating relations between Bob Alpert's Lakeway Company and community residents. After meeting with the Lakeway Civic Corporation, Alpert agreed to form the LRA to "inform the community about practical decisions affecting the community, [maintain] a free flow of communications, and [introduce] a new and improved package of recreational resources." The LRA board consisted of eleven directors, six appointed by the Lakeway Company and five by members of the LCC and the Lakeway Yacht and Country Club. Included also was a representative of the Lakeway Ladies Golf Association. It was arguably a step in the right direction, but because the Lakeway Company still called the shots, residents wanted an organization that better represented their personal and community interests.

***

On May 22, 1978, approximately sixty Lakeway residents met and organized the **Homeowners Association of Lakeway**, which challenged Bob Alpert's Lakeway Company on issues such as changing homeowner policies, uncontrolled expansion, higher taxes, the Lakeway MUD, and a continued lack of communication. All meetings were to be open, with no business conducted in closed sessions. Membership was open to all Lakeway homeowners and dues were initially set at $15. The first elected officers were President Juanita Porter, Vice President Vic Dias, Secretary Kathy Goldsmith, and Treasurer Herb Walton. The Homeowners Association also planned a new publication for its members.

Bob Alpert and his Lakeway Company had published their in-house *Lakewaves* under the editorship of Byron Varner, who had also named the publication. Although *Lakewaves* was meant to foster better relations between the developer and homeowners and prospective buyers, Varner later admitted it was "too developer-oriented," leading him to help launch the Homeowner Association's ***Homeowners News*** in 1978. In its first issue, dated July 10, 1978, the *Homeowners News* promised to be a genuine "voice of Lakeway, to obtain and disseminate a wide range of subject matter in a factual, comprehensible and readable format [and] to dispel rumors, educate, and, hopefully, better equip our residents to enjoy living, working, playing and progressing in our unique community." Its editors did such a good job that in 1991 the Lakeway Civic Corporation presented its Meritorious Service Award to the *Homeowners News* editorial staff for its distinguished service to the community. The *Homeowners News* remains a monthly publication for Lakeway residents.

In 2006, the Homeowners Association changed its name to the Homeowners Association of Greater Lakeway, because of its desire "to reach out to new residents in our community." Two years later, it merged with the Lakeway Yacht and Country Club and became the **Greater Lakeway Residents Association (GLRA)**. New responsibilities included activity groups such as the Newcomers Alumni Club, language classes, bridge groups, the Greater Lakeway Play Group, the Travel Group, the Holiday Ball, and the Wine Club. The GLRA also took over the responsibility for the Lakeway Activity Center's lending library, as well as sponsoring Town Hall meetings, Meet the Candidates Night, the Info Fair, golf tournaments, Breakfast with Santa, and an annual meeting with the Lakeway Civic Corporation. All Lakeway residents are eligible and dues were set at $30 per year.

***

In addition to the aforementioned community organizations, there are more than thirty social, political, and service organizations in Lakeway. Some are local chapters of national or regional organizations, such as Alcoholics Anonymous & Alanon, the Daughters of the American Revolution, the Boy and Girl Scouts of America, Lake Travis Democrats, Lake Travis Republican Club, Lake Travis Lions Club, the Highland Lakes Group, the Lake Travis Crisis Ministries, and the Lakeway/Lake Travis Rotary Club. Others are expressly local organizations, including Friends of the Lake Travis Community Library, Friends of the Parks, Lake Travis Arts League, Lake Travis Thrift Shop, Lake Travis Youth Association, Lakeway/Hills Solos Club, Men's Breakfast Club, Newcomers Club, Newcomers Alumni Club, Service League of Lakeway, the Women's Club of Greater Lakeway, and the Lakeway Players, the only community theater group in Lakeway.

CHAPTER EIGHT

A COMMUNITY AND GOVERNMENT OF VOLUNTEERS

I believe that most of what made Lakeway great is more the product of the residents' efforts than the developers.

Byron Varner

From the beginning, Lakeway was blessed with an outstanding quality of retirees who willingly lent their time and expertise for the betterment of the community. . . . [They] dramatically reduced the cost of government, which is reflected in the amount of taxes paid by the citizens. In addition, tasks performed by volunteers promote a sense of community and retain the small town atmosphere that has characterized Lakeway since its beginning.

Sue Wright

Bob Young was ninety years old when fellow Lakeway resident Ernie Conine interviewed him in 2000. Bob and his wife, Leonore, were among Lakeway's first property owners when in 1965 they bought a lot at 105 Atlantic. Bob vividly described early yard parties attended by as many as 100 people. They shared beer, barbeque, and lots of friendly conversation. At one such party a new resident, who had been a vice president of a large oil company, wanted everyone to know the importance of his former position. After listening patiently, Bob Young said, "Yes, it certainly sounds as though you have had an impressive career, but after you've been around here for awhile you'll realize that Lakeway is just a bunch of old farts having fun." The ex-oilman was not particularly happy with Bob's comments, but a few weeks later at another yard party he had undergone an obvious transformation. He came up to Bob, threw his arm around his shoulder, and announced, "Well, from one old fart to another, I want to wish you a happy Fourth of July."

Lakeway, however, was about something more than just retired folks relaxing and having fun. Most residents wanted to build a community based on mutual respect and congenial relationships, but they also wanted to establish a political framework that would guarantee individual rights and controlled community growth. To accomplish these objectives, they established a government and social framework using almost exclusively volunteers.

***

The year 1971 marked a critical watershed in the development of Lakeway. The original founders had invested millions of dollars in building the Lakeway Inn and Marina, laying out streets, and installing a water system. They had developed approximately 1,000 acres of their original land purchases, on which there were now some 300 homes. They had, however, seen comparatively little return on their massive capital investment and they were ready to sell.

Robert Alpert

On April 26, 1971, the Lakeway Land Company sold the inn, the marina, and its residential properties to Robert Alpert, the president of the Dallas-based Alpert Investment Corporation, which had financial backing from the Connecticut Mutual Life Insurance Company. The price was a reported $4.5 million.

Alpert changed the corporate name to the Lakeway Company and promised "to honor all previous commitments, both written and implied [and] to build the finest recreational community in the Southwest." He then opened an impressive new sales office next to the Tejas Building on Lakeway Drive, increased the size of the marina, added sixty rooms and another swimming pool to the inn, and announced an agreement with Lamar Hunt to build a championship tennis complex, which became The World of Tennis.

Lee Blocker agreed to stay on to ease the transition, as did inn manager Pierre Caselli. Alpert, however, brought in Ralph Hutchinson as his chief executive officer. When Hutchinson left shortly thereafter, Alpert appointed retired Air Force Colonel Jim Gribble as president. Unfortunately, this rapid turnover of executive officers continued well into the future, and the Lakeway Inn did not always enjoy amiable relationships with the surrounding community. To be fair, Robert Alpert's objective was to make money rather than to please the people of Lakeway. As local historian Doris Besperka put it, "Robert Alpert was a businessman whose main priorities were new amenities, subdivision expansion, and selling lots. He had very little interest in developing a community."

Another significant and controversial development for the young community occurred in February 1972 when the Texas Water Rights Commission approved a Lakeway Municipal Water District (LMUD). The State of Texas had recently authorized these municipal utility districts to provide developers with a financing vehicle to pay for the installation of water and wastewater utilities where no such services existed. According to Byron Varner, "Texas laws governing MUDs in the 1970s were heavily weighted in favor of land developers. A MUD could issue bonds to finance construction of utilities and a developer could then use his own funds for other amenities." The developer could also control MUD policies by placing his own employees on the board of directors, which Robert Alpert initially did. When the Texas legislature eventually restricted such practices, board members were elected by the residents. There are now more than 850 MUDs in Texas, several of which are within or surrounding Lakeway.

The Lakeway MUD purchased the Lakeway Company's water system in September 1972 for $870,000 and took over its operation. When

Early World of Tennis promotion

it extended its water services to newly opened areas, its costs were greater, in part because development was slower than anticipated. As a result, these so-called "out-of-district" areas had to pay higher rates. On the other hand, the more recently opened areas had sewers, whereas the older sections were stuck with septic tanks. These differences would lead to several bitter legal suits and countersuits.

Another point of contention was the location of the Lakeway MUD's facilities. Not surprisingly, most residents did not want MUD structures or recycling reservoirs anywhere near their homes. A particularly nasty and protracted legal battle broke out after the MUD decided to expand its water treatment plant on Sailfish Drive. After Lakeway was incorporated as a general law village in 1974, it could define residential areas, protect golf courses and parks, and control building standards for business use within the village. One piece of land zoned as parkland included the area where the Sailfish plant was located. Not until 1988, after fifteen years of acrimony and legal suits, did the MUD agree to remove its Sailfish Park facility, thus ending its ongoing dispute with the neighborhood organization, Citizens for Sailfish Park (CSP). The MUD also agreed to pay CSP members for all legal expenses incurred since 1980 and to restore the park to its original condition by 1992.

Over the years, there have also been disputes with the MUD over its assessment of fees and its storage and disbursement of wastewater effluence, particularly after a major leak into Hurst Creek and the spraying of treated wastewater on trees adjacent to Lakeway Elementary. Frequently these disagreements resulted in expensive court battles, in which the MUD, the city, and its citizens all ended up losers.[1]

With Lakeway steadily annexing surrounding areas, the question also rose as to how best to expand water services to its new residents. Some voices urged the city to take over the Lakeway MUD and perhaps some of the neighboring MUDs as well. A few argued for the reverse, that the Lakeway MUD should absorb the city.

Despite these contentious disputes, the Lakeway MUD's rates have remained competitive and the quality of its drinking water has won numerous awards. Then, too, the MUD board was made up of citizen volunteers, as were its advisory committees, all of whom were not paid for their long hours of conscientious and challenging work.

***

Over the years of the Lakeway Company's existence, Lakeway residents increasingly realized they could not depend on Robert Alpert and his staff to make decisions in their best interests. They were especially concerned about having their own fire and police protection, the overall maintenance of their community, and the need to fund such services. Additionally, because the community was still under Austin's Extra Territorial Jurisdiction (ETJ), the possibility remained that Austin might decide to annex Lakeway, which under Texas law it could then do without the permission of its residents.

A 1972 committee formed by the Lakeway Civic Corporation, and chaired by Newt Herndon, concluded that to protect its independence Lakeway needed to become an incorporated community. Over Robert Alpert's opposition, the Austin City Council granted its unanimous approval in 1974, with the stipulation that it retain its ETJ over "all areas outside of and adjacent to the Village city limits."

Lakeway solidified its newly achieved independence by holding its first election on July 13, 1974. By a margin of 243 to 85, residents approved incorporating as a general law village, with taxing powers and the right to control police and fire protection, street maintenance, building and zoning codes, and sundry other operations. They also elected N. C. "Newt" Herndon their first mayor, along with commissioners Jim Gribble and Bob Derby. Their initial term was for only eight months and, as was the case with all subsequent volunteer city leaders, there was no salary. The Lakeway Civic Corporation

1. A more detailed chronological description of the MUD's battles with residents and the city appears in the Lakeway Time Line, beginning on page 175.

then requested a voluntary property tax consisting of 25 cents per $100 of the Travis County tax valuation to get the village started until a formal tax structure could be established. Lakeway conducted its new government in the Tejas Country Store Building.

In 1983, new challenges brought on by an economic and population spurt led voters to approve an aldermanic form of government, which consisted of five aldermen and a mayor. Ken Shepherd was elected mayor and Ed Smith and Sam Huser were voted in as aldermen, all for two-year terms. James R. Hastings, J. Sloan "Tony" Leonard, and Kenneth W. Kennedy were elected for one-year terms. Once again, all were unpaid volunteers. To show its appreciation of "the critical importance of volunteerism to the growth and development of Lakeway," the Civic Corporation began granting its Outstanding Citizen of the Year Award, a practice that continues to the present day.

In April 1989, Lakeway's population exceeded the 5,000 inhabitants needed for home rule eligibility. On May 5, Lakeway citizens voted 622 to 137 to become a Home Rule City. Included among the many advantages were better control over platting and zoning regulations. Ken Shepherd was elected mayor and Ken Kennedy, Nat S. Kendall, Veronica Bennett, Roger J. Schuler, and Guy Brown, Jr. were voted in as city councilmembers. In September, the new city council approved a five-year master plan to guide the community on such issues as land use, roads, utilities, police, fire, recreation, health care, organizations, education, and village management. Above all, the plan promised "to manage growth by quality controls in keeping with city standards to maintain a residential-recreational community."

Lakeway's new status as a Home Rule City also renewed the debate over whether the MUD and the City of Lakeway should be consolidated. When the state legislature approved the formation of MUDs, some lawmakers argued they could be dissolved when municipal governments were sufficiently developed to run their own utility. Proponents of unification also thought the city might get better bond ratings than the MUD itself could.

Those serving as mayor or councilmembers under the Home Rule City model remained volunteers, but in February 1994, Lakeway added a city manager and an assistant to the mayor, and both were paid positions. Retired Air Force officer

Dedication of the new Lakeway City Hall, June 18, 2005. Signing, from left to right, are Assistant City Manager Steve Jones, City Manager Dave Denson, Mayor Steve Swan, former mayor Gerry Astorino, and former mayor Charles Edwards.

Dave Benson became Lakeway's first city manager, a position he would hold for the next ten years, and Terence Harkin became the administrative assistant to the mayor and the city manager.

***

HELP WANTED: Financially independent, agile, young-at-heart go-getter type individual wanted to fill executive position at Lakeway. Must have sincere desire for service to community, good sense of humor, willingness to work long hours at no pay, and to be on call 24 hours a day in any kind of weather. Duties will include coordinating work of volunteers, removing bats from cathedral ceilings, jump-starting cars, rescuing cats, pulling drunks' cars out of ditches, answering false alarms and, on rare occasions, putting out a fire. Qualified persons should apply at once for the job of Chief, Lakeway Volunteer Fire Department, Village of Lakeway. Hurry!

The above tongue-in-cheek advertisement was the creation of Byron Varner in the June 1980 edition of the *Homeowners News*. Facetious, to be sure, but over the years Lakeway has increasingly depended on volunteers, without whom the city would certainly have trouble functioning.

After Cole Rowland became mayor in 1991, the city mailed out a short questionnaire asking for volunteers in specific areas. When more than 100 individuals signed on, Mayor Rowland concluded, "One of Lakeway's strengths has been the willingness of its citizens to take an active part in their municipal government."

In 1993, Mayor Burton Barnes pleaded for more volunteers, pointing out that "Lakeway uses more than 100 volunteers in some twenty-three boards, commissions, committees, and positions."

Three years later, newly elected Mayor Jack O'Neill honored the city's 125 volunteers for their approximately 30,000 hours of donated time. He estimated their labor was equal to 14.4 full-time jobs, which saved the city an estimated $360,000 annually. By 1997 the number of volunteers had grown to 180, and new estimates suggested they were saving the city as much as $1 million a year.

By 2009, the Lakeway Civic Corporation listed more than 400 names in its recently established volunteer database, many of whom served on several committees, organizations, boards, clubs, commissions, or the city council. The mayor's wife, Jean O'Neill, alone served on thirteen different entities and Bill Chandler on eleven. Little wonder that Mayor Gerry Astorino (2003–2005) could say, "To be a successful mayor, you just surround yourself with the most talented people you can find and get out of their way. In Lakeway this has meant fellow volunteers." Salaried fire chief Dwight Clark had used different words back in 1993 to say the same thing: "Volunteers do for nothing what I don't get paid enough to do."

The case for the late Byron Varner as Lakeway's all-time champion volunteer is a strong one. Among his many contributions were helping begin church services in 1971, creating and editing the Lakeway Company's monthly newsletter *Lakewaves* in 1972 and the *Homeowners News* in 1978, on which he served as editor for its first three years. He organized the Men's Breakfast Club in 1974, serving as program chairman and emcee for five years. He also started Lakeway's first post office in 1975. He served as president of the Lakeway Civic Corporation and was a board member of the MUD, where he worked to end the long-running controversy over conflicting rates. He was also the driving force behind the creation of the Lakeway Historical Society, and in 1988 he published his superb *Lakeway: The First 25 Years*. Fittingly, the Lakeway Civic Corporation named him Lakeway's Outstanding Citizen in 1992.

In an April 28, 1994, letter to the *Lake Travis View* urging people to vote for the planned Activity Center, Byron Varner posed a series of questions about how different Lakeway might have been if its residents, when asked to volunteer, had said, "No thanks, I came here to retire, not to get involved."

What if the Lakeway Company had been in control of the community when it

> went under? What if all those who organized and built the Lakeway Church, the school, the Homeowners Association, the *Homeowner's News,* the Hamilton Greenbelt, the Service League, the Women's Club, the Men's Breakfast Club, the Historical Society, and the many other things that make Lakeway a special place to live, had not had the vision, creativity or desire to serve?

A year and a half before he died in 2006 in St. Petersburg, Florida, an increasingly disillusioned Byron Varner sent an e-mail to Lakeway archivist Mike Boston expressing his final thoughts on volunteers:

> When I first decided to write *Lakeway - The First 25 Years,* I learned that naysayers outnumber doers about 10 to 1. While Lakeway had an abundance of volunteers that made the community into what it had become, when we left there seven or eight years ago, my own experience was that one percent of the people do all the work and the other 99% complain about it.

Perhaps Varner's frustration was warranted, but even the most cynical of critics would admit that much of Lakeway's uniqueness is due to the ongoing efforts of its volunteers. After all, it was also a younger Byron Varner who wrote, "Perhaps no other community of its size anywhere can boast of the volunteerism and citizen activism with which Lakeway has been blessed."

CHAPTER NINE

THE LAKEWAY ECUMENICAL CHURCH

Keeping the spirit of ecumenism, mutual respect and consideration has not always been easy. Misunderstandings and occasional whiffs of jealousy have occurred. In spite of these, charity has prevailed. Without charity the ecumenical church at Lakeway would never have been started.

MONSIGNOR RICHARD E. MCCABE, 2001

CHRISTIAN WORSHIP DID NOT MIRACULOUSLY FIRST appear on the Lakeway scene after the opening of the Lakeway Inn in 1963. Indeed, there had long been an active spiritual life for residents of western Travis County. A few church buildings went back to the nineteenth century, but the earliest services were more commonly held in schoolhouses and private homes. The majority of worshipers were Baptists, and there were early Baptist congregations in both Hudson Bend and Bee Cave. Bee Cave also had a number of Presbyterians who held their services in the Beck Store and a local schoolhouse. To the north, in what is now Lakeway, there was a Methodist congregation, as well as a Church of Christ, which held its services both in the open and in the Teck School.

During these early years, revivals and regional prayer meetings were popular, with many western Travis County residents traveling long distances in wagons, on horseback, or by foot to gather in the open or around brush arbors for spiritual and social activities. These meetings proved especially compelling during hard times, natural disasters, or when the country was at war.

With the emergence of Lakeway as a budding community in the 1960s, many of its new residents wanted their own churches, although initially their places of worship were creative and unconventional.

***

In 1958, a twenty-nine-year-old Austin priest named Richard E. McCabe drove west on unpaved RR 620 to administer to the few pre-Lakeway Catholic families that lived in what Father McCabe called "depleted sheep and goat country." These were particularly hard times for those raising such animals, as the miracle fiber of nylon was steadily gaining favor over traditional wool, mohair, and angora fabrics. Five years later marked the opening of the Lakeway Inn and the beginning of a new community. Father McCabe, who was by then the head of Catholic Charities for the Diocese of Austin, admired the new development and praised its founders' willingness to invest great sums of money in an exciting new venture. Not surprisingly, he responded positively when a small group of new resident Catholics asked him to hold local services. Father McCabe held his first Catholic Mass in the Lakeway home of Walter Jenkins, who at the time was Lyndon Johnson's top administrative assistant. When sixty-five worshipers showed up a week later for a second service, Father McCabe knew he needed more spacious accommodations, and he found them in the Lakeway Inn, although this occasionally meant using the Yacht Club bar for his Sunday services. Billie Caselli, the non-Catholic wife of inn manager Pierre Caselli, accompanied the services on a portable piano provided by the inn.

According to one account, the first organized Protestant services in Lakeway were held in late 1969 in the home of Mr. and Mrs. LeRoy Deaton at 307 Comet Cove. The following January, Marcus Mauritz and his wife, along with Ralph and Eloise Keller and a few others, moved their Sunday services to the inn. Catholic services were held at 10:00 a.m., followed by the Catholic mass at 11:15. Father McCabe joked, "The Baptists did not always appreciate attending services in the Inn's bar."

While the Lakeway Inn was being renovated in 1972, Catholics and Protestants held joint services in the new Lake Travis Elementary School, as did a small group of Christian Scientists, whose leading spokesman was Lakeway co-founder Lee Blocker. This impressive show of ecumenical cooperation inspired Catholic and Protestant parishioners to ask Ralph Keller and Father McCabe to seek funding for their own church building. The result was a board of trustees consisting of four Catholics, four Protestants, and one Christian Scientist. Ralph Keller was elected the first president of the board, which then hired Austin's O'Connell & Probst architectural firm to build a church capable of holding 300 parishioners at an estimated cost of $200,000.

The Lakeway Company had initially offered a piece of land at the corner of Sailmaster and Lakeway Drive, but when this property appreciated too much in value, it offered several other sites. In 1973, the Lakeway Company donated the present 3.5-acre lot at the intersection of Lakeway Drive and Lakeway Boulevard, with the stipulation that a building would have to be constructed by 1975. The Lakeway Company also mandated that there could be no food service unless catered by the Lakeway Inn and no form of lottery or bingo, although these restrictions were later lifted.

The groundbreaking ceremonies for the Lakeway Ecumenical Church took place on December 17, 1973, and the dedication of its first building followed on June 9, 1975. This first building was completely paid for within eleven months, in large part because three Protestant members contributed more than half of the cost. Separate services were held for its Protestant and Catholic members.

Ralph Keller, who also served as the church's first president, designed and made all the chandeliers in his home workshop. His son built the first pews. The organ was donated by another church member. Overseeing the construction and administration of the new church were

Groundbreaking ceremonies for the Lakeway Ecumenical Church. From left to right: Ralph Keller, Father Richard McCabe, and Colonel James T. Gribble, who was then president of the Lakeway Company.

The Lakeway Church, 2011

trustees Walter G. Beach, Marcus Mauritz, Rick Szukalla, Father Richard McCabe, and Harold Hoefgen, who also served as chairman of the Building Committee.

The Christian Scientists, who initially held their own services in the church sanctuary, opened the Christian Science Reading Room in Suite 2 of the Lakeway Village Square in 1984. They now hold their services in the Third Church of Christ, Scientists, at 3575 RR 620S.

In 1989, at the instigation of now Monsignor Richard McCabe, the Lakeway Church's six-month-old Women's Club opened a local chapter of the Ladies of Charity, an international organization founded in the sixteenth century by St. Vincent de Paul. Its motto was "to serve, rather than be served." The following year, the Ladies of Charity opened the Lake Travis Thrift Shop in the 620 Mall, next door to the Crisis Ministry. By 1995, more than sixty ecumenical volunteers ran the Lakeway Thrift Shop, including forty-one members of the Ladies of Charity. On April 1, 2008, it moved to its current location at 1508 RR 620.

June 21, 1995, marked a fateful turning point for the Lakeway Church. After twenty years of shared worship, Catholics and Protestants decided to go their separate ways. According to Monsignor McCabe, it was "a congenial separation" brought on by the need for more space. Dr. Harold D. Edwards, the Protestant pastor, said, "Neither congregation wanted to separate, but we had to face the reality of the growth of Lakeway and the Lake Travis area."

At the time, the church was servicing 353 Protestant and 397 Catholic families. The Protestant congregation retained the Lakeway Church property and compensated the Catholic congregation for its equity. The Catholics then sought a new site for their planned church.

Monsignor McCabe took five years to find the property and then design and build the Church of the Resurrection of the Lord at Emmaus, which was dedicated in January 2001. Of his new church, which towers high above Lakeway like a medieval cathedral, Monsignor McCabe wrote, "It stands as a testimony of our faith, the same sentiment of the church builders of the 11th, 12th, and 13th centuries of France and England. The Romanesque still flourishes, but nothing touches the Gothic. We stand back now, in the symphony of design and execution, enjoying the latest testimony to the glory of God."

When Monsignor McCabe died on July 10,

2010, both Protestants and Catholics reminded each other of the role he played in encouraging the unique ecumenical spirit of the Lakeway Church. LaNell Edwards fondly recalled when Monsignor McCabe and Reverend Tom Carroll, then the Protestant minister of the Lakeway Church, "decked out in some fabulous garb and calling themselves the Righteous Brothers, rode together in the annual Lakeway Fourth of July Parade." Of Monsignor McCabe's leaving the Lakeway Church, Reverend Carroll said, "I hated to see him move out. . . . That man lived a life that personified his Christian faith. He included everybody in his life. . . . You could never tell in [our] church who was Catholic and who was Protestant, except on Sunday when we broke off into our separate groups."

***

The Lakeway Church has greatly expanded over the years, both in terms of parishioners and buildings. A $280,000 renovation in 1980 more than doubled its seating and added additional classroom space. An educational building was added in 1983, which was enlarged in 1988. A two-story, 18,000-square-foot Fellowship Hall opened in 1999. Its most recent building is a $4 million, 14,000-square-foot Student and Children's Center, which opened in January 2010.

The fourteen churches now listed in the Lakeway Residents Directory certainly fulfill the spiritual needs of a wide range of parishioners. Yet, one reflects fondly on the legacy of the original Lakeway Church, which was open to all and unquestionably transcended doctrinaire dogmatism.

Monsignor Richard E. McCabe and the Emmaus Catholic Church

CHAPTER TEN

LAKE TRAVIS INDEPENDENT SCHOOL DISTRICT

Send your teachers, your preachers, your churches and schools. . . . The great Lone Star State will be then as the brightest evening star in the United States. But there is work to be done.

John Milton McCoy,
First city attorney, Dallas, 1870

Johnnie Fields, "Lake Travis High School Rendering"

In February 1969, Ernest C. Stewart wrote a letter to the *Lake Travis News* calling for a new bridge to be built across Lake Travis that would connect Leander and Lakeway. The old Lohman's Crossing low-water bridge across the Colorado River had sunk to the bottom when the Mansfield Dam created Lake Travis in the early 1940s. Fearing that six-year-old Lakeway might be forced to become part of the Austin School District, Stewart hoped that it might instead join Dripping Springs, Eanes, and Leander to form an independent school district, but a bridge was needed if Leander was to participate. The bridge was never built, but Lakeway did become part of the Dripping Springs Independent School District. When this proved unsatisfactory, largely for reasons of logistics and perceived unfair taxation, Lakeway joined other disgruntled residents of western Travis County to form the Lake Travis Independent School District (LTISD) in 1981. Unfortunately, the relationship between residents of Lakeway and those of western Travis County has not always been harmonious with each other or with the LTISD.

***

As described in Chapter 3, pre-1963 children in the general area where Lakeway would emerge attended small country schools. Hirsh [sic] Creek and Hudson Bend were nineteenth-century schools that consolidated in 1890 to form the Teck School, close to the present corner of Debba Road and RR 620. To the south, the children might have attended one of several schools, such as the Little Yellow Schoolhouse in Bee Cave or the Fitzhugh School even farther south. These one-room schools dotted the landscape, especially after 1855 when the Texas legislature agreed to pay $1.50 per year for each enrolled child. By the time Lakeway became a reality in 1963, area schools had become part of the Dripping Springs Independent School District (ISD).

The Dripping Springs ISD could trace its roots back to the centennial year of 1876. Over the ensuing decades, it had grown so large that by 1981, when the Lake Travis Independent School District broke away, the Dripping Springs ISD covered 368 square miles in Hayes and Travis Counties. The longest bus route covered 123 miles during its two daily round-trips, which meant that some children in Travis County were spending as much as four hours a day on a school bus. Current Lakeway Parks and Recreation director Andra Dearing, who as a youngster lived in Pace Bend Park where her father was the director, recalls her eleven-hour school day:

> I was picked up at 6:00 a.m. and I was on the bus for a little more than two hours and then two more hours in the afternoon. I would not get home until 5:15. When I was in elementary school, the bus would not come all the way into Pace Bend Park so my mom would drive me to meet it at Old Ferry and Bee Creek Roads, right at the entrance of Briar Cliff. Later, we got picked up at the Briar Cliff Marina, maybe three-quarters of a mile from our house. Eventually, when I was in junior high, the bus came down to my road, but I still had to walk a good half mile.
>
> For someone who got carsick, as I did, this was pure misery. I would just lean against the window because it was nice and cold. When we were a little older, the girls would get on the bus in their curlers, and proceed to do their hair and makeup.
>
> We also got very creative. We would sing songs, commercials, anything we could think of, everything from "Rudolf the Red-Nosed Reindeer" to "I Wish I Were an Oscar Mayer Wiener." We played games and threw things around, although we were not supposed to do that.

Transportation problems for distant students also made it extremely difficult for them to participate in any after-school activities, although an Activity Bus left school at 5:30 p.m.

The opening of Lake Travis Elementary on RR 620 on November 20, 1972, ended the long bus rides for the youngest children living in or near Lakeway, but their older siblings and all children living in the far reaches of western Travis County continued to spend several hours each day on a school bus.

Many of the parents, and especially those living in Lakeway, also wanted to sever ties with the Dripping Springs ISD because their county was furnishing up to 80 percent of the financial support for the school district. There were also conflicts over school board elections, bond issues, and the school site selection process.

A 1975 vote to divide into two districts failed when Hayes County voters overwhelmingly rejected the proposal. Three years later a petition containing more than 1,000 signatures mandated another election, and this time voters approved the division. The Dripping Springs School Board responded by taking legal action to block the split, but after the Circuit Court of Appeals denied the suit in November 1980, the Lake Travis Independent School District became a reality.

The newly formed board of trustees chose Dr. Frank Jennings to be LTISD's first superintendent. The board also introduced a $7.3 million bond issue to finance a permanent junior and senior high school. After the bond issue passed on August 15, 1981, twenty-four portable classrooms were moved onto the grounds of Lake Travis Elementary to serve the anticipated 225 middle and high school students expected for the opening of the 1981 fall semester. Andra Dearing, who was then entering ninth grade, remembers the overcrowded conditions:

> The junior high portables were located on the south side of the elementary school, with the high school on the north. Initially, we had no lockers, no covered areas to speak of, although they would be added later in the year. We were also served lunch out of a portable building.
>
> In the fall of 1984, the high school students were relocated to the new campus on RR 620, but the junior high students were left behind, although they moved into the portables on the north side.

In the fall of 1982, the Lakeway Company donated fifty-five acres on RR 620, some two miles south of Lake Travis Elementary, for the planned junior and senior high school complex, and the

LTISD purchased an additional fifteen acres on its own. Classes began on September 4, 1984, in the new but yet unfinished building. Less than five years later, on April 2, 1989, the LTISD dedicated a new and separate high school building and field house on the same campus.

***

All new school districts face challenges, but those confronting the LTISD were particularly daunting. An early problem originated with many older Lakeway residents, who considered Lakeway a weekend retreat or a retirement locale rather than a growing, multifaceted community. Most no longer had school-age children, and, although Texas school taxes were frozen at age sixty-five, they seemed determined to defeat the school bond proposals, especially in the early 1990s when leaders of the Homeowners Association led the opposition.

After the defeat of two bond proposals in 1990, letter writer Carl Russell described the enormous "gorge" that existed between younger and older citizens of Lakeway. "The message," he said, "was young people take your kids and go away." Nevertheless, he pleaded for better understanding for what it takes to have a viable community and excellent schools. Other local supporters pointed out that someone had paid taxes for their children when they were raising young families and that good schools increased property values. In the ensuing years, as Lakeway became more of a mixed-generational community, its voters became much more willing to support school funding proposals.

There were also long-standing disagreements between families who lived at the far western edge of the district and the Lake Travis School Board. These residents wanted an elementary school of their own so their children could avoid the several hours they spent on school buses each day, often on dangerous and heavily traveled Highway 71. Typical was a 1998 letter that urged western Travis County voters to reject a $41 million school bond proposal because at least $7 million was targeted for sports- or entertainment-related projects and for a new elementary school in Bee Cave. The writer also complained of a lack of representation on the school board. The bond issue passed, but the breakdown of the vote highlighted the conflict: Lakeway residents voted approval by a three to two margin, whereas

Lake Travis High School

those residing in the Briar Cliff and Pedernales areas voted against its passage. This geographical conflict remains unsolved. As of 2011, all five of the district's elementary schools are located within a few miles of the junior high and high school campus on RR 620.

The fact that the LTISD had five different superintendents during its first twenty years of existence also proved unsettling, and several acrimonious financial disputes did little to enhance the reputation of the new district.

On February 11, 1985, the Lake Travis Board of Trustees hired Superintendent Dr. Walter Marks to a three-year contract at an annual salary of \$72,000. Marks used a \$19 million bond issue to build a separate high school building, which included an ornate entrance and rotunda, and an elaborate and expensive administration building, which critics dubbed the Taj Mahal. Unfortunately, many future voters cited this perceived excessive spending to oppose subsequent school bond campaigns. Marks left the LTISD in 1987 to accept a superintendent's position in Richmond, California, where he gained further notoriety, and this time on a national scale. In 1995, ABC's news magazine *Primetime* and CBS's *60 Minutes* featured stories on Marks for his extravagant and possibly illegal expenditures of public funds at two additional school districts. Regrettably, these exposés once again reminded area residents of Marks's immoderate expenditures while serving as LTISD's superintendent.

A very positive, noncontroversial innovation in 1985 saw the creation of the Lake Travis Educational Foundation, which grants college scholarships to deserving graduates of Lake Travis High School. It also presents mini-grants to teachers to enrich their basic curriculum and administers a "Special Care" fund to help children with extraordinary needs.

Dr. Marks's replacement, Dr. Walter Howard, also had a stormy tenure as superintendent, primarily because school board and community critics wanted to curtail his spending. The Lakeway Homeowners Association became involved when in April 1990 it appointed Glenn Williams to head up a committee to investigate whether the LTISD was spending more per child than comparable nearby districts. The Williams committee eventually concluded that "costs can be reduced by improvements in operating efficiency and productivity with no adverse impact on quality." Unfortunately, no one on the committee suggested comparing LTISD's spending to the top-rated school districts in the state.

Superintendent Howard argued that as a young district, which had more than tripled its student body in less than ten years, the LTISD had a higher debt service because of initial building costs and the introduction of comprehensive educational programs. Howard also wanted to hire twenty-three new teachers, but the board argued that seven were sufficient to keep the district in compliance with state mandates and comparable neighboring school districts. Howard again disagreed, contending that the LTISD should strive to emulate Alamo Heights, Highland Park, Eanes and other top-rated statewide districts rather than comparing itself to small and often rural nearby communities. Howard also emphasized that future national priorities demanded better educated students. The majority of residents, however, clearly sided with the board. Two letter writers thought the district should be laying off teachers rather than hiring them and another suggested returning to the country schoolhouses that he had attended. One resident proposed using volunteers in the classroom and another suggested not feeding students on athletic or field trips, except for football.

Dr. Howard was fighting a losing battle. His bond issues did not pass, and on January 11, 1993, the board forced his resignation, buying out the remaining seventeen months on his contract for \$80,000. Bob Hart, the director of Business and Finance, agreed to serve as interim superintendent, which he did until Dr. Gloria Berry was hired on July 1, 1993. Dr. Berry served nine years before retiring and being replaced on July 1, 2002, by Dr. Donald Rockwell "Rocky" Kirk, whose nine years of stewardship were marked by relative calm, a growing student body, some academic gains, and a great deal of success on the athletic fields.

***

Although sports generally play an important role in Texas scholastic circles, this has especially been true of football. Lake Travis High School's tenure at the Division 2 and 3 level was marked by mediocrity in most sports, but especially on the gridiron. When it moved up to Division 4, however, its fortunes rapidly began to change. New coach Jeff Dicus won state championships in football in 2007 and again in 2008, when starting quarterback Garrett Gilbert was voted national high school player of the year. After Coach Dicus left for Ducanville, his successor, Chad Morris, won a third straight title, and a year later Coach Hank Carter added a fourth successive state title. Julie Green's girls' volleyball team also won a state championship in 2010. This athletic success may have quieted those critics who thought that some of the millions of dollars spent on an indoor practice facility and a state-of-the-art weight room could have been better spent on academic and cultural endeavors.

Lake Travis's academic standing has improved over the years, although not at the rate witnessed in sports. For example, in 1986, the average Lake Travis High School SAT score was 878, some 28 points below the national average. By 1995 it stood at 950, which was 30 points higher than the national average and 57 points higher than the Texas average.

LTISD's annual results on the Texas Assessment of Knowledge and Skills tests (TAKS) have been inconsistent and unpredictable. Administered by the Texas Education Agency, the four possible ratings for school districts and individual schools are Exemplary, Recognized, Acceptable, and Unacceptable. In 1994 and 1996, the LTISD received an overall rating of Exemplary. Only 3.2 percent of the more than 1,000 districts received this rating. Nevertheless, shortly thereafter voters defeated a $44 million bond issue. Unfortunately, the district's rating fell to Recognized or Acceptable in subsequent years, until it again achieved an Exemplary rating in 2010. During these interim years, several of its elementary schools and one of its middle schools continued to be recognized as Exemplary.

Lake Travis has also produced between one and four National Merit Scholars annually over the past several years, although these numbers fall far short of such regional schools as Anderson, Westlake, and Westwood.

In 2010, *Newsweek* rated the top 1,600 public high schools in the country, and Lake Travis High School came in at 862. This was an admirable achievement, although for sake of comparison, nearby Westlake stood at 58, Westwood at 90, and Anderson at 321. *Newsweek* based its ratings on "how hard school staffs work to challenge students," measured in part by the number of advanced tests given at a school.

What does the future hold for the LTISD? We know its student body and physical plants will continue to grow. There were just over 500 students and one building in the district when it enrolled its first students in September 1981. By 2005, that number exceeded 5,000, and the projected figure for 2015 is 11,500. Growth for growth's sake is not necessarily a positive, but if accompanied by rising intellectual achievements, the Lake Travis Independent School District has the potential to join the finest school systems in the state and even the nation.

PART III

THE ESSENCE OF LAKEWAY

Bill Hawkins, "The Creation"

CHAPTER ELEVEN

LAKEWAY PAINTERS AND PHOTOGRAPHERS

Creativity is within you. I can't teach creativity.

JOHNNIE FIELDS, CREATOR AND
INSTRUCTOR OF THE LAKEWAY PAINTERS

Dallas Gorman, "Welcome to Lakeway"

Johnnie Fields, "Evening Walk in Lakeway"

Johnnie Fields, "Lake Travis" and "Hurst Creek Marina"

Janet Campbell, "Lake Travis Marina"

Janet Campbell, "Lake Travis Sunset"

Linda Wells, "Ducks at City Park"

Linda Wells, "The Cliffs at the Park"

Linda Wells, "Foot Bridge - Smith Greenbelt"

Judy Hazen, "The Chapel of Four Seasons"

Cole Rowland, "From the Deck"

Dallas Gorman, "Activity Center Fountain" and "Eagle at City Hall"

Bill Hawkins, "Sunset" and "The 18th at Yaupon"

Cal Rice, "Deer vertical"

Bill Hawkins, "Rainbow"

BIOGRAPHICAL NOTES ON PAINTERS AND PHOTOGRAPHERS

Janet Campbell has been painting professionally for thirty years. Her strong impressionistic style of watercolors employs the "wet-in-wet" technique and features the bold use of color. Her primary subjects have been scenes in Central Texas and images from her travels to Central America, England, Italy, Japan, and Mexico. Architectural and historical structures, cityscapes, florals, landscapes, and lake scenes have inspired her work. She is especially drawn to the light and shadow on a building or the colorful reflections and patterns in glass or on water.

Johnnie Fields, who painted the cover for this book, studied architecture at the University of Texas after his discharge from the U.S. Navy in 1945. He and a friend started their own architecture firm in 1955 in Odessa and opened an Austin office in the 1970s, which became Fields & Associates Architects. He built his Lakeway home in 1978. Fields says his love of architecture stems from "its design and creativity." His firm has designed several Lake Travis school buildings, including Hudson Bend Middle School and Lakeway Elementary. He always loved to draw, but he was approaching fifty when he began to take his watercolor painting seriously. He now admits that "watercolor is really my first love." Although he has done some work in oils, he much prefers watercolors because "you can create much more sparkle and much more liveliness in watercolor than in oils." Over the past several years, he has taught more than 100 aspiring local artists, of whom he says, "Some of them are now really good painters."

Dallas Gorman started visiting Lakeway in the mid-seventies and fell in love with its beauty and small-town charm. She moved here permanently in 1990 and began working for the City of Lakeway's Parks and Recreation Department in 2005. She is currently Programs Coordinator for the Lakeway Activity Center. Her photos won top honors at the State Fair of Texas in 1989 and 1999. She has also won awards at the Annual Lakeway Photo Fest, sponsored by the Arts Committee.

Bill Hawkins published his first photos at age seventeen. His photography has won numerous awards, including a second place at the State Fair of Texas in 2009 and Best in Show at the Lakeway Photography Contest in 2007, 2008, 2009, and 2010. His photographs have graced the covers of the Lakeway Residents Directory in 2006, 2007, 2008, 2010, and 2011. He also excels at image editing and photo restoration.

Judy Hazen was introduced to watercolor painting in classes taught by Jan Witten Sewell and Johnnie Fields. Among her many Lakeway activities, Judy is "the beekeeper" for Ladies of the Lake Quilting Bee, a group that makes charity quilts for indigent children and wounded soldiers returning from Iraq and Afghanistan. She also leads the volunteers of the Lakeway Garden Club in maintaining the Hamilton Greenbelt Garden, also known as the Chapel of Four Seasons.

Cal Rice is a professional photographer who writes, "I like creating an image that visually shares the desired 1,000 words." Cal's artwork also "strives to create memories which will last beyond one lifetime and images which can be felt and understood on multiple levels." Before Cal left Lakeway some ten years ago, he took a number of photographs that certainly fulfilled his professional objectives.

Cole Rowland received the Lakeway Civic Corporation's Outstanding Citizen Award for 2000 for his many civic contributions, including serving as mayor in 1991–1993, being a driving force behind the acquisition of City Park, and as Lakeway's leading spokesman on local and Highland Lakes water issues. Cole developed his watercolor skills in classes with local artists Virginia Grumbles and Johnnie Fields.

Linda Wells' artwork clearly displays her love of nature's full range of colors, from the subtle to the vibrant. As she puts it, "There is abstract beauty in realistic art and in response, realistic beauty in the abstract." Wells, who now prefers oils and pastels, was art director for two companies and an illustrator/designer for Texas Parks & Wildlife, for whom she painted several hunting and fishing stamps. In addition to her own work, she also teaches art.

CHAPTER TWELVE

GREENBELTS, CANYONLANDS, AND FRIENDS OF THE PARKS

One touch of nature makes the whole world kin.

William Shakespeare

Its red rock path meanders for 1,700 paces along Hurst Creek, into and back out of the preserve. The path cuts through a slice of natural history that traces its origin back 135 million years.

John Redford Taylor, describing the Hamilton Greenbelt

Nothing has contributed more to the unique beauty of Lakeway than its magnificent greenbelts, parklands, and numerous walking trails, but their creation did not happen overnight or accidently. In December 1974, the Lakeway Company deeded to the Lakeway Civic Corporation (LCC) the five areas it had designated as parkland: Dragon Park, 3.5 acres (later enlarged); Lakeway Drive Parkway, a small strip of land in the 100 block of Lakeway Drive; Rebel

Sailfish Park

Park, a 5.6-acre nature trail at the dead end of Rebel Drive extending to the lake; Porpoise Park, a 1.68-acre greenbelt area on Porpoise Drive; and Sailfish Park, 3.4 acres off Sailfish Drive.

Predictably, these five small pieces of land could not meet the needs of a growing community, even after the Lakeway Civic Corporation turned them over to the Village of Lakeway in 1987 because of maintenance costs and liability issues. Clearly, there was a need to set aside additional parkland, but the Lakeway Company was not so inclined. As would so often occur in the history of Lakeway, a couple of special residents stepped up to meet the challenge.

***

Jack and Myrtle Hamilton moved to Lakeway in 1975, after he retired as president of an Amoco Oil subsidiary in Iran. "We were looking for a Shangri-La," said Jack, "and we found it in Lakeway." The Hamiltons built a home next to the eleventh tee on the Live Oak Golf Course, where they occasionally greeted thirsty golfers with a refreshing drink. On New Year's Day they were even known to serve eggnogs. And because their home was near the airstrip, they frequently offered telephone and taxi service to arriving guests. Not surprisingly, they also became involved in a wide variety of additional community activities.

While Jack was serving as president of the Lakeway Civic Corporation, the Lakeway Company's Bob Alpert agreed to sell eighty-four acres along Hurst Creek, downstream from Lohman's Crossing. When Jack discussed the $44,000 asking price with members of the LCC board, they agreed they would have to start a fund drive. Jack called a recess and went home for lunch. When he returned, he told the board he had already raised the money.

"How?" was their incredulous response.

"Well," said Jack, "I asked Myrtle."

As Myrtle later explained, "We wanted to do something for Lakeway. We didn't want to take a cruise or something just for ourselves." The Hamiltons later bequeathed a large sum of money in their will to develop and maintain this new parkland, but before their generous gift officially became the Hamilton Greenbelt, critics had to be convinced that this wonderful gift would not create social and security problems for neighborhood residents.

The original plans for the Hamilton Greenbelt included hiking, bicycling, and nature trails, with the possible addition later of a children's playground, ballfields, and a picnic area. Several nearby homeowners responded with threatened legal actions because they feared the greenbelt would jeopardize their privacy and lead to trespassing, vandalism, noise, drugs, crime, and unnamed "immoral" activities. As one *Lake Travis View* letter writer put it, "We do not wish to create locations in Lakeway which will enhance crime, and, in particular, give the newly-arrived teenagers opportunities for practicing obscure activities." Other faultfinders insisted it would raise taxes and force the community to hire more police. Someone suggested the land instead should be turned into a wildlife and nature preserve. The Lakeway Civic Corporation and several local homeowners made separate studies of the best possible use of the land. When they compared notes, they discovered their findings were not all that different. Everyone agreed the trails should be at least 200 feet from any private properties, and motorized vehicles, toilets, and picnic tables would be prohibited. In addition, there would be only two parking areas, and the two nature trails would follow the land's natural contours. Finally, as few trees as possible would be cut down and the greenbelt would be left in its natural state. Declaring the greenbelt a bird sanctuary and nature preserve also meant neighbors would be protected from overuse and the wrong kind of development.

Jack and Myrtle Hamilton

Nature writer John Redford Taylor might also have swayed sentiment with an article in the August 16, 1990, *Lake Travis View.* Calling the greenbelt "a pocket of primeval tranquillity," he reminded readers what this land looked like millions of years ago when "Tyrannosaurus Rex loped through the area, terrorizing other smaller and larger reptiles."

> You walk atop a limestone cap that descends 380 feet below the thin, Hill Country top soil. Called the Glen Rose formation, the limestone cap was formed during the geologic period known as the Lower Cretaceous. Its red rock path meanders for 1,700 paces along Hurst Creek, into and back out of the preserve. The path cuts through a slice of natural history that traces its origin back 135 million years.
>
> Through a surprising variety of trees and shrubs, 23 of which are conveniently labeled, you walk atop a limestone cap that descends 380 feet below the thin, Hill Country top soil. . . . [On] the inbound

path of the greenbelt . . . you find a clear pool below a grotto carved out by creek waters that washed away softer formations. The pool is still fed by the trickle of Hurst Creek, growing weaker as upstream dams and lowered water tables prevail. The reed-framed, weedy pool is alive with fathead minnows and killifish that scurry in and out of dark shallows, eating small insects and practicing their getaways for when the resident green-backed heron arrives to dine.

If you look closely at the limestone layers below the falls and the boulder-studded slope across the pool, you can see half a million years of stony history. Cricket frogs, salamanders, and brown snakes thrive there. . . .

There are two bison-sized Indian mounds along the pathways: one near the grotto falls and the other on the back-leg path. They remind us of the horseless, gunless Tonkawas who were native to this area. . . .

The Hamilton Greenbelt grows mulberry trees, agaritas, persimmons, river willows, bumelias, sycamores, bottle-brushes, parsley law, button bushes, flameleaf sumacs, and other broadleafs, all trying to turn this cedar brake into a deciduous woodland. . . .

The greenbelt hosts killdeer, belted kingfishers, whitetail deer, raccoons, skunk, and nine-banded armadillos. You can see wagtails on rocks in the creek, snipping insects with their sharp little beaks; spotted sandpipers mining the stream for worms and small crustacean, blue heron stalking frogs, fish and snakes in the smorgasbord at water's edge; and a hundred other species of Hill Country flora and fauna. . . .

The Hamilton Greenbelt I officially opened on April 21, 1990, the day before National Earth Day. After its dedication, LCC President A. P. "Block" Olbrich invited everyone "to take a hike on the 4,200-foot-long marble-chip trail." Hamilton Greenbelt II was completed and dedicated in May of the following year. It included a second trail that went primarily along Yaupon Creek and could be accessed from a new entrance on Palos Verde Drive. In 1996, after obtaining an easement from the Lakeway MUD, the LCC donated $35,000 to complete a connecting trail between Hamilton Greenbelts I and II. A primitive trail, designed by George Blume, was added in 1998–1999 through the efforts of Friends of the Park, city funds, and a matching grant from Texas Parks & Wildlife. This primitive trail, which could also be accessed from Squires Drive, reached all the way to the Hurst Creek inlet into Lake Travis, thereby increasing the total distance of the Hamilton Greenbelt trails to approximately six miles.

When Jack Hamilton died in 1993, three years after Myrtle, the LCC learned it would receive $260,000 from the Hamilton estate for maintaining the Hamilton Greenbelt. It used the money to "establish an inviolate and perpetual Greenbelt Trust Fund," which later became a part of the Lakeway Community Foundation, when it was created in 1997 as "a tax-free legal entity to accept tax deductible donations for various civic purposes." Of the Hamiltons, LCC President John Brodnax said, "Jack and Myrtle lived so as to leave things better than they found them. Their love for Lakeway and their desire to improve it is an inspiration to all of us."

In July 1995, the LCC deeded the Hamilton Greenbelt to the City of Lakeway, where it came under the city's Parks and Recreation Commission, which since its creation in 1991 has overseen all parklands.

Friends of the Parks built this Hurst Creek overview in the Hamilton Greenbelt in 2010.

THE SMITH GREENBELT

In 1997, community activists Coleman and Mary Smith donated $125,000 to the Lakeway Community Foundation for the acquisition and development of 4.6 wooded acres along Hurst Creek. Located between Lohman's Crossing and Lakeway Drive, the Smith Greenbelt was named in their honor. The city had apparently traded 1.5 public acres on Lakeway Drive to developers Jim Rasnick and Joe Longton, who built the Santorini Villas on the property. In return, they sold land along Hurst Creek to the Lakeway Community Foundation.

In 2002, the Lakeway Civic Corporation funded a $12,000, 350-foot concrete walkway connecting the Hamilton and Smith Greenbelts. Now one could walk on a public path all the way from the northeast end of the Hamilton Greenbelt to the end of Lakeway Boulevard, a distance of almost five miles. Even more impressive is the fact that Lakeway now has more than ten miles of trails, with twenty-two additional miles planned for the Highlands over the next several years.

Cal Rice, "Hurst Creek and the Smith Greenbelt"

Smith Greenbelt Reflecting Pond

Bill Hawkins' prize-winning photographs depict Lakeway and its parklands as a nature lover's paradise.

TRAILS OF THE HAMILTON GREENBELT AND THE SMITH GREENBELT, CIRCA 2009

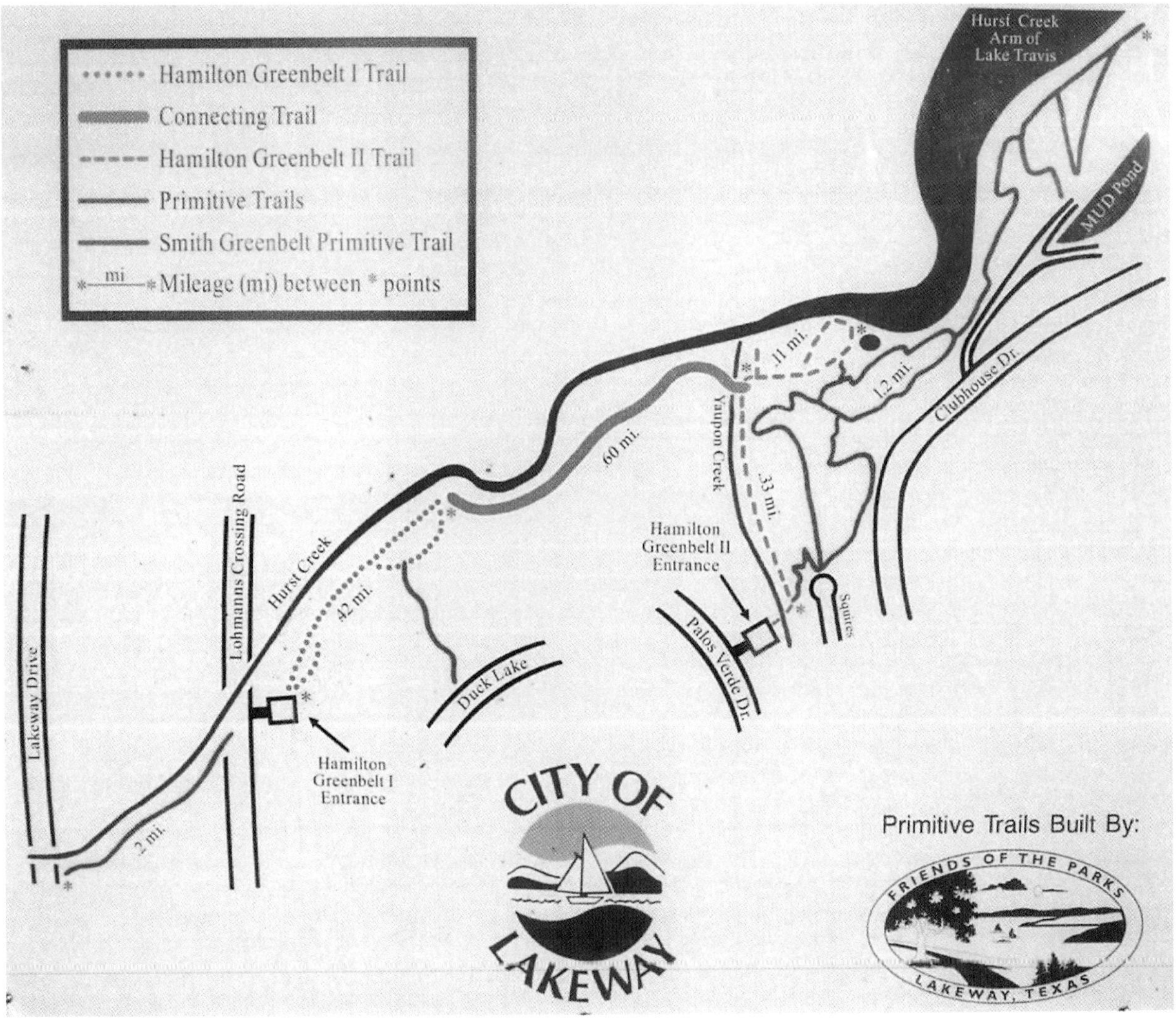

FRIENDS OF THE PARKS

The idea of Friends of the Parks is not so much to save money as it is to develop volunteer activities.

Peg Hein, co-founder and chair of Friends of the Parks

Friends of the Parks is a group of citizens who enjoy the rewards of volunteer service in the parks and greenbelt areas of Lakeway. Monthly Saturday morning work sessions provide opportunities for all levels of service, whether it is tree maintenance, general clean-up or tending the memorial gardens at City Park. A few of the hardier members help build and maintain hiking/biking trails in the Greenbelts and Canyonlands Natural Area. Still others provide food for monthly workday picnics.

Fred Hazen, Chair, Friends of the Parks, 2002–2003

On June 21, 1996, the Lakeway Parks and Recreation Board approved the formation of Friends of the Parks (FOP), a volunteer group that would care for, improve, and beautify parks and greenbelts, including the construction of literally miles of trails and several bridges. FOP's first meeting was held at the new City Park Pavilion on August 28, 1996. The twenty-eight founding members elected Marv and Peg Hein as co-chairs for the first two years. Subsequent chairs were George Blume, 1998–1999; Fred Roth, 2000–2001; Fred Hazen, 2002–2003; Jesse Gutierrez, 2004–2005; Mickey Wright, 2006–2007; George Ferrie, 2008–2009; and Bill Freas, 2010–1011. There are currently more than 150 members.

The Friends of the Parks's first major project focused on the recently acquired City Park property, which included a general cleanup, the trimming and thinning of cedars, and the laying out and building of trails. Other early City Park projects were the Barnes and Kathryn's Corner Memorial Gardens, the Butterfly Garden, the Dewitt Ira Smith Cactus Garden, and the planting of native trees. A grant from the National Tree Trust resulted in the planting of more than 300 native varieties in Lakeway's parks, greenbelts, and along Lakeway Boulevard.

Friends of the Parks did not build the original trail in the Hamilton Greenbelt, but its members extended and improved the trails, which enabled the FOP to host an annual 5K and 10K run/walk.

George Blume was the first to recommend land along Hurst Creek Road for a city park. In addition to being a city councilmember and chairman of Friends of the Parks, Blume designed and built primitive trails and bridges in the Hamilton Greenbelt and the Canyonlands.

Peg and Marv Hein founded Friends of the Parks in 1996 and served as co-chairs for the first two years.

Beginning in 1999, Friends of the Parks sponsored the annual 5K/10K Wilderness Run/Walk in the Hamilton Greenbelt.

THE CANYONLANDS

As part of a Texas Parks & Wildlife $500,000 grant for its new Swim Center Park, the City of Lakeway agreed to keep the Canyonlands in its natural state in perpetuity; however, nature trails, benches, and other limited improvements were permitted. Consisting of twenty-four acres of spectacular scenery and rugged terrain, the Canyonlands exists at the upper reaches of Rough Hollow Cove. The rim trail provides breathtaking vistas, particularly during autumn colors, and other trails, all built by Friends of the Parks, take hikers down into the canyon and along both sides. Friends of the Parks has also built bridges and water erosion dams to make the Canyonlands safe and accessible for hikers and nature lovers.

The Canyonlands

Autumn in The Canyonlands and the Reflecting Pool

Lakeway Mayor Dave DeOme and two additional Friends of the Parks volunteers prepare concrete supports for a Canyonlands bridge.

TRAILS OF THE CANYONLANDS

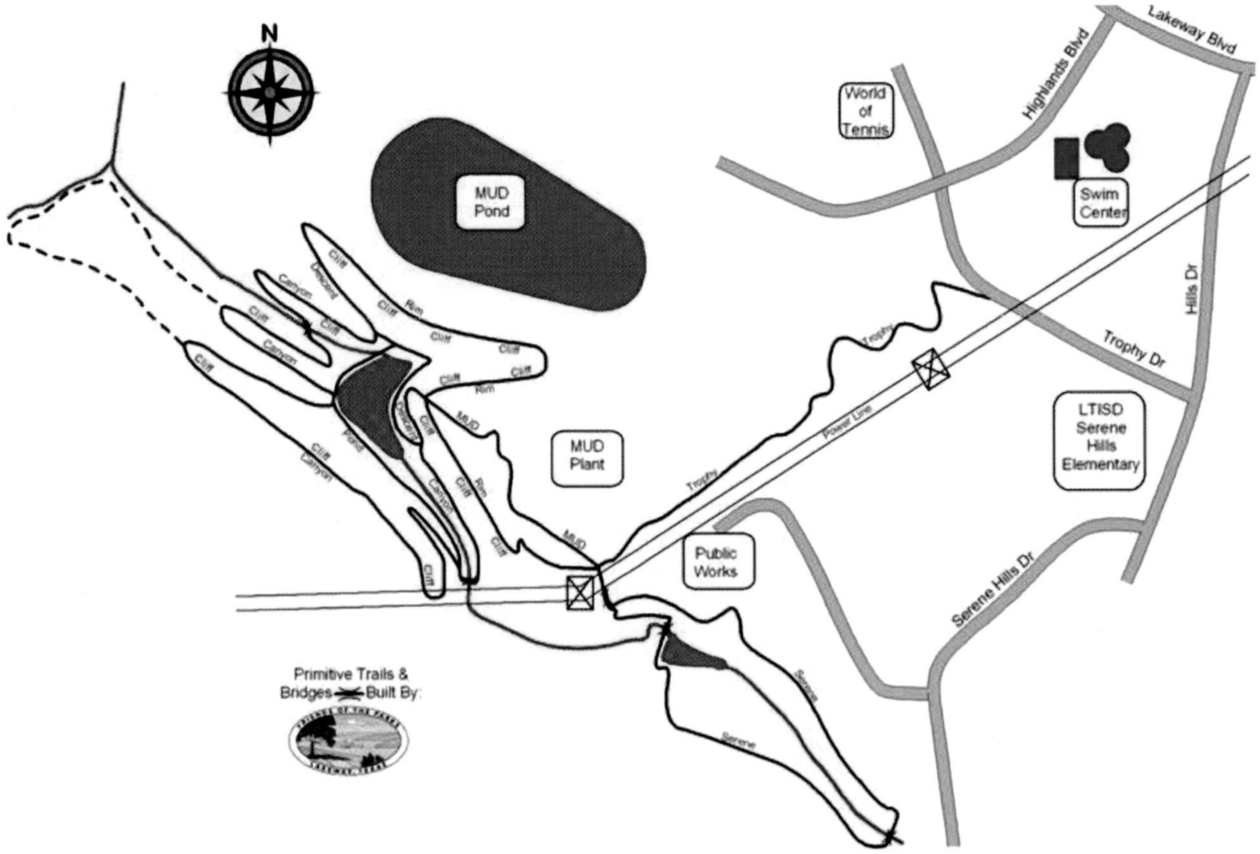

CHAPTER THIRTEEN

THE BATTLE OVER CITY PARK

Isn't it conceivable that 25 years from now Lakeway residents will be grateful that a parcel of land on Lake Travis was saved and made into a city park?

BEA SMITH, *LAKE TRAVIS VIEW*, JUNE 18, 1992

[My wife and I] envision a park full of 500 or so gays and lesbians sunning their fannies on the ledges and shore as they do in Hippie Hollow.

ROBERT WEEST, *LAKE TRAVIS VIEW*, JULY 30, 1992

City Park's wildflower meadow

THE RELATIVELY MILD DEBATE OVER ACQUIRING the Hamilton Greenbelt paled alongside the full-blown brouhaha surrounding the announcement that Lakeway planned to purchase fifty-four acres of waterfront land for a future city park. The controversy became so heated, even splitting up old friends, that one Lakeway dinner hostess allegedly warned her guests that anyone talking about either the park or abortion would be served no dessert. Opponents warned of uncontrolled mobs of people, gridlocked traffic, giant tax increases, and Lake-

The future Lakeway City Park as it looked in 1991

way becoming another Hippie Hollow, where folks shed their clothes before dipping into Lake Travis. There were also those who preferred to use the land for commercial purposes, including rumors of a possible six-story hotel and marina or a multi-unit condo development. Proponents argued that a growing city needed a public park for its families and that this particular property, with more than 2,000 feet of water frontage, represented the community's last chance to obtain land with such potential.

Early in 1991, George Blume, who was then a member of the Lake Travis Chamber of Commerce, was looking for parkland. He had approached the Lakeway MUD concerning property on Lohman's Crossing, near where the round water tank now stands; fortunately, the MUD turned him down. George was disappointed, but his mood changed when he saw a sign on Hurst Creek Road advertising a sixty-four-acre, waterfront property. The original asking price was $677,000, which was less than its appraised value of $714,900. George spoke with Mayor Cole Rowland, Councilmember Veronica Bennett, and City Administrator Sam Huser, all of whom were enthusiastic about the purchase. Bennett, who was also chairman of the Land Acquisition Committee, declared, "This is the last piece of property for Lakeway to acquire. Even if we did nothing with it, we could protect it from having a six-story hotel built on it." She also pointed out that an increase in taxes would only amount to $20 to $30 per year for the average homeowner.

Years later, Mayor Cole Rowland explained how the city purchased the land for slightly more than one-half of its original asking price. A councilmember who strongly opposed purchasing the land suggested offering $375,000, believing that such a ridiculously low bid would surely be rejected. He was wrong. At the time, the country was still suffering the aftereffects of the Savings and Loan debacle, which had forced the federal government to form the Resolution Trust Corporation (RTC) to liquidate the assets of defaulting banks and S&Ls. Because the Lakeway property had been repossessed, the RTC was willing to accept Lakeway's lowball offer.

Before the offer could be consummated, it had

to be put to a vote, which triggered an intense community debate, often via letter-writing campaigns in the *Lake Travis View*. Former mayor Ed Smith referred to "a written policy that no public lands should be on the Lake" and suggested instead taking a piece of the Hamilton Greenbelt. Smith also warned that it would cost as much as a million dollars to develop the park and that one-fifth of the land was underwater. Ed Nelson, who was vice president of the Park Homeowner's Association, said there were concerns about "increased traffic, a surge in muggings, assaults and rapes, harassment of pedestrians by motorists since there are no sidewalks, and an increase in trespassers, drunk drivers and drug traffickers." Former mayor Jim Gribble proposed the area behind the Village Square, although those sixteen acres were then being offered for approximately three times the asking price per acre of the Hurst Creek parkland, and with no water frontage. Gribble also suggested acreage on Lohman's Road south of Retama Courts, stressing that both these properties would be more secure because of nearby police facilities. Another former mayor, N. C. Herndon, also opposed the purchase of parkland on Hurst Creek, insisting that it would be "inviting to people of all classes, some of whom might be very undesirable [and] may have unsanitary habits, some may be foul mouthed, some may be dope users, and some may be generally obnoxious. . . . Would you want them to use the public restrooms and portable facilities?" Park opponents then circulated this ominous warning:

WARNING!!

VOTE NO TO LAKEWAY'S HIPPIE HOLLOW!!

Saturday, June 22, 1991, an election will be held to determine if the City of Lakeway should acquire land to establish a public park on Lake Travis.

The Facts are:

THIS "PARK" and its improvements could RAISE LAKEWAY TAXES by $5,000 per family

THIS "PARK" could become another Hippie Hollow.

THIS "PARK" could attract NUDE SUNBATHERS, DRUGS, AND TRASH to Lakeway.

THIS "PARK" could result in MASSIVE TRAFFIC JAMS on Hurst Creek, Lohman's Crossing, and Lakeway Drive.

VOTE NO

AT CITY HALL ON SATURDAY, JUNE 22, 1991
(ABSENTEE VOTING JUNE 10-21, 1991)
AND PRESERVE THE QUALITY OF LIFE IN LAKEWAY

George Blume countered the worst fears of the critics, pointing out that "Hamilton Greenbelts I and II have trails going through heavily wood areas, with numerous secluded and remote areas. . . , [but] drugs, drinking, and other mischief are not a problem." Councilwoman Veronica Bennett also attempted to allay fears that a city park might become another Hippie Hollow: "Can you imagine a Hippie Hollow in Lakeway? Everyone has to drive past the police station to get into Lakeway." Lorraine Kyle Stryjak argued that "most of us would be paying less in one year to purchase the park than we do to receive cable TV for one month." She then added, "The ownership of this proposed parkland offers this generation of Lakeway residents the opportunity to contribute lasting beauty to the community." John Daniels put it even more succinctly, "If it turns out only half as nice as the Hamilton Greenbelt projects, it will be a tremendous boost to our community." An older citizen, who admitted she had changed her mind about voting against the park after taking a tour of the property, wrote, "I think I'll like taking my great-grandchildren to fish there."

On June 22, 1991, the measure to purchase the property passed by the narrow margin of nineteen votes, although today scarcely anyone will admit to having voted against the park.

After the successful vote, the Lakeway City Council authorized Mayor Cole Rowland to seek park planning from the Texas Parks & Wildlife Department, which offered this free service for municipalities under 7,500 residents. The city council also created an eleven-member, all-volunteer Parks and Recreation Commission to assist and advise on the maintenance and operation of the city parks, greenbelts, and recreational facilities and to establish rules and regulations for the use of these amenities. Chairman John "Ken" Pettigrew and his commission members began by sending questionnaires to 1,738 registered voters soliciting their input on what they wanted in their park. Of the 497 responses, only 37 were negative. Walking trails, picnic tables, and benches led the list, while gaming tables, shuffleboard, and rental canoes were the least desired. A majority also objected to alcohol and lighted ballfields.

The commission held more than twenty open meetings to obtain further citizen input. A few respondents continued to worry about noise, congestion, crime, and falling property values, but most participants now wanted to create the best possible park. Of the twenty-one items requested by citizens, the only rejections were a boat ramp, amphitheater, tennis courts, outdoor and indoor pools, and canoe rentals.

Protracted legal battles brought against the city by Houston-based oilman and part-time resident Jeff Sandefer greatly complicated planning for the park. Sandefer had at one time owned the park property, but had sold it for more than $2 million to Austin developer Doug Fike, who, before the Savings and Loan collapse, reportedly was planning to build seventy condos on the property. Sandefer, who still owned a vacation house at the edge of the parkland, now brought suit because the planned ballfields would allegedly devalue his property. When he lost this suit, Sandefer hired environmental experts to find evidence that the park would also destroy the potential habitat of the endangered golden-cheeked warbler. Unfortunately, no warblers were available to help settle matters, as they were wintering in Central America. Nor did the warblers appear in the spring, when Horizon Environmental Services spent three days searching for them.

Sandefer next accused the city of polluting the ground with sediment from burning asbestos construction materials while clearing the land for the ball diamond. Sandefer sent his "findings" to state and federal environmental agencies, but the Texas Air Control Board told him he was wasting its time. Sandefer also triggered the wrath of George Blume, who wrote a letter asking how Sandefer knew the city was burning toxic waste. Blume also asked if Sandefer himself had dumped the toxic waste there when he owned the property. If so, explained Blume, he was legally obligated to inform those to whom he had sold the property. Blume also walked the Sandefer property, where he discovered a discarded automobile battery, gasoline cans, and an assortment of environmentally unsound plastic objects.

Because the vote to purchase the parkland had passed by such a narrow margin, opponents now insisted that another vote be held to support putting the newly acquired parkland up for sale. There were also heated arguments on what the proposed park should look like. Elsa Hopkins, who was less than enthusiastic about a city park and who would win a seat on the city council in 1992, asked, "Are we really talking about a lake-front park or is it a backwater flat down in an arm of Lake Travis?" She also warned, "Residents' security has been usurped," evidently referring to those living near the park.

In July 1992, George Blume filed complaints against Jeff Sandefer and Elsa Hopkins with the Texas Ethics Commission, Sandefer for not filing as "a specific purpose committee" when he paid for newspaper ads urging readers to vote against the purchase and retaining of the city park, and Hopkins for filing a final report as treasurer of the Keep Lakeway Private Committee that contained "incomplete or false information" on the amount of money Sandefer had spent on newspaper ads and legal expenses.

Estimates of how much Jeff Sandefer spent on his war against the city park project range from $50,000 to $100,000, mostly for legal fees. He did eventually withdraw his request for a permanent court injunction to halt park construction and settled his ballfield suit by making an offer of $100,000 to the Lake Travis Youth Association to move their planned baseball diamond to Highway 71, where it and several other ballfields became known as the Field of Dreams.

By early 1992, former mayors Ed Smith and Jim Gribble, along with Jeff Sandefer and several other citizens who had also opposed buying the park, had formed the Keep Lakeway Private Committee, which circulated a petition to restrict park usage to Lakeway residents. Although the committee successfully gathered 638 names, the city refused to accept the petition, arguing that it violated the city charter and a state law that prohibited a municipality purchasing land for a public park and then making it private. Smith's response was quick and to the point: "See you in court." At the time, the city was seeking a $350,000 matching grant for the development of the parkland from the Texas Parks & Wildlife Department, which meant the park had to be open to the public. The suit brought by Keep Lakeway Private cost the city $15,000 in legal fees, but the district court ruled in its favor.

The next step for park opponents was to push for a public vote to sell the parkland, which led some pro-park individuals to declare that what the opposition really wanted was to develop this choice piece of real estate exclusively for commercial purposes.

In May 1992, Ray Norris, Burt Folsom, and Elsa Hopkins won seats on the city council. Folsom and Norris wanted to move or sell the park, whereas Hopkins, at the very least, urged keeping the land in its natural state. The three of them pushed through a council motion calling for a special election on August 8, 1992, to determine if the city should now sell the parkland. Not surprisingly, this campaign launched another spate of letters to the *Lake Travis View* and the *Homeowners News*.

Peg Hein, who would later co-found Friends of the Parks, urged voters to keep the park because "in all probability Lakeway residents will never again have access to the lake." Former mayor Richard McLaren was also supportive: "People would not believe that a place called Lakeway did not have access to the beautiful lake from which it took its name." Marten and Cheryl Davies, who were born in England, wrote that they were "horrified that there is even the remotest possibility that our American-born children may find part of their great heritage cast aside for the green and greedy dollar of development. . . . Let it not be said after the battle has raged and the votes have been cast, Remember the park! This is Lakeway's Alamo!"

Fred and Donna Schmidt responded by creating the Lakeway Enrichment Organization (LEO). With its $2,000 operating budget, the LEO membership divided Lakeway into forty-two areas and then went door-to-door passing out literature. They launched telephone and letters-to-the-editor campaigns, phone banks, voter registration drives, yard signs, and fund-raising.

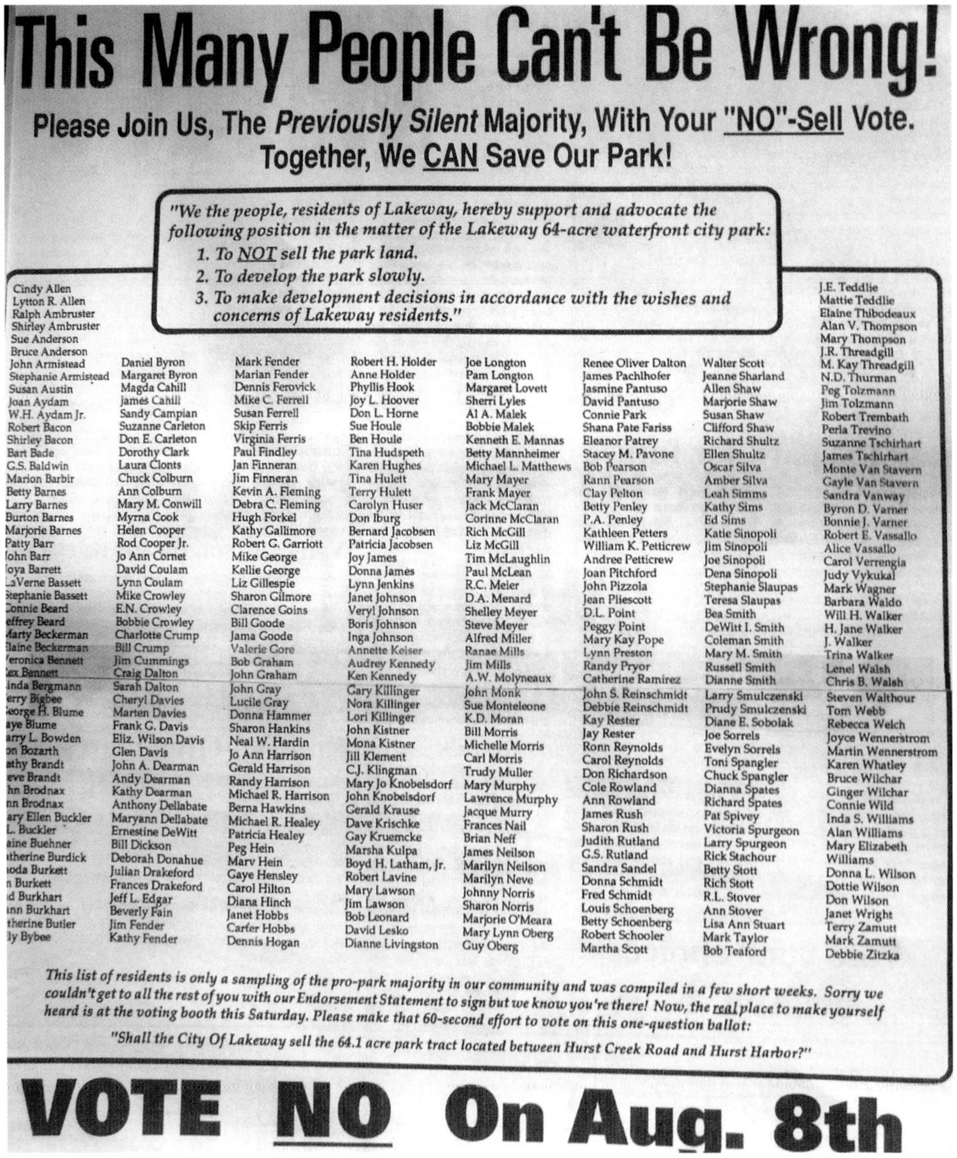

This Many People Can't Be Wrong!

Please Join Us, The *Previously Silent* Majority, With Your "NO"-Sell Vote. Together, We CAN Save Our Park!

"We the people, residents of Lakeway, hereby support and advocate the following position in the matter of the Lakeway 64-acre waterfront city park:

1. *To NOT sell the park land.*
2. *To develop the park slowly.*
3. *To make development decisions in accordance with the wishes and concerns of Lakeway residents."*

Cindy Allen
Lytton R. Allen
Ralph Ambruster
Shirley Ambruster
Sue Anderson
Bruce Anderson
John Armistead
Stephanie Armistead
Susan Austin
Joan Aydam
W.H. Aydam Jr.
Robert Bacon
Shirley Bacon
Bart Bade
G.S. Baldwin
Marion Barbir
Betty Barnes
Larry Barnes
Burton Barnes
Marjorie Barnes
Patty Barr
ohn Barr
oya Barrett
LaVerne Bassett
Stephanie Bassett
Connie Beard
effrey Beard
Marty Beckerman
laine Beckerman
eronica Bennett
ex Bennett
inda Bergmann
erry Bigbee
eorge H. Blume
aye Blume
arry L. Bowden
on Bozarth
athy Brandt
eve Brandt
hn Brodnax
nn Brodnax
ary Ellen Buckler
L. Buckler
aine Buehner
therine Burdick
oda Burkett
n Burkett
d Burkhart
nn Burkhart
therine Butler
ly Bybee

Daniel Byron
Margaret Byron
Magda Cahill
James Cahill
Sandy Campian
Suzanne Carleton
Don E. Carleton
Dorothy Clark
Laura Clonts
Chuck Colburn
Ann Colburn
Mary M. Conwill
Myrna Cook
Helen Cooper
Rod Cooper Jr.
Jo Ann Cornet
David Coulam
Lynn Coulam
Mike Crowley
E.N. Crowley
Bobbie Crowley
Charlotte Crump
Bill Crump
Jim Cummings
Craig Dalton
Sarah Dalton
Cheryl Davies
Marten Davies
Frank G. Davis
Eliz. Wilson Davis
Glen Davis
John A. Dearman
Andy Dearman
Kathy Dearman
Anthony Dellabate
Maryann Dellabate
Ernestine DeWitt
Bill Dickson
Deborah Donahue
Julian Drakeford
Frances Drakeford
Jeff L. Edgar
Beverly Fain
Jim Fender
Kathy Fender

Mark Fender
Marian Fender
Dennis Ferovick
Mike C. Ferrell
Susan Ferrell
Skip Ferris
Virginia Ferris
Paul Findley
Jan Finneran
Jim Finneran
Kevin A. Fleming
Debra C. Fleming
Hugh Forkel
Kathy Gallimore
Robert G. Garriott
Mike George
Kellie George
Liz Gillespie
Sharon Gilmore
Clarence Goins
Bill Goode
Jama Goode
Valerie Gore
Bob Graham
John Graham
John Gray
Lucile Gray
Donna Hammer
Sharon Hankins
Neal W. Hardin
Jo Ann Harrison
Gerald Harrison
Randy Harrison
Michael R. Harrison
Berna Hawkins
Michael R. Healey
Patricia Healey
Peg Hein
Marv Hein
Gaye Hensley
Carol Hilton
Diana Hinch
Janet Hobbs
Carter Hobbs
Dennis Hogan

Robert H. Holder
Anne Holder
Phyllis Hook
Joy L. Hoover
Don L. Horne
Sue Houle
Ben Houle
Tina Hudspeth
Karen Hughes
Tina Hulett
Terry Hulett
Carolyn Huser
Don Iburg
Bernard Jacobsen
Patricia Jacobsen
Joy James
Donna James
Lynn Jenkins
Janet Johnson
Veryl Johnson
Boris Johnson
Inga Johnson
Annette Keiser
Audrey Kennedy
Ken Kennedy
Gary Killinger
Nora Killinger
Lori Killinger
John Kistner
Mona Kistner
Jill Klement
C.J. Klingman
Mary Jo Knobelsdorf
John Knobelsdorf
Gerald Krause
Dave Krischke
Gay Kruemcke
Marsha Kulpa
Boyd H. Latham, Jr.
Robert Lavine
Mary Lawson
Jim Lawson
Bob Leonard
David Lesko
Dianne Livingston

Joe Longton
Pam Longton
Margaret Lovett
Sherri Lyles
Al A. Malek
Bobbie Malek
Kenneth E. Mannas
Betty Mannheimer
Michael L. Matthews
Mary Mayer
Frank Mayer
Jack McClaran
Corinne McClaran
Rich McGill
Liz McGill
Tim McLaughlin
Paul McLean
R.C. Meier
D.A. Menard
Shelley Meyer
Steve Meyer
Alfred Miller
Ranae Mills
Jim Mills
A.W. Molyneaux
John Monk
Sue Monteleone
K.D. Moran
Bill Morris
Michelle Morris
Carl Morris
Trudy Muller
Mary Murphy
Lawrence Murphy
Jacque Murry
Frances Nail
Brian Neff
James Neilson
Marilyn Neilson
Marilyn Neve
Johnny Norris
Sharon Norris
Marjorie O'Meara
Mary Lynn Oberg
Guy Oberg

Renee Oliver Dalton
James Pachlhofer
Jasmine Pantuso
David Pantuso
Connie Park
Shana Pate Fariss
Eleanor Patrey
Stacey M. Pavone
Bob Pearson
Rann Pearson
Clay Pelton
Betty Penley
P.A. Penley
Kathleen Petters
William K. Petticrew
Andree Petticrew
Joan Pitchford
John Pizzola
Jean Pliescott
D.L. Point
Peggy Point
Mary Kay Pope
Lynn Preston
Randy Pryor
Catherine Ramirez
John S. Reinschmidt
Debbie Reinschmidt
Kay Rester
Jay Rester
Ronn Reynolds
Carol Reynolds
Don Richardson
Cole Rowland
Ann Rowland
James Rush
Sharon Rush
Judith Rutland
G.S. Rutland
Sandra Sandel
Donna Schmidt
Fred Schmidt
Louis Schoenberg
Betty Schoenberg
Robert Schooler
Martha Scott

Walter Scott
Jeanne Sharland
Allen Shaw
Marjorie Shaw
Susan Shaw
Clifford Shaw
Richard Shultz
Ellen Shultz
Oscar Silva
Amber Silva
Leah Simms
Kathy Sims
Ed Sims
Katie Sinopoli
Jim Sinopoli
Joe Sinopoli
Dena Sinopoli
Stephanie Slaupas
Teresa Slaupas
Bea Smith
DeWitt I. Smith
Coleman Smith
Mary M. Smith
Russell Smith
Dianne Smith
Larry Smulczenski
Prudy Smulczenski
Diane E. Sobolak
Joe Sorrels
Evelyn Sorrels
Toni Spangler
Chuck Spangler
Dianna Spates
Richard Spates
Pat Spivey
Victoria Spurgeon
Larry Spurgeon
Rick Stachour
Betty Stott
Rich Stott
R.L. Stover
Ann Stover
Lisa Ann Stuart
Mark Taylor
Bob Teaford

J.E. Teddlie
Mattie Teddlie
Elaine Thibodeaux
Alan V. Thompson
Mary Thompson
J.R. Threadgill
M. Kay Threadgill
N.D. Thurman
Peg Tolzmann
Jim Tolzmann
Robert Trembath
Perla Trevino
Suzanne Tschirhart
James Tschirhart
Monte Van Stavern
Gayle Van Stavern
Sandra Vanway
Byron D. Varner
Bonnie J. Varner
Robert E. Vassallo
Alice Vassallo
Carol Verrengia
Judy Vykukal
Mark Wagner
Barbara Waldo
Will H. Walker
H. Jane Walker
J. Walker
Trina Walker
Lenel Walsh
Chris B. Walsh
Steven Walthour
Tom Webb
Rebecca Welch
Joyce Wennerstrom
Martin Wennerstrom
Karen Whatley
Bruce Wilchar
Ginger Wilchar
Connie Wild
Inda S. Williams
Alan Williams
Mary Elizabeth Williams
Donna L. Wilson
Dottie Wilson
Don Wilson
Janet Wright
Terry Zamutt
Mark Zamutt
Debbie Zitzka

This list of residents is only a sampling of the pro-park majority in our community and was compiled in a few short weeks. Sorry we couldn't get to all the rest of you with our Endorsement Statement to sign but we know you're there! Now, the real place to make yourself heard is at the voting booth this Saturday. Please make that 60-second effort to vote on this one-question ballot:

"Shall the City Of Lakeway sell the 64.1 acre park tract located between Hurst Creek Road and Hurst Harbor?"

VOTE NO On Aug. 8th

The LEO also published its own broadbill, urging voters to "Save Our Park!"

On August 8, 1992, Lakeway residents convincingly rejected selling the park by a vote of 1,286 to 736. Shortly thereafter, the city council accepted the bid of $399,800 from Keystone Construction and Fred Tillman Construction to build the park, although that figure was later reduced when the city slightly modified its specifications for trails and other aspects of the park and agreed to do much of the clearing and leveling itself. In addition, Lakeway residents were encouraged to help defray expenses by donating money toward picnic and pavilion tables, grills, park benches, and other park amenities.

Lakeway volunteers also exceeded the minimum of $10,000 worth of labor, equipment, and materials needed as part of the campaign to obtain a Texas Parks & Wildlife matching grant. Calling themselves SAMBA in the Park (Saturday Morning Bushwhacker Assembly in the Park), the volunteers devoted two Saturday mornings each month during late 1993 and all of 1994 chopping and sawing, raking and hauling, and determining which trees and plants should be retained. In doing so, the SAMBA volunteers anticipated the more permanent Friends of the Parks organization, which began caring for the parks and greenbelts in 1996.

The Lakeway City Park was officially dedicated on April 9, 1994. In his comments commemorating the acquisition and building of City Park, Parks and Recreation Commission chairman Alan Williams singled out George Blume, city administrator Sam Huser, and Fred and Donna Schmidt for special praise: "If it weren't for their special efforts we would not be standing here today." He also praised former mayor Cole Rowland, who had vigorously supported the park during his administration. As for his own contributions, Williams, who, along with the Schmidts, had been active in the fund-raising campaign to help the city match the Texas Parks & Wildlife's $420,000 grant, jokingly mentioned his need for a bulletproof vest during some of the heated meetings.

***

With the battle for City Park having finally been won, Lakeway citizens could now concentrate on building the best possible park, which they have done with admirable resolve, imagination, and the strong backs of literally hundreds of volunteers, many of whom became members of Friends of the Parks.

Five months after its official opening, roughly 100 cars a day were entering City Park, and there had been no reports of vandalism. On July 12, 1994, the Lakeway City Council approved spending $63,500 on park improvements, as had been requested by the Parks and Recreation Commission. Fortunately, the city had cleared $70,000 from the sale of water taps that were on the original property. Private donations had also brought in several thousand dollars. According to the October 1994 issue of the *Homeowners News*, which initially had not been enthusiastic about the park, "CITY PARK IS A REAL SUCCESS STORY!"

City Park is indeed a magnificent creation, combining its natural blessings with the human touch of those who have worked so diligently to make it attractive. Nevertheless, some things cannot be controlled, especially the capricious whims of Mother Nature. In July 2007, heavy rains, including nineteen inches in a single day in Marble Falls, pushed Lake Travis to 701.6 feet,

City Park's Upper Trail

an increase of over twenty feet in one week. In the Lakeway area, water reached the second floor of some homes in Graveyard Point. The torrential rains and the fast-rising Lake Travis also left City Park's major trails underwater and usable only by web-footed creatures.

An early criticism of the park was that it was being built primarily for children in what some residents still considered a semi-exclusive, retirement community. Nothing could be further from the truth. On any given weekday, one will find more adults than children in City Park, although happily all ages take advantage of the facilities, including many of their canine family members.

In 1998, Ellen Ybarra asked the city council to build a dog park so "dogs can run free, socialize, do their business, and play with their canine friends." The city built and opened the Dog Park in 2000. All dogs are welcome, regardless of parentage, breed, or color.

The City Park's Butterfly Garden, which opened in 1999, was made possible by a donation from the Bernard M. Jacobsen Memorial Fund. Professional butterfly garden designers donated their expertise to the project and selected appropriate plants and trees. The Butterfly Garden contains at least two special plants that appear to be weeds to the uninitiated, but actually provide nectar for the Monarch butterflies during their normal mid-October migration. One is called frost weed, whose small, white flowers remain until the frost, and the other is the poverty or Roosevelt bush, which in October is covered with clusters of small, white flowers. Other plants in the Butterfly Garden attract different varieties of butterflies and provide their own nectar, as well as places for the laying of eggs.

Friends of the Parks's members clearing brush and building a kayak and canoe ramp in City Park. That's Mayor Dave DeOme with the pickaxe.

Special events such as this hot-air balloon rally have proven enormously popular in City Park. In 2010, for example, an estimated 6,700 visitors collectively attended Eggstravaganza, the Fourth of July Celebration, Movies in the Park, and Goblin Blow. Yet, everyday activities are of greatest value to most families. On any given day, several hundred people will enjoy the simple pleasures of walking the two miles of park trails, picnicking, playing basketball or volleyball, chasing canines in the dog park and children on the playscape, or simply sitting on a bench chatting with friends.

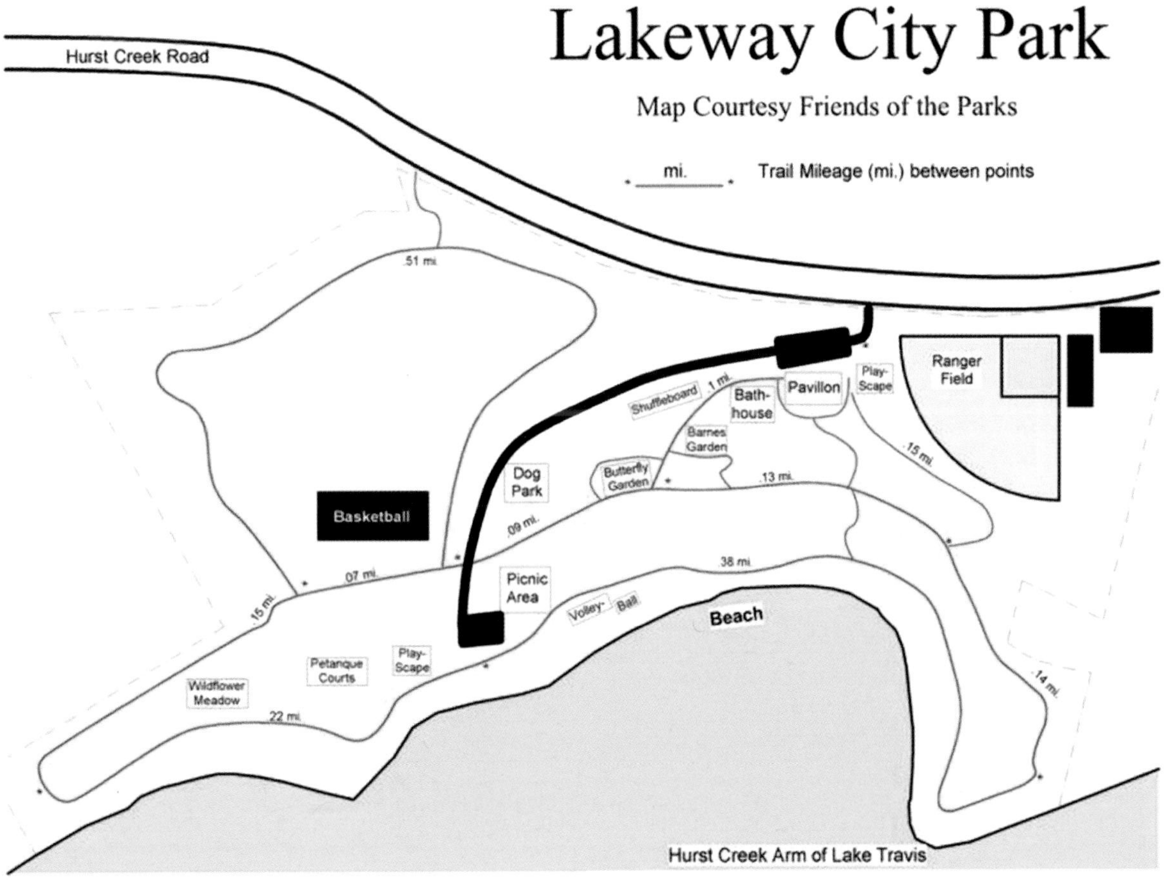

CHAPTER FOURTEEN

THE LAKEWAY ACTIVITY CENTER

All taxpayers of the city will be required to fund a facility that will be used regularly by only about 10% of the residents.

KEN KENNEDY, LAKEWAY ALDERMAN AND COUNCILMEMBER

We have the opportunity to create a place where we can all be together, young and old, enhancing our community's quality of life and pulling together towards a common goal.

SHELLEY MEYER, COMMUNITY CENTER COMMITTEE

DISCUSSIONS CONCERNING THE NEED FOR A community center had been ongoing since the beginning of Lakeway in 1963. Early residents used the Lakeway Inn and the Property Owners Clubroom at the Live Oak Golf Club for public meetings, at least until the Clubroom burned down in 1982. They then turned to the auditorium in the Village Hall, but the growing community needed a larger facility for its public and social meetings. Unfortunately, the wheels of progress often roll at an agonizingly slow pace.

***

In a 1986 commissioned report, architects Stuart L. Rothman and Richard E. Wall presented several reasons why Lakeway should build its own community center:

> Civic and community centers are social structures, user-friendly, warm and inviting, pleasant to look at and be in, and symbolic of the "good life."
>
> [They] are unique urban places intended to generate community pride and promote the vitality of the image of the city they are in. . . .
>
> There now exists a fair number of clubs and associations encompassing a wide and fascinating diverse range of activities in [Lakeway]. Give them a place to flourish and they will.

The architects also suggested a wide range of possible governmental, recreational, social, and commercial possibilities, including meeting rooms for up to 500 persons that could be divided into smaller spaces for music and dance classes, card games, exercise rooms, a library, food service, and even a health club.

The following May, the *Homeowners News* supported a community center, which would become "the hub of civic, government, cultural, recreational, and religious activities." The editors pointed out that normally the developer sets aside land for such a building but unfortunately that had not been the case for Lakeway.

On March 31, 1988, Mayor C. Ed Smith appointed the first of what would eventually be three Community Center Committees, all of which concluded that Lakeway should have some kind of building to house its various social and community organizations. That year, the Lake Travis Chamber of Commerce also endorsed the idea of a community center. With a steadily increasing population, which optimistic planners predicted might well reach 10,000 residents by 2005, something clearly had to be done.

In September 1992, Mayor Cole Rowland appointed the second Community Center Committee to review past campaigns and to recommend where a center might be built and what it should contain. Under the guidance of chairman Bob Stover, the committee sent out questionnaires seeking input on two qualitatively different activity centers, with one costing approximately twice as much as the other. Of the 664 respondents, 223 voted for the more expensive version, 170 for the cheaper plan, and 252 wanted neither.

On March 3, 1993, the *Austin American-Statesman* announced, "Lakeway May Build Million-Dollar Center." Unfortunately, this triggered a negative reaction among more conservative elements of Lakeway. Nevertheless, in December Mayor Burton Barnes, who had come into office the preceding May, recommended a very ambitious structure to be built on a ten-acre tract that the city had recently purchased behind the Village Square. The 15,000-square-foot main floor was to include "a combination of fixed and flexible meeting rooms." A lower level of some 9,600 square feet would provide "high impact" space for youth and adults, including an indoor, 45- by 75-foot heated swimming pool. The committee recommended $20 to $30 annual fees for adult members, plus an additional $30 to $40 for an adult pool membership. Non-taxpayers could become members by paying higher fees. The committee estimated the cost of the facility at just under $3 million, to be financed by municipal bonds, which would require voter approval at the regularly scheduled election on May 7, 1994.

As had earlier occurred in disputes over the Hamilton Greenbelt and City Park, residents once again expressed impassioned opinions in the *Lake Travis View*. Those opposed usually cited high building and operating costs, especially those connected with the indoor pool, which they feared would result in sizeable property tax increases. Mike Bowens's objection covered several points: "The city council needs to return to their basic charter of providing law enforcement, maintenance of infrastructure, and enforcement of regulations, and leave the empire building, monument production and misplaced social activism to our neighbors to the east." Former councilmember Ken Kennedy added that the city "should not be getting into the entertainment business." As a member of the Community Center Committee, Shelley Meyer predictably supported the proposed plan: "We have the opportunity to create a place where we can all be together, young and old, enhancing our community's quality of life and pulling together towards a common goal." Councilmember Elsa Hopkins, who actually was willing to accept a scaled-down version of what she initially labeled "a tax-funded country club," opined, "Societies which have invaded the storehouse to eat the seed grain have always perished."

Supporters of a community center formed the Lakeway Enrichment Organization, which on April 28, 1994, ran the following bold-print notice in the *Lake Travis View:*

You're Being Deceived

By uppity Community Center OPPONENTS with poor research, bad financial data, misinformation and misrepresentation, and a clear inability to place the needs of the broad Lakeway Community above their own special interests, financial stinginess, and visible fear of "the public" (i.e., anyone—Lakeway residents and outsiders alike—not circulating within their private social circles).

You're Being Robbed

Of the best opportunity Lakeway has ever had to finally build its much needed Community Center, including a reasonable selection of facilities to service the recreational needs of today's resident population.

VOTE FOR! THE COMMUNITY CENTER. NOW.

Opponents responded by creating the Concerned Citizens of Lakeway, which stressed building costs, which they insisted would be at least $700,000 more than the city's new estimate of $3,500,000, resulting in an even greater jump in property taxes. The most contentious issue was clearly the indoor pool, and when Mayor Barnes and a majority of the Lakeway City Council insisted on an all-or-nothing vote, which included the pool, any hope for passing the bond issue was gone.

On May 7, 1994, voters soundly rejected the bond issue needed to pay for the proposed Activity Center by a margin of 1,621 to 508. Two days before the election, Concerned Citizens of Lakeway took out a full-page ad in the *Lake Travis View* that clearly highlighted the main issue for the majority of voters: "VOTE AGAINST THE BOND ISSUE! SAY NO TO HIGH TAXES!"

Shortly after the defeat, John Reagan, who had opposed the previous bond issue, coordinated a private committee, which proposed a more modest building that included no swimming pool or exercise facility. The Reagan committee also suggested a privately financed facility or one possibly underwritten by the Lakeway Civic Corporation and its Property Maintenance Trust Fund. When the LCC showed no interest, it was back to the drawing board.

Mayor Jack O'Neill appointed the third Lakeway Activity Center Committee on February 5, 1996, consisting of eleven volunteers, including Frank Black as chair. After once again carefully researching the subject, the committee recommended a 13,000-square-foot building, faced with stone or brick, that would include a 375- to 400-seat auditorium, smaller meeting rooms, and no swimming pool. The new estimated cost was $1.6 million, or approximately one-half that of the previously designed building, which the voters had so resoundingly rejected. The Lakeway City Council aided the cause when it declared that there was insufficient space to house the more than 1,300 meetings and social gatherings then being held annually in Lakeway.

On January 18, 1997, voters finally approved the building of an activity center by a margin of 868 to 507. Sadly, only 27 percent of registered citizens bothered to vote in what had been an eleven-year struggle. Nevertheless, future councilmember Ann Gribble proudly announced, "We will step into the millennium with the Lakeway Activity Center."

***

Designed by Robert Jackson Architects, work began on the Activity Center building in November 1997. Two months later the Lakeway Activity Center Committee launched its "Let's Pave the

Way Together" campaign to raise the $180,000 needed to furnish and equip the building and to landscape the property. In July 1998, the Lakeway City Council approved $117,000 to help pay for furniture, a sound system, kitchen equipment, and other incidentals. The Lakeway Civic Corporation also donated $125,000 to help defray expenses. By the end of the summer, 423 individuals, thirty-seven organizations, and ninety-two businesses had contributed more than $116,000. The names of contributors were inscribed on the tiles that line both sides of the walkways in the courtyard. They came in four sizes: 4 by 8 inches for $125, 8 by 8 inches for $250, 8 by 12 inches for $375, and 8 by 16 inches for $500. Winston L. McGinnis, Jr. was appointed director of the new Activity Center on August 17, 1998.

After additional controversy and many delays and threatened legal actions, the Lakeway Activity Center officially opened its doors on November 13, 1999, with former mayor Jack O'Neill thanking the many civic organizations, local businesses, Lakeway officials, and community volunteers who had finally made this day possible.

The Greater Lakeway Residents Association and the Lakeway Civic Corporation lease office space in the Activity Center. The main auditorium regularly hosts plays, concerts, special speakers, and large community meetings and dinners. On any given day, smaller rooms may feature photographic or painting exhibits and workshops, meetings of the Boy Scouts and the Girl Scouts, or classes in yoga, dance, bridge, arts and crafts, gardening, and Spanish. Numerous youth organizations also take advantage of the facilities.

The Activity Center is currently so pressed to meet the demands for its facilities that manager Darline Foshee recently declared, "We could easily double our space and still need more room." The Activity Center is now the most used building in Lakeway, and, as has been the case with the Hamilton Greenbelt and City Park, no one now questions its role in the community.

The Lakeway Activity Center

CHAPTER FIFTEEN

THE FOURTH OF JULY: A COMMUNITY CELEBRATION

Linda Wells, "Fourth of July in Lakeway"

UNLIKE THE CONTENTIOUS AND DIVISIVE BATTLES fought over the Hamilton Greenbelt, City Park, and the Activity Center, Lakeway's Fourth of July celebrations have always united individuals, families, and the community in the most joyous of ways.

***

Lakeway was only thirteen years old in 1976, when the United States celebrated its 200th birthday. Nevertheless, in anticipation of this venerable event, Lakeway formed its own Bicentennial Committee. The resultant tribute set an admirable precedent for all the Fourth of July celebrations that were to follow. Central to these annual commemorations have been parades, music, patriotic speeches, family activities, and stirring tributes to those who fought and died for our country.

A brief sampling of Lakeway's Fourth of July pageants reveals certain things held in common, but each also has had its own special flavor: The 1992 edition, for example, featured a parachute drop, booming cannons, a color guard marching smartly up the Live Oak fairway, and a special tribute to "Lakeway's Americans from Far and Near." Foreign-born residents who had become U.S. citizens included individuals from Latvia,

Germany, Holland, Norway, Lithuania, England, Canada, Columbia, and Peru.

The 1993 celebration featured the Austin Symphony Orchestra and a student essay contest on the theme of "Education: Foundation of Freedom and Independence." The day also included a presentation of the fifty state flags and the judging of floats, which, over the ensuing years, have become increasingly more elaborate and competitive.

In 1994, Lakeway held its Fourth of July Celebration for the first time in the new City Park. The following year, George Blume, who had first identified the City Park property back in 1991, planned the festivities as president of the Arts League. The theme was "Victory—50 Years Later—Remembering the Price of Freedom." Included were a P-38 flyover, the music of the Austin Symphony Orchestra, fireworks, and lots of food and games for a crowd of more than 3,000. Ticket sales covered the $30,000 cost. The parade marshal was U.S. Air Force Colonel Hank Potter. As a young lieutenant, Potter was the navigator on Lieutenant Colonel James Doolittle's surprise bombing raid on the Japanese homeland, just four months after Pearl Harbor.

The 1997 edition focused on "America's Future—Our Youth." It also included Lake Travis School District's student-winning essays, as well as flyovers by Lakeway's own pilots.

Deborah Davidson organized the 2001 activities, which featured Lakeway's four retired generals: Tommy Thompson, George Edwards, Ken Kennedy, and Dick Drury. The parade marshal was retired Colonel Roy Doran, who had survived the World War II Bataan Death March. More than 3,000 attended the evening fireworks display in City Park.

The following year, in accordance with Mayor

WELLS FARGO & COMPANY
U.S. MAIL

Charles Edwards' proclamation that July 4, 2002, was "Celebrate Freedom Day," Lakeway honored World War II veterans, more than forty of whom rode in the morning parade.

The year 2003 marked the fiftieth anniversary of the Korean War Armistice, and Lakeway honored the so-called Forgotten War's 1.8 million veterans. Parade marshals were Lakeway founders Lee and Kay Blocker, Frank Denius, and John and Kay Crooker. Austin's Civic Wind Ensemble and Mormon Choir provided appropriate music. By now, it was common for the annual parade to feature more than 100 floats competing for first prize.

Ann Neighbors was the organizing force behind the 2004 celebration, "Freedom Is Not Free," the music for which was provided by the Capital City Highlanders Bagpipe Band. The Texas National Guard and Lakeway's Police Color Guards' Vietnam veterans served as parade marshals. Approximately 1,000 attended the day's activities and 5,000 the evening's patriotic program featuring the Austin Civic Wind Ensemble and local church choirs.

Susan Bowers coordinated the planning for the 2007 theme, "Land of the Free and Home of the Brave." Rear Admiral and astronaut Stephen S. Oswald served as Grand Marshal and featured speaker. The evening entertainment again featured the Austin Civic Wind Ensemble, several church choirs, and the usual spectacular fireworks.

The following year headlined former Navy SEAL and Medal of Honor winner Lieutenant Commander Michael Thorton, along with four recipients of the Lakeway-funded Patriot Fund's iBOT motorized wheelchairs for men and women injured in Iraq and Afghanistan.

"Military Service—A Family Affair" was the theme for Lakeway's 2010 celebration, featuring Grand Marshals Rosie Babin and her son, Corporal Alan "Doc" Babin, Jr., a combat medic who had been badly wounded in Iraq.

Over the years, patriotic themes have become the norm and are even honored by some of Lakeway's youngest participants.

442

CHAPTER SIXTEEN

HERITAGE PARK

THE LAKEWAY HISTORICAL SOCIETY AND HERITAGE CENTER

When Lakeway celebrates its 100th birthday in 2063, it may be one of the nation's best historically documented cities. At least, that is the intention of the Lakeway Historical Society.

BYRON VARNER

In 1992, Austin watercolor artist Joan Salvant permitted the above sketch to be used as the logo for the Lakeway Historical Society. As Byron Varner explained, "The windmill seemed most fitting of all symbols because of its use by pioneers who settled this area and the ranchers who followed them and preceded Lakeway's developers."

AS HAS BEEN THE CASE WITH SO MANY CREATIONS OF enduring value in Lakeway, Byron Varner, who in 1988 published *Lakeway: The First 25 Years*, was the driving force behind the Lakeway Historical Society, which in 2001 became the Lakeway Heritage Commission.

Inspired by Lakeway's twenty-fifth anniversary in 1988, Varner, who was then president of the Lakeway Civic Corporation, formed a committee to consider creating a historical society. The result was a nonprofit, tax-exempt corporation, which elected its first board of trustees in January 1989. Board members were President Coleman Smith, Vice President Rella Giammalva, Second Vice President Travis Porter, Treasurer Kay Light, and Secretary Byron Varner.

The board's immediate objective was to find temporary office space where it could hold its meetings. Its long term goal was to locate a permanent home where it could collect, preserve, catalog, and display Lakeway's past, including ongoing governmental and civic organizational records. The board also hoped to develop pride in Lakeway's heritage and growth and to inform young people of the community's historical significance. Finally, it planned to raise funds for a series of historical markers to be placed throughout the community. With such ambitious aspirations, the Historical Society clearly needed a financial angel.

Byron Varner was having lunch with Charles McCoy when his old friend informed him he was planning to donate a couple of lots on Lakeway Drive to his church. Knowing that McCoy had already been very generous to his place of worship, Varner suggested he might instead consider making a gift of these two properties to the Historical Society. On October 16, 1992, Charles and Nancy McCoy did just that because, as Charles explained, "I wanted to give back some of what I have received in the form of this land to a group who are 'givers' and not 'takers'."

The sale of one of the lots allowed the Historical Society to purchase the two-acre property at the corner of Lohman's Crossing and Hurst Creek, which eventually became Heritage Park. The only structure on the property was a small, dilapidated building that had originally been a bunkhouse on Gus Mauermann's ranch. The sale of the second lot provided $134,000 in seed money to tear down this old building and construct the Lakeway Heritage Center.

The Historical Society had initially stored its artifacts and archival materials in the old bunkhouse, but this soon proved disastrous. According to Caroline Ryals, an early member of the Historical Society and later chair of the Heritage Commission, "The stone foundation was cracking, the termites were tearing away at the structure, the septic system failed, and we had to battle rats for the premises." When asked why the members did not simply move into one of the city's newer buildings, Ryals responded, "History! That building is the second oldest structure within Lakeway's city limits." Doris Besperka, who also served on the Heritage Commission and has penned a series of "Bedtime Stories" about Lakeway's early history, remembers when "termites

The old Mauermann Ranch bunkhouse was the real estate office for Phillips Properties between 1971 and 1985. A local Boy Scout troop also used this building before it became the temporary home of the Lakeway Historical Society in 1994.

Tearing down the old bunkhouse in preparation for the new structure. Only the old "Rock Room" on the right would survive.

chewed through an outside wall, attacked a picture frame, and made a meal of a photograph of the members of the first Quarter-Century Club." Besperka also recalls that the last straw was the ceiling collapsing on their only computer and the septic system backing up, forcing the city to rent a porta-potty.

When the old bunkhouse was declared uninhabitable in 2004, the Heritage Commission moved its materials into storage and began raising funds for the construction of a new building. The sale of the second McCoy lot had brought in $134,000. The Lakeway Civic Corporation donated $20,000 for the restoration of the "Rock Room" portion of the old bunkhouse, and private sources provided additional funds, including $10,000 from developer Haythem Dawlett, who also did the landscaping. The City of Lakeway, which had taken over the ownership and administration of the newly named Heritage Commission on September 17, 2001, pledged the final $41,315 on February 21, 2005, but not without considerable debate. Councilmembers George Blume and Karl Ansbach voted against the appropriation, largely because of cost and a perceived lack of community support for the project. Mayor Gerry Astorino, Mayor Pro-Tem Steve Swan, and Councilmembers Mike Doherty and Glenda Foreman voted for the funding.

Lakeway architect Jim Little volunteered his time and expertise to design the 1,500-square-foot Lakeway Heritage Center, which was dedicated on November 8, 2005.

***

A major development for the original Historical Society occurred in September 1999, when it hired University of Texas graduate student Matthew Darby as its first professional archivist. Darby's responsibility was to organize the Historical Society's collection of letters, publications, photos, maps, oral histories, and other artifacts. Mike Boston, who replaced Matthew Darby in 2005, is the Heritage Center's current archivist and has further indexed its greatly expanded holdings.

In addition to its archival responsibilities and public exhibits, the Heritage Commission has sponsored Memorial Day and Veterans Day celebrations, as well as the yearly Quarter Century Club picnic for residents who have lived in Lakeway for at least twenty-five years. Furthermore, as has been the case with the Hamilton Greenbelt, City Park, and the Activity Center, all of which encountered considerable initial opposition, the Heritage Center and Heritage Park have become proud community treasures.[1]

1. When the Lakeway Historical Society deeded its land, structures, and archival materials to the City of Lakeway in 2001, it included the following covenant: "The property may only be used, developed or improved to:
   1) further the collection, preservation, storage and display of Lakeway historical items
   2) be a repository for official and historical records regarding the geographic area of Lakeway
   3) develop a pride in Lakeway's heritage, growth and development
   4) educate youth and adults about Lakeway's historical significance
   5) promote Lakeway's historical sites and legends
   6) reasonably further the purposes set forth in 1) through 5)."

THE SPIRIT OF FREEDOM MONUMENT

The Lakeway Historical Society dedicated its Spirit of Freedom Monument at a public ceremony on Veterans Day, November 11, 1995, which also marked the fiftieth anniversary of the end of World War II. The keynote speaker was Brigadier General Ken Kennedy, a longtime Lakeway resident and former councilmember, who had served in World War II, Korea, and Vietnam.

Byron Varner had spearheaded the efforts to raise $50,000 for the sixteen-foot, five-sided granite monument. The five sides signify the five services, the five years of World War II, and the five-sided Pentagon. At the top of the monument is a five-pointed stainless steel star symbolizing the Silver Star, the Bronze Star, the Gold Star Mothers, the star of each state in our national flag, and the Lone Star of Texas. Engraved on each side of the monument is the seal of each service branch, under which are the names of local residents who served, inscribed without rank in alphabetical order. The three flagpoles behind the monument display the Lakeway, United States, and Texas flags.

In 1997, the names of 318 Korean and Vietnam veterans were inscribed on two new granite panels, joining the 512 World War II names already listed on the monument.

The September 11, 2001, attacks on the World Trade Center and the Pentagon led to the dedication of a new granite panel on November 11, 2006, honoring the names of veterans from the First and Second Gulf Wars, Iraq, Afghanistan, and other foreign campaigns.

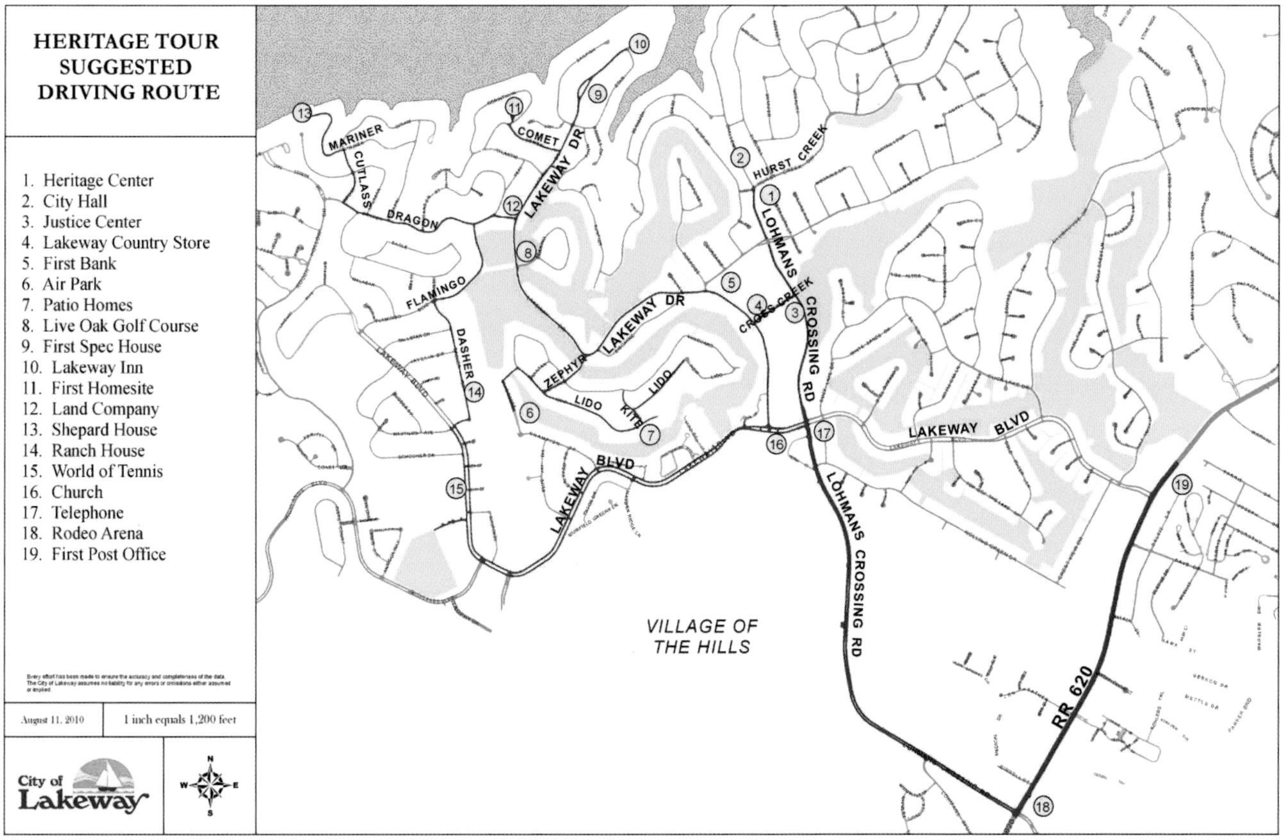

LAKEWAY HISTORICAL MARKERS

The City of Lakeway contains a single State of Texas Historical Marker. It is located at the southwest end of Ladin Lane and honors German immigrant John Henry Lohmann, who was one of the earliest settlers in the area. Lohmann was recognized for his road construction projects, especially his Lohman's Ford Road, which crossed the Colorado River. (See the historical marker photo on page 36 of Chapter 4)

In 1991, Historical Society President Byron Varner launched a plan to document Lakeway's "historical significance for perpetuity" by placing local historical markers at various sites throughout the city. The first markers were unveiled on June 25, 1991, and Varner planned to add at least twenty-nine more of these silver-cast, aluminum plaques in the future. As of 2010, there were nineteen markers. The initial cost of the first markers was approximately $250, financed by donations from Lakeway residents and businesses.

Your tour begins at the Heritage Center located at the corner of Lohman's Crossing Road and Hurst Creek Road.

1. In Appreciation—This marker honors Austin residents Charles H. and Jean McCoy, who donated two valuable commercial lots to the Lakeway Historical Society, the proceeds of which made possible the purchase of this two-acre tract, refurbishing of the old ranch house, and seed money for the History Center building. (Lohman's Crossing @ Hurst Creek Road)

1. Early Ranch House—Erected in the 1930's by Gus Mauermann, this building served as quarters for the ranch hands of the Mauermann Ranch, later known as the Josey Ranch before it became Lakeway. (Lohman's Crossing @ Hurst Creek Road)

1. Early Ranch House Water-Well—This water-pump marks the location of an actual water well, where a windmill was used to draw water from the well and transfer the water to a wooden storage tank beneath the adjacent oak tree. (Lohman's Crossing @ Hurst Creek Road)

2. Lohmann's Ford Road—German Immigrant, John Henry Lohmann established his homestead near a sandbar on the Colorado River bed in 1861, about one-half mile downhill from 1001 Challenger. Pioneer families who forded the river here called the trail Lohmann's Ford Road. When Travis County built a bridge here some years later, an unknown map maker dropped an "n" from Lohmann's name, and the old trail became Lohman's Crossing Road. (1001 Challenger)

3. Old Village Hall - (now the Justice Center) - On April 12, 1982, with the words, "I christen thee Village Hall," Village Clerk Petrea Sodke broke a bottle of champagne against this building to complete opening ceremonies. (105 Cross Creek Road)

4. Lakeway Country Store—Built in 1969, the Tejas Country Store Building provided the community's first grocery store, apartment units and the Ole' Boutique, a ladies fashion shop. (1204 Lakeway Drive)

5. First Bank—This site was first occupied by the Lakeway Land Company as its headquarters and sales office in June 1971, until a fire destroyed it in 1979. It also housed Lakeway Bank, Kivlin Construction Co., the Lakeway MUD office and Ann Petty's Beauty Salon. (Corner of Lakeway Drive and Porpoise)

6. Airfield Ranch—This land was part of a small ranch owned by the Clifton George family from 1929-1936. They used this site as a landing strip. Lakeway Company built a 3,200 ft. runway here in 1964 and extended it to 4100 ft. in 1986. (115 Flying Scot)

7. First Condominiums—Construction was completed on the Lakeway Patio Home Condominiums, Section 1, in 1971 and they became the first condominiums in Texas. (Kite St. @ Lido Circle)

8. Live Oak Golf Course—George King was the first golf-pro at Lakeway's first golf course. Nine holes were opened in 1965; eighteen-holes, with a permanent pro-shop, opened in 1967. (510 Lakeway Drive)

8. Lakeway Flag Pole - Donated in 1977 by local patriots George and Mary Coale to celebrate the 4th of July. (510 Lakeway Drive)

8. First Fire Station—A volunteer fire department was established and located on Live Oak Tee Box #10. It moved to Village Hall in 1982 and then to its current location on Lohmans Crossing Road in 1988. (510 Lakeway Drive)

9. First Spec House—Located at 126 Lakeway Drive, this house was built in 1963 by Lakeway developer Flint Sawtelle and was the first one constructed for sale.

10. Lakeway Inn—Completed and opened on July 12, 1963 as the Lakeway Inn. The grand opening ceremony was attended by Mrs. Lyndon B. Johnson and Governor John Connally. It became the Lakeway Resort & Spa when a day spa, crystal ballroom and two pools were added in 2005. (101 Lakeway Drive).

11. Indian Mounds—Lakeway's first inhabitants were the prehistoric and latter day natives whose remnants have been found in numerous Indian mounds here along Comet Street as well as in many other areas in Lakeway. (Lakeway Drive @ Comet Street)

11. First Homesite Purchased—Shortly after Lakeway opened in 1963, Louis and Irene Hamilton became the first residential homesite owners when they purchased the Lot 226, Section 2. They built the house in 1965 and sold it to Walter and Marjorie Graham in 1976. (303 Comet Cove)

12. Lakeway Land Company Office—One of six houses built for sale by the Lakeway Company in 1963-65, this structure was occupied as its company headquarters and sales office from 1965 until completion of a large commercial building at 1200 Lakeway Drive in 1971. (413 Lakeway Drive)

13. 818 Mariner—Built in 1966. Original owners were Alan and Louise Shepard. In 1961, Alan became America's first astronaut in space and later landed on the Moon during his second space flight in 1971. Before entering the lunar craft to end that successful mission and return to the orbiting space capsule, Shepard delighted golfers everywhere by unfolding a specially-made driver and hitting two golf balls from the Moon's surface.

14. Lakeway Stables—When Lakeway opened in 1963, horseback riding was one of the main recreations along with swimming, fishing and boating. For 15 years, stables operated on this site to entertain visitors. (425 Dasher)

15. Lakeway World of Tennis—Opened in 1973, this facility hosted several major professional tournaments from 1974-1980. Notable professionals who played on the stadium court were Rod Laver, Ken Rosewall, Ilie Nastase, Jimmy Connors, Chris Evert, Billie Jean King, Evonne Goolagong and Martina Navratilova. Lakeway Company headquartered here in 1979. Athletic and spa amenities were added in 2005. (1 World of Tennis Square)

16. Lakeway Ecumenical Church– Father Richard McCabe started Catholic services in Lakeway in 1963. Ralph Keller started Protestant services in 1969. Services were held at the Lakeway Inn until 1975 when both groups completed this edifice in 1975. (Lakeway Blvd @ Lakeway Drive)

17. Lakeway's First Telephone—In 1962, Lakeway's founders started development here without telephone service. Southwestern Bell Telephone Company installed a coin-operated telephone on this site late that year. Lines were extended to Lakeway Blvd. in 1963. (Southeast corner of Lakeway Blvd. @ Lohman's Crossing Rd.)

18. Lakeway Rodeo Arena—The sport of horseback riding was a natural for the Lakeway area in 1964, when the remoteness of ranchland was plentiful and easy access was available for visitors to the Lakeway Inn through the Lakeway Airpark. On August 18, 1978, a rodeo arena opened on land that was formerly part of the Schramm Ranch and that is now the Randall's parking lot on RR620. For nearly 8 years, the community enjoyed professional rodeos, concerts, dances, children's riding clinics and western barbeques. (2301 RR620 South)

19. First Post Office—Bonnie and Byron Varner operated Lakeway's first sub-station until 1977 when postal services moved to the Lakeway Inn. (801 RR620 South)

CHAPTER SEVENTEEN

CHILDREN IN THE GARDEN OF EDEN

The Lakeway Sculpture Garden

W. C. Fields was once asked how he liked children. "Parboiled," snapped the cantankerous comedian, who once got three-year-old Baby Leroy drunk on a Hollywood set. Does Fields stand alone? After all, who could possibly object to those cute little nippers or their equally adorable counterparts in the animal kingdom?

There are, of course, at least two sides to every story, even when the story is set in pristine and idyllic Lakeway. Many of the folks who first built here were thinking of vacation homes, but when they retired, they thought in more permanent terms. Few wanted a Sun City, where visiting children had to vacate the premises by sundown, but most also did not anticipate a community of young families or paying hefty school taxes.

The question of what to do with our four-footed children, who so delicately and efficiently browse our gardens and lawns, has been even more controversial—and of much greater duration.

***

Once upon a time, a curious tourist walked up to a reservation Indian and asked, "Hey, Chief, what did you call this continent before we arrived?" The old Indian looked at him, sadly shook his head, and replied, "Ours." More recently, a cloven-hoofed Lakeway resident snorted his agreement with his fellow Native American: "We go along with our Indian friends. We should never have allowed such a lax immigration policy."

Strangely enough, there were few deer in the Lakeway area in 1963, when the Lakeway Inn opened its doors. Over the succeeding decades, developing neighborhoods eliminated most natural predators, while manicured lawns, abundant plants and flowers, and spreading golf courses provided excellent habitat for the deer.

In a 1988 public meeting, Texas Parks & Wildlife Department (TPWD), specialist Horace Gore

The critter on the left seems sincerely curious about his Lakeway neighbors—the one on the right, not so much.

Jackson, *Lake Travis View*, July 9, 1986

estimated the herd had grown to approximately 1,000, which was double the size he recommended. Gore advocated netting the surplus deer and transporting them to East Texas in trucks, using a safe and humane procedure. The following year, the TPWD trapped and relocated 102 Lakeway deer to the outskirts of Palestine, Texas.

When the deer continued multiplying at far too rapid a pace, the Homeowners Association sponsored another public meeting in 1996, again presided over by a representative of the Texas Parks & Wildlife Department. The extremes of opinion ranged from those who believed there should be no organized controls to those advocating Lakeway deer hunts. The TPWD representative explained that the only surefire way to control the Lakeway herd was to build a deer resistant fence around the entire city. He also recommended not feeding the deer, because corn has less food value than grass and often contains alpha-toxins that promote undersized and unhealthy deer. Tom Priddy, who later headed a deer control committee, suggested the city investigate sterilization procedures to control the herd.

In a 1997 election, 86 percent of Lakeway voters agreed that the city suffered from an overpopulation of deer. Two years later, the Lakeway City Council formed the Lakeway Deer Control Committee, which once again sought help from the TPWD, which now estimated the Lakeway deer population at 3,000 to 5,000 animals. It also announced that Lakeway had the worst deer overpopulation of any Texas community and that if nothing were done the numbers would double every two to five years. The question still not answered was how best to reduce the herd and control or eliminate its future growth.

By the late 1990s, traffic accidents were eliminating approximately 200 deer a year, which did less to dent the herd than it did the involved automobiles. The city also continued to net, tranquilize, and transport deer to various TPWD-approved state ranches and even to a few Mexican ranches, but such options ended when these relocation sites dried up.

In 2000, the Lakeway Deer Control Committee recommended that the city seek a Travis County depredation permit, and in November residents approved lethal measures for thinning the deer herd by a vote of 1,614 to 1,573. The city council subsequently agreed to remove 500 to 600 deer annually by one means or another. The following February, the city council also passed an ordinance forbidding the feeding of deer, with guilty parties subject to a fine of not less than $1.00 or more than $500.

Not surprisingly, the "Bambi syndrome" kicked in, which over the next several years led to a stream of heated letters on both sides of the controversy. In fact, during the spring and summer of 2003, there were more letters in the *Lake Travis View* on the deer depredation issue than on the possibility of a Lakeway "Big Box" store named Wal-Mart. Semantics entered the fray when one letter writer pointed out that "depredation" meant "to plunder, ravage, or lay waste." Lakeway and The Hills tried to soften the blow for their joint deer depredation program by insisting that the actual killing of the deer would be done after the animals had left the premises. At least no one called for reconsidering a previously suggested bow-and-arrow campaign. After all, seeing Bambi with an arrow sticking out of its ribs would scarcely have had a salutary effect on Lakeway's other children.

In the late summer of 2003, the Texas Department of Criminal Justice (TDCJ) blocked an attempt to trap and ship Lakeway deer to Texas prisons where they were to be slaughtered and fed to the inmates. The TDCJ explained that it had no holding pens and that the animals might also be dangerous to those handling them. Only if Lakeway wanted to field dress the animals would the TDCJ accept them. City Manager Dave Benson concluded that Lakeway did not have the facilities to trap and field dress deer or to transport their carcasses in refrigerated trucks. In the previous year, Lakeway had hired a trapper to net deer, load them onto a trailer, and take them to a processing plant in Johnson City, where the ground-up venison was donated through the Travis County Food Bank to a charity in Johnson City.

The struggle to manage the deer herd continues, although Lakeway's annual trapping nets no longer stir up much controversy, other than an occasional column by John Kelso in the *Austin American-Statesman*. In the meantime, there remain some noncontroversial tales of Lakeway's deer. At one time, a legendary black buck, who sired many dark-furred progeny, roamed Lakeway. Alas, his ebony offspring seem to be slowly disappearing from the flock. Another famous buck managed to get tangled up with a discarded mop. It eventually flopped over his head, where it became permanently lodged. Naturally, he became known as "Old Dread-Locks."

***

Despite the wishes of a few recalcitrant older citizens, the trapping and removal of children was never seriously contemplated in Lakeway. In truth, most of the earliest residents were older and possessed mature families. Many were retired military officers, including several generals, numerous colonels, and even an astronaut. They were joined by a considerable number of former oil executives, many of whom had lived and worked in the Houston area. The Lakeway Land Company's national and international advertising campaign brought in additional buyers, but they too were often retirees whose children had long left the nest.

The paying of school taxes became an issue for some of these older residents, especially after the Lake Travis Independent School District became a reality in 1981. Covering approximately 800 square miles, the LTISD served increasing numbers of school-age children, a comparatively small percentage of whom lived in Lakeway during its early years. This issue, however, predictably faded after many of Lakeway's early residents were replaced by young and growing families.

***

School battles aside, Lakeway has become a marvelous place for children to grow up, and frequently older residents have worked alongside younger families to make this happen. Not only is Lakeway a safe community, where youngsters can safely walk or ride their bikes almost anywhere, but there are also countless amenities for the entire family to enjoy. A weekend stroll in City Park will find great numbers of children enjoying the playgrounds, fishing, riding their bikes, playing basketball, romping with their dogs on the trails or in the Dog Park, wiggling their toes in the Hurst Creek outlet, or simply enjoying a picnic with their parents.

The battle over making City Park a reality has been discussed elsewhere, but it is important to note that the Children's Playground, which was dedicated on September 19, 1998, was made possible by a gift from the Abigail Elaine Hendrix and Bernard M. Jacobsen Memorial Fund.

In December 1999, the Lakeway Homeowners Association hosted a town meeting on a proposed swimming pool complex. More than 100 residents offered their opinions, and an organization called Friends of the Pool was formed to make the Swim Center a reality. The Parker Kerby Development Company offered to donate $250,000 toward the project if Lakeway agreed to annex its planned 371-acre Flint Rock development, which it did.

On May 5, 2001, Lakeway residents voted 1,210 to 1,122 in favor of a $2 million bond issue to help fund the Swim Center. The Lakeway MUD added its support by donating twenty acres of its Canyonlands holdings. In 2002, the city received a $500,000 Texas Parks and Wildlife grant for the project. The Lower Colorado River Authority also donated $100,000 as part of its Partnerships in Parks Program. These grants, in addition to the $2 million bond issue, paid for the Swim Center, which features a six-lane, heated fitness/lap pool and a 5,000-square-foot family recreation pool.

When the Lakeway Swim Center officially opened on May 24, 2003, it also included a bathhouse and picnic area outside the pool fence, in part financed by families that purchased hand-painted ceramic tiles as part of a "Splashdown" fund-raising campaign.

The most recent attraction for the young people of Lakeway is the 9,000-square-foot Skate Park, which opened in July 2006, adjacent to the Swim Center. Haythem Dawlett and his Las Ventanas developers generously donated approximately $60,000 to the project.

Many of the programs at the Lakeway Activity Center have also targeted young people. For example, the winter of 2010 featured art classes for children of all ages and various after-school sports programs. There were also dance and cooking classes for the young and even a teen supper club. Indeed, one would be hard-pressed to identify a Lakeway family whose children have been unable to find something to keep them busy and entertained.

***

At one time older residents might have resented young families moving into Lakeway, but those days are far in the past. Today, the Lakeway community is a healthy mix of young families and those, euphemistically speaking, who appear to be more chronologically advantaged. Even the deer have endured, although in far fewer numbers than in the past.

The Swim Center and Skate Park Complex also includes volleyball and basketball courts.

PART IV

WHAT DOES THE FUTURE HOLD?

Bill Hawkins, "Blue Crane Flying"

CHAPTER EIGHTEEN

AS THE HOUSES GREW LARGER, THE PEOPLE BECAME SMALLER: THE BATTLE OVER EXPANSION AND DEVELOPMENT

They paved paradise and put up a parking lot.

SINGER, SONGWRITER JONI MITCHELL

Construction of Fine Homes Tame Area.

JOHN RENFORD TAYLOR, *LAKE TRAVIS VIEW,* APRIL 25, 1991.

WHY DO SOME OF US CHOOSE TO LIVE IN EVER larger houses as we slip into our golden years? Is it only because we can afford to do so? I know our first house was "only" 1,600 square feet, which made it 50 percent larger than the home in which I was born and twice as large as the house in which my grandparents raised six children. Now that our own children and most of our pets have escaped the nest, we have moved into a 3,000-square-foot home, which is certainly not considered large by Lakeway standards. Nevertheless, we are now pygmies living in a castle, surrounded by inherited furniture and various other accouterments of an advanced stage of civilized life. We scarcely know our neighbors who also live in impressive edifices that certainly look nothing like those that typified the Hill Country throughout most of its human history. I am not sure what all this means, but I do recall novelist Edward Abbey writing, "Growth for the sake of growth is the ideology of the cancer cell." Yet, towns, like the people who reside in them, never stay the same, but change also brings inevitable controversy.

The mid-nineteenth century Wunneberger Cabin is the oldest structure in Lakeway.

This home under construction is one of the newest in Lakeway.

***

When Lakeway was still a village, everyone knew each other. Not surprisingly, many of these early homeowners wanted to retain the quiet serenity of small-town life. Others, and especially developers, pushed for Lakeway to become a vibrant, expanding city with a growing tax base. Such diametrically opposing views quite naturally led to conflicts.

***

In 1971, a group of concerned residents, fearing that Lakeway might be annexed by the city of Austin, asked the Lakeway Civic Corporation to help the community become a corporate village. Three years later, the Austin City Council transferred its Extra Territorial Jurisdiction (ETJ) rights to the Village of Lakeway; however, Austin retained its ETJ rights to lands adjacent to the village boundaries.

Over the ensuing years, Lakeway sought to expand its ETJ. Many of the affected properties were relatively small and were later annexed with little opposition. Such was not the case with several large parcels of land that fundamentally changed the nature of Lakeway. The time line that begins on page 176 chronicles many of these annexations; yet, some were so controversial that they deserve special mention.

In April 1989, the Lakeway Village Council requested that Austin transfer its ETJ over The Hills of Lakeway, Lakeway West (later called the Lakeway Highlands), Brook Hollow, Rough Hollow, the Schramm Ranch (later renamed Vista Royale), and footage along RR 620, all of which would have more than doubled the size of Lakeway.

In the fall of 1994, the Lakeway City Council specifically proposed annexing a 1,000-foot strip along RR 620 from Vineyard Bay on the north almost to Lohman's Crossing Road. At two public meetings, dissenters stated that they had moved to Lakeway for what it was, not what it might become. Nevertheless, on December 12, 1994, the city council voted 4 to 2 to annex the RR 620 strip, thereby enlarging Lakeway proper by more than 25 percent.

In December 1995, Lakeway once again requested that the City of Austin transfer Rough Hollow, Lakeway West, and the Schramm Ranch to its ETJ. Ross Perot, Jr.'s Hillwood Development Corporation, which had purchased these lands from the bankrupt Lakeway Company earlier in 1995, had requested the action. In return for the support of its residents, Lakeway agreed to allow The Hills to incorporate as a separate municipality. After Austin agreed to the transfer in December 1996, Lakeway was free to annex these lands, which, with the exception of The Hills, it did, but not without considerable opposition from many Lakeway residents.

The pro-annexation advocates naturally included developers, some of whom were also Lakeway residents. Several mayors and city councilmembers, along with longtime City Manager Dave Benson, also supported annexation in order to increase the tax base and to control development. When Benson announced in 1996 that the annexation of Lakeway West, Rough Hollow, and the Schramm Ranch would allow Lakeway to increase its boundaries by approximately 40 percent and to expand to 25,000 inhabitants, several residents expressed their opposition in the *Homeowners News* and the *Lake Travis View*. Ernie Conine warned that Central Texas did not need "another overcrowded urban blob," while suggesting, "There's something charming about living in a town where the most burning issue is what to do about the deer grazing in our yards, and where city government is run by unpaid friends and neighbors. . . . The larger the population, the larger and more remote the city bureaucracy will become, and the more politics will be dominated by commercial and developer interests." Richard Springer said simply, "It will forever change Lakeway as we know and love it."

Others questioned the need for extra tax revenues if the community chose not to expand to 25,000 inhabitants, while extolling the virtues of small-town living and a minimum of commercial establishments. Interestingly, one of the early opponents of annexation was real estate owner Guy Oberg, who in 1993 created BABY (Bigger Ain't Better Y'all).

Proponents argued that growth was inevitable and that by absorbing these adjacent areas, Lakeway could control and regulate development through its zoning and building codes, while greatly increasing needed tax revenues. The ancillary issue of multifamily living units, while also controversial, received little support from anyone except developers.

Many of the ensuing hard feelings over growth and development might have been alleviated if residents had been allowed to vote on the major properties in dispute, but in May 1994, Lakeway voters had passed a series of eight proposals meant to streamline the governing process, including one that allowed the city to annex adjacent territory with or without resident consent.

***

The annexation and subsequent development of Rough Hollow and Lakeway West were particularly contentious, exacerbated by the fact that the succession of developers who purchased the rights to these lands either changed or did not adhere to their announced plans for these areas.

Already in 1985, Bob Alpert's Lakeway Company had announced its intention to develop Rough Hollow, and had even platted the area in 1987. The Lakeway Company, however, fell into deep financial trouble, leading to a four-year, multiparty bankruptcy fight before the Eagle Development Corporation, a joint venture between Ross Perot, Jr.'s Hillwood Development Corporation and the GE Pension Trust, briefly took over the properties in 1994.

In 1996, Lakeway Partners, LLC, headed by local restauranteur Rocky Piazza, Steve Dallas, Jack Lieberman, and South Korean financier Danny Kim, purchased the rights. At the time, Piazza proudly announced, "For the first time in its history, the people who control the land in Lakeway will live in the area."

On June 16, 1997, Lakeway city councilmembers voted unanimously to annex Rough Hollow. Mayor Jack O'Neill, who had wanted to negotiate a better deal with the developers, cast a lone dissenting vote. Five months later the city council again unanimously approved the Lakeway Partners Development Agreement covering Rough Hollow, the Lakeway Highlands, and Vista Royale for a period of ten years. This agreement, which was at least the fifteenth version, covered density, building codes, construction and residential traffic, the donation of two acres in Vista Royale and five acres in Lakeway Highlands for governmental use, and an elementary school site of between ten and twelve acres in the Highlands. The Rough Hollow section called for a minimum of 4.5 miles of improved trails, recreational areas of 3.5 acres per 1,000 estimated population growth, and a four- or five-acre waterfront park suitable for swimming on Rough Hollow Cove. Also promised was a ten-acre park for organized sports and the completion of a road to Highway 71 before more than 50 percent of the subdivision was platted. The agreement also allowed Sections 37 and 38 to be gated.

This would not be the final plan for these properties, and critics continued their fight, insisting that Mayor Jack O'Neill, the city council, and City Manager Dave Benson should demand much more from the developers. The opposition also objected to a private marina and any gated sections that would block Lakeway residents' access to Lake Travis. In addition, they challenged the Lakeway Partners' plans for an unspecified number of multifamily dwellings and expressed their concern over water and environmental issues, especially after a couple of yellow warblers were sighted in the Highlands. Finally, they asked for a public referendum before the city gave its final approval to any developers agreement.

The Lakeway Partners' plans for Rough Hollow and the Highlands became irrelevant in 1998, when financier Danny Kim, who had insisted his love for Lakeway was so intense that he planned to become a resident, withdrew his financial backing after his Seoul-based Dong Ah Construction Company crashed, along with the South Korean stock market.

That same year, Credit First Suisse of Boston purchased the rights, but in 2004 it sold out to California-based Las Ventanas Land Partners and its local manager, Haythem Dawlett, who remains one of the current developers.

Dawlett immediately announced ambitious new plans for Rough Hollow. Included were "2,000 homes, a little commercial development, parkland and a swim park with a public beach in the back of Rough Hollow Cove." First on his list, however, was a "yacht club style" marina. The Lakeway City Council responded by annexing the twenty-nine acres of Rough Hollow Cove and approving a zoning change to allow a marina with 280 covered slips, as well as a members-only yacht club and ship store. City Manager Dave Benson announced his approval, saying, "This isn't like Hurst Creek Marina or Lakeway Marina or any of the others we have in the area. You're not going to see any boats on trailers heading through Lakeway to this marina."

***

Although the controversy over "Big Box" development in Lakeway was not as long-lived as the contentious debates over the annexation of Rough Hollow, the Highlands, and Vista Royale, it was even more intense. In fact, the *Lake Travis View* called it "the biggest crisis ever to hit the City of Lakeway." The issue of Big Box development would rage for eleven months in 2003 before the Lakeway City Council, bending to pressure from residents, decided not to change its ordinance that limited commercial buildings to 100,000 square feet.

In January 2003, the Rio Development Corporation announced its proposed 74-acre Avenue of the Lakes project to be built near the Lohman's Crossing entrance to Lakeway. The developers' plans called for a Wal-Mart, a Lowe's, a high-end restaurant, two 24,000-square-foot office buildings, and several speciality shops. Rio also promised a greenbelt and park that would cover 30 percent of the area, featuring existing ponds and wildlife, and a site on which to build a city or regional library. The property, however, first needed to be re-zoned commercial by the Zoning and Planning Commission (ZAPCO). Over the ensuing months, an intense debate boiled over among residents and city officials over the advantages and disadvantages of Big Box stores within Lakeway. The opposition cited Wal-Mart's track record of driving out small businesses, vacating its nonproductive older stores, increasing noise and traffic, lowering surrounding property values, and adversely changing the atmosphere of Lakeway. Proponents insisted this was a golden chance for the city to gain much needed tax revenues.

On February 13, 2003, opponents created the LakewayFirst organization. Headed by John Hoopingarner and Bill Schweitzer, its mission was "to help the citizens of Lakeway, Texas, to preserve and enhance their quality of life."

LakewayFirst cited Lakeway's 1998 Comprehensive Plan, which stated, "Aesthetic appearance greatly influences the perceptions both residents and visitors have about a community. Because of Lakeway's natural beauty and small town character, the city's urban image is appealing."

News that a Wal-Mart Superstore might be going up at the entrance to Lakeway also triggered a spate of letters to the *Lake Travis View*, most of them negative. Typical was Nellie Symm-Gruender, who wrote, "A Wal-Mart in the middle of Lakeway attacks every reason that I live in this area." She was writing as a citizen although she was also on the Lake Travis Chamber of Commerce Board of Directors, which worried about protecting Lakeway's small businesses. Yvonne C. Connell asked, "Why does Lakeway have to follow the craze, which seems to be sweeping the nation, for mega-box stores? Why can't Lakeway be a little unique and not follow the cookie cutter plan for Anytown, USA?" Among those supporting Big Box stores were letter writers Mike C. Ferrell and Rob and Toni West, who stressed increased tax revenues and the advantage of not having to drive to Austin to shop.

Rio co-partners Robert Walker and Larry Stauffer estimated that additional annual city revenues would be as high as $2 million from collected sales taxes and another $2 million from property taxes, both of which could lower residents' property taxes. In addition, they argued that because change was inevitable Lakeway was better off being involved in it. They also warned that other developers were seeking to build government-sponsored, low-cost apartments on the property.

Letter writer Steve Brown dismissed the tax advantages, pointing out that the promised $500,000 drop in property taxes would factor out to a reduction of $62.50 for each household, but even that might be lost with the need for extra police and fire equipment and the upgrading of Lakeway MUD facilities.

On April 21, the Lakeway City Council voted unanimously to re-zone the land in question, known as the Wunneberger and Witt tracts, from agriculture to office and light retail, as ZAPCO had already recommended. This decision cleared the way for Rio Development formally to present its plan for the property, which by this time very much focused on its planned Wal-Mart Superstore, because Lowe's had withdrawn its interest in the project.

LakewayFirst responded to the city council's decision by circulating a petition requesting that voters be allowed to determine Big Box commercial development. City Manager David Benson responded that if the petition was legal it would be placed on the agenda for the council's June 16 meeting. At the meeting, however, Lakeway attorney Tom Buckle argued that it was illegal to put the petition to a vote, although a referendum might be legal.

In July, resident Mary Kay Davis filed a class-action lawsuit against Lakeway officials in district court, stating that a Wal-Mart Superstore would do irreparable harm to her home on Rolling Green Drive. Her lawsuit maintained that the re-zoning of the involved property failed to comply with city ordinances, that the city had blocked a petition drive, had held no public hearing on the zoning change, and that "Office/Light Retail" certainly did not apply to Wal-Mart.

In September, ZAPCO sent two possible plans for Big Box structures back to the city council, one calling for a limit of 100,000 square feet, which even LakewayFirst agreed to, and the other 200,000 square feet, which Wal-Mart needed for its Superstore. The city council scheduled a vote on the matter at its September 15 meeting.

Facing an overflow crowd in the Lakeway Activity Center, the Lakeway City Council voted to let residents decide the fate of the zoning change in a non-binding referendum to be held on November 4, 2003. This decision also put Mary Kay Davis' lawsuit against the city on hold.

In the meantime, a November *Homeowners News* editorial railed against citizens who attacked the volunteers who made up Lakeway's government. It argued for "an atmosphere of debate and free expression of ideas, versus a Lakeway dominated by those who choose to impose their political preferences through intimidation." Clearly, the *Homeowners News* did not approve of the tactics of those who opposed Wal-Mart or any kind of Big Box development and who loudly objected when they were not allowed to speak or were strictly limited in how long they could address the city council. As a witness to many heated exchanges in the public meetings, I did observe acrimonious accusations and a general lack of goodwill, but these transgressions occurred on both sides of the issue.

At the November 4 election, 72 percent of the 2,629 voters rejected Big Box development, after which Mayor Gerry Astorino announced, "It's something the City Council will clearly have to take into consideration when it comes up later this month." Three weeks later, the city council voted unanimously to reject any commercial buildings over 100,000 square feet.

There is a fascinating footnote to this story. On October 30, 2003, attorney Ted Stewart published a letter in the *Lake Travis View*. Stewart represented Gwendolyn and Joe Wunneberger, who owned most of the land Rio Development was planning to purchase for its Avenue of the Lakes project. Stewart wrote that the Wunnebergers were willing to sell 30 of their 44.3 acres to the City of Lakeway for $3 million, although it was currently listed at $4.9 million. The Wunnebergers also agreed to take a note for 90 percent of the price at a competitive interest rate, which would have made the down payment only $300,000. Stewart argued that the front section along RR 620 could be C-1 zoned, and the land behind this section, which also contained a stream, could then be used for ballparks, a library, an art center, or green space. The Wunnebergers also offered to give their historic log cabin, which is the oldest structure in Lakeway, to the city as a gesture of their goodwill.

***

Annexation battles in the Lakeway City Council and among residents of both Lakeway and the areas to be annexed have been an integral, and often controversial, part of Lakeway's history. Names such as Casa Verde, the Air Park, The Hills, World of Tennis, Estates of Lakeway, the 620 Strip, Coves of Lakeway, Flint Rock, Schramm Ranch, Cardinal Hills, Cherry Mountain, Clara Van, Travis Oaks Trails, Masonwood, the Chandler Tract, and the Heard Tract come to mind, and their individual fate can be followed in the Lakeway Time Line. Annexation debates certainly will continue until Lakeway reaches the outer boundaries of its ETJ, which appears to be in the very near future.

CHAPTER NINETEEN

VISIONARIES: THEN AND NOW

Like the ancient Roman deity, Janus, whose two faces looked backward to the past and forward to the future, having reviewed the past, we find ourselves wondering what the future holds for Lakeway.

LAKEWAY'S *HOMEOWNERS NEWS'* COMMEMORATIVE SILVER ANNIVERSARY ISSUE, 1988

Bill Hawkins, "The Moon and Venus at Dawn"

In April 1988, Lakeway's *Homeowners News* dedicated its *Commemorative Silver Anniversary Issue* "to the past, present, and future of a Dream Community in Unity." The editors began by reminding their readers of the uniqueness of Lakeway:[1]

> We who live here know we have a community with a unique style of life which is the envy of outsiders. But sometimes we may forget, it did not just happen. It started when four men, impressed with the idea of a lake front resort/hotel, began a dream which expanded into a community harmonizing with the beauty of the Texas Hill Country.

The editors also encouraged several leading citizens to project Lakeway twenty-five years into the future. Lee Blocker, who was one of the original founders of Lakeway, began his comments with a caveat:

> Please realize that the ideas expressed are not wishful thinking on my part, since some of the items represent development contrary to my desires.
>
> The population will grow significantly. It will at least triple the growth rate of the City of Austin. The boundaries of the Village of Lakeway will increase in size.
>
> The identity of the two MUDs will disappear. The Village of Lakeway will take them over. . . .
>
> The Village of Lakeway will gradually begin to control the deer population. This will be done in a manner that will satisfy the citizens interested in keeping the deer.
>
> There will be another major marina built in the Rough Hollow area.
>
> At the present time Lakeway enjoys a fine mix of ages in its citizenry. As time goes on, this mix will broaden to include an even more representative blending of all age groups.
>
> The Lakeway Ecumenical Church will continue to expand its facilities; however, this will not match the percentage growth of the Village of Lakeway because there will be an increase in the number of denominational churches in the area, not necessarily in Lakeway.
>
> Local area shopping and dining will improve rapidly, though not necessarily within Lakeway Village. There should be a local theater for movies as close as Oak Hill within five years. . . .
>
> Lakeway is one of the loveliest developments in the world. Every time my wife and I come home from vacation, we sit on our deck and wonder why we ever left.

Co-founder G. Flint Sawtelle told Byron Varner in 1986 that he never expected Lakeway to prosper to the extent it had:

> I am just amazed at the continuing change and progress I see each time I visit Lakeway. I remember that Lakeway wasn't even one year old when two people whose opinion I valued highly told me it was a big mistake to locate here. . . .
>
> I don't think any of the original group ever thought that Lakeway would become as large as it is today. I personally thought maybe it would be 1,500 to 2,500 acres maximum when we first conceived the idea. . . . I have no idea how large it will eventually become but it has great future possibilities, that's for sure.

The last of the three co-founders, John Crooker, described how the tragic assassination of John F. Kennedy in 1963 implausibly contributed to the initial success of Lakeway. Crooker also acknowledged the contributions of Bob Alpert, who purchased Lakeway from its original investors in 1971:

1. In addition to the *Homeowners News Commemorative Silver Anniversary Issue,* the other major source for the quotations pertaining to 1963–1988 is Byron Varner's *Lakeway: The First 25 Years,* 173–178.

> Lakeway had been in development only a few months when tragedy in Dallas made Lyndon Johnson President of the United States. Perhaps no other area in Texas benefitted more from his presidency than Austin and the Hill Country. His interest in Lakeway through frequent visits and property ownership, as well as use of the Inn for several stopovers by the White House Press Corps, gave us publicity we otherwise would not have had and it helped us greatly in our sales efforts. . . .
>
> Bob Alpert foresaw the future of resort communities and came into the game with major financial backing, which would see him through the changing times.

Jim Gribble, who constructed the Tejas Building and ran the Country Store in the Village Square before serving as a commissioner (1974–1975) and then mayor (1975–1983), understood the importance of water to the growth and well-being of the community:

> Lakeway can be a budding Austin. We could be the west corner post of this complex [but] water will be the critical problem. I can envision a day when if you take three gallons of water out of Lake Travis, you must put two back in. The issues will be how clean is the water and not to use too damn much of it.

Jim Gribble's wife, Ann, started a gift shop in the Lakeway Inn in 1966 that she later moved into the Village Square. Ann, who served as a Lakeway councilmember (1998–2000), called Lakeway "a special corner of the world, made up of a heterogeneous group of people who come from everywhere. It has a cosmopolitan feeling to it while retaining its small town, hometown feeling. To me that is a real nice, rare quality."

C. Ed Smith, Jr., who served as commissioner, alderman, and mayor (1981–1989), was prescient as he gazed into his crystal ball:

> Looking down from above, hopefully, I would expect to see the Village of Lakeway encompassing the present Greater Lakeway area and beyond. . . .
>
> It may be more urban than resort, but high standards of building requirements and ordinances will keep it the high class community it is today.

David Lewis, who moved into Lakeway in 1979 and purchased the Village Square in 1985, praised the natural beauty that Lakeway residents so appreciated:

> Lake Travis stands as one of the great monuments of man working in harmony with nature. The builders and leaders of Lakeway have always been cognizant of the task and responsibility to measure up to that monument. . . .
>
> The future Lakeway I see is a continuation of the very essence of our community—a feeling of quiet, casual elegance. I see a generation of native-born Lakewayites who will not want to leave. I see a mixture of people much like our architecture, with wide variations of age, economics and ethnic backgrounds—but they will be harmonious, with a common bond of love for Lakeway.

Veronica Bennett, who was president of the Homeowners Association when Lakeway celebrated its twenty-fifth birthday, and later served as an alderwoman and councilmember (1989–1993), understood that Lakeway would continue to grow, but she also urged citizen involvement in molding its future development:

> The past is interesting; it has made us what we are; however, we cannot bring it back to savor the pleasant times or to correct regretted errors. The present is today, and we should all strive to learn from the mistakes of the past and not allow them to be a part of the "here and now." It is also imperative we keep and cherish all that was good, and nurture it

> for the future well-being of the community. The future of Lakeway is bright, but it will take a caring, voting, volunteering citizenry to help it meet its full potential as "A Dream Community in Unity."

At the time of the Silver Anniversary, Jean Blocker, the wife of co-founder Lee Blocker, succinctly summed up the sentiments of that first generation of Lakeway residents:

> I loved Lakeway in the beginning, and I still love it today just as much. This is right where I want to be.

***

How have the predictions and hopes for Lakeway changed over the past twenty-five years? Certainly most current residents continue to acknowledge that future growth is inevitable, but not all welcome the prospect. Some fear losing the friendliness and small-town life that has characterized most of Lakeway's first fifty years. All agree, however, that projects such as the new Lakeway Regional Medical Center will have a tremendous impact on the city and the surrounding area.

Robert C. "Bob" Laws has lived in Lakeway for forty years. As a member of the old Historical Society and the current Heritage Commission, he certainly has the advantage of perspective:

> After college and the army I was working for IBM sales in Austin in 1968 when I purchased a golf course lot on Lakeway Drive for $3,000. Three years later we moved into our home. My uncle, Jack Laws, who came from Houston with the original developers as one of the first real estate salesman, told me that it would be a good investment, and it was.
>
> Living in Lakeway as thirty-year-olds with children was awakening to say the least. The average age was at least sixty-five and the men wore their military rank on their golf hats. Most of the retirees did not want children next door. If our children left a toy in the front yard, we often received a friendly reminder.
>
> A few friendly older neighbors did invite us to cocktail parties, and we soon learned that when they said 6:00 p.m., they were serious. We would show up fashionably at 6:30. The martinis would be consumed shortly thereafter and the host and guests would retire.
>
> Please do not misunderstand, the retired folks that started Lakeway were quality, successful and high class. I was privileged to be around them and learn from their experiences. Their proven talents most of the time moved our village in the right direction. Until recently this meant no growth, low taxes, and restrictive ordinances and building codes. The idea was we moved here but we don't want you to follow. If you do, do not bring your "Big Box" businesses with you. Today, we have fourteen banks and are building the second largest hospital in Austin. Our city government has traded "no growth" for "a larger tax base."
>
> The Hill Country will explode in the next twenty-five years. In fifty years, Lakeway, Dripping Springs, Spicewood, Johnson City, Blanco, and Marble Falls will all be touching. I also envision a bridge across Lake Travis connecting the north and south shores.
>
> Not unlike the old West and its barbed wire range wars over water, there will be fights over the Highland Lake reservoirs. With the continued growth on and around Lake Travis and the expanding need for water for homes and irrigation, there will be a crisis. The legislature and courts will get involved, especially with San Antonio's on-going attempts to replenish its depleted source of ground water and the Lower Colorado River Authority's standing contracts with downstream rice farmers.
>
> The neighborly attitude that existed when I moved here no longer seems to be

the norm. We had "neighbors" that may have lived five blocks away and we still related sociably. Today, I notice a lack of interacting with the people next door. Whether it's the sign of the times or of a population approaching 15,000, I miss the small village attitudes. I do not, however, want to sound negative concerning our good city. I could not have chosen a better place to live and raise our three children. I came here as a young man of thirty and will leave only one way.

Like Bob Laws, Steve Swan has deep roots in Lakeway. His parents moved to Lakeway in 1972, and Steve and his wife, Linda, did so in 2000. Both as a councilmember (2003–2005) and a two-term mayor (2005–2009), Steve worked to improve Lakeway's tax base through carefully orchestrated growth:

During the foundation years of Lakeway, citizens and their elected officials set high standards for development, and established an irresistible living environment which will always be a challenge to sustain. As one of the many volunteers who have followed our "pioneers" in civic positions, this strong foundation still provides the guidance we need, and gives us the courage to strive for excellence.

It was a privilege to serve as mayor. I tried to keep my focus on planning for the future development and living environment of our city. I am proud to have encouraged and aggressively supported the development of the Lakeway Regional Medical Center and the annexation of a large parcel of land on Highway 71 known as the Heard Tract, and now being developed as Cinco Hills. This southern-most part of our city, in addition to residential development, provides new commercial revenue opportunities now that the Lakeway portion of RR 620 is approaching full development.

Time will tell how these major steps affect the long term attractiveness and financial well-being of Lakeway. As I look into the future, it will be important that the Lakeway staff and elected officials participate effectively in formulating mobility decisions regarding the 620 corridor. I believe that this one issue will greatly affect the livability of our community in the future.

Former councilmember (2006–2009) and current Lakeway Mayor Dave DeOme (2009–) also tackles the question of inevitable growth, while expressing confidence that Lakeway and its residents will continue to savor the quality of life they have so long enjoyed:

Hopefully, the Lakeway of the future will not look much different from today's Lakeway. Of course, we can expect the City will be bigger and more modern. The question, as always, will not be IF Lakeway will grow, but HOW it will grow.

Following years of planning, we will all soon benefit from the first class Lakeway Regional Medical Center, which will attract more healthcare professionals to live in the City. This facility and the new residents will, in turn, attract additional businesses and services to the area, which will make it less and less necessary to travel into Austin to satisfy shopping or service needs.

Even with the new Regional Medical Center, I do not believe that Lakeway will move far from its heritage as primarily a residential community. Some of the vacation homes built in the 60s and 70s will probably be torn down or significantly remodeled. Such a transition should be expected, and the City's zoning and planning organization is prepared for such an eventuality. I do not foresee a transition to greater housing density. In Lakeway, the single family, detached home will remain the rule, rather than the exception.

I strongly believe the attractiveness of Lakeway is rooted in its many greenbelts, parks and golf courses. The strong zoning ordinances and building controls are also a major contributor to Lakeway's charm. Over time, these cornerstones of Lakeway's beauty will not diminish.

Why will they not diminish? It is really all about the residents of Lakeway. Those already here and those yet to come choose Lakeway for many reasons. Once here, they quickly begin to appreciate that the underlying depth of Lakeway's uniqueness rests with its residents. They are active, gregarious and involved. They come to love Lakeway and they commit to making the City better. They soon learn that the Lakeway they moved to is even better than they originally anticipated. They will not let it change, at least not in any fundamental way.

Former Mayor Cole Rowland (1991–1993), who in 2001 received the Lakeway Civic Corporations's Outstanding Citizen Award and who also served as president of the Highland Lakes Group, comments on the challenge of providing sufficient water to meet the rapidly expanding needs of Central Texas:

Over the next twenty-five years there will be both favorable and unfavorable factors affecting lake levels. As the population grows in Central Texas, there will be less water left in the reservoirs by cities which own water contracts but which do not need the water to meet current demands. The rice industry will have seen its supply of cheap "interruptible" water diminish, so it will be forced to switch to strains of rice, or other crops, which do not require flooding the fields. The net result of these two trends will be lower average highs and lows for lake levels, but the seasonal lows, that are traditional now during the rice season, will fade.

The City of Lakeway and the Lakeway MUD will merge, with complex results for both entities and for consumers. Both floods and droughts will tend to be more severe than in the past.

The "free" water right owned by LCRA, on the yield of Lakes Buchanan and Travis, is about sold out. It will have to be supplemented by very expensive water obtained from groundwater, desalination or downstream off-channel reservoirs. The technology exists today to convert wastewater into drinking water. As water becomes much more valuable, only the "yuck" factor on the part of consumers will have to be overcome. That may take longer than twenty-five years.

As a former city councilmember (2002–2006) and current president of the Lakeway Municipal Utility District Board, Karl Ansbach also foresees a rapidly growing city absorbing the LMUD, while at the same time seeing its pool of citizen volunteers greatly diminish:

The opening of the new Regional Medical Center will prove to be a big impetus for business activity in Lakeway and Bee Cave. Additionally, we will see more and more residents wanting to "move west" into our area, and I see the Lakeway population hitting 25,000 by the year 2035.

The Lakeway MUD will sign a contract to take over the maintenance and operation of water and wastewater services for Rough Hollow and the Highlands development. This will more than pique the interest of Lakeway City officials and, once again, the City will attempt to take over the LMUD. Eventually, much to the chagrin of LMUD customers and many non-LMUD customers, the city will succeed in its endeavor. Hopefully, this process will be one that is thoroughly thought out by both sides and results in a centralized water/wastewater service that is fairly priced. As part of the Rough Hollow/Highlands agreement, LMUD will be able to sell the Cedar Tract on Lohman's Crossing to the City and the much awaited Town Center will become a reality.

The city has always relied on its many volunteers to serve in so many capacities. However, as more and more younger "work force" families move into the area, the pool of retired volunteers will dwindle and the city will be forced to look at other alternatives, such as paid workers. Sounds like the next 25 to 50 years will be very interesting. I wish I could be here to see it.

George Blume, who moved to Lakeway in 1986, has been one of the community's most active and accomplished volunteers. He deserves major credit for obtaining and developing the property that became City Park. He also served as president of the Lake Travis Arts League and the City of Lakeway Arts Committee. He was chair of Friends of the Parks and served as a Lakeway councilmember (2001–2005). Despite his enviable record of working to make Lakeway a better place to live, Blume refuses to see himself as a visionary:

I do not like using the word "Visionary." Fifty years ago the Visionaries were talking about Flying Cars and Space Colonies; no Visionary foresaw the Internet, email, and the World Wide Web.

My hope is that in the future the City of Lakeway will continue to expand its network of Greenbelts and natural areas like the Canyonlands. In the past the Lake defined the character of the City. In the future the protection of these natural areas will augment the Lake in preserving the character of Lakeway.

My hope is that the City of Lakeway will establish an independent Organized Recreational Athletics Program, not only for our youth, but also for all citizens.

My hope is that the City will become more "walkable" to promote good exercise, health, and social interaction with our neighbors.

My hope is that Gated Communities will disappear from our landscape, to allow greater social interaction within the community.

My hope is that the many building restrictions will be refined to allow more architectural freedom for our homes and buildings and allow for greater individualism, creativity and imagination within our citizens.

Judy and Fred Hazen have also been among Lakeway's most active volunteers. They have been members of Friends of the Parks for the past twelve years and both served on the board. Judy also organized the FOP workday picnics. Fred served on the Lakeway Arts & Beautification Committee, the Heritage Commission, and as chair of the Photo Festival. In addition, he coordinated numerous Veterans' Roundtables:

We've been fascinated with Lakeway since first coming to visit our daughter and family on Star Street near the Lakeway Inn in 1991. As many of you know, grandchildren hold the greatest influence on picking retirement locations.

Just getting to Lakeway was then an adventure: Coming out of Austin on FM 2222 as it opened into hill country vistas, driving across the top of Mansfield Dam and negotiating the road work on widening RR 620, and then spotting the famous golf ball water tower!

Lakeway's "small town feeling" welcomed us with its July 4th parade, concerts and picnics at our "new" City Park and the boat parade-of-lights at Christmas time. Friends of the Parks was our first involvement in community service. It is amusing to list all the things Lakeway didn't have in the early years. We recall life with a one-clerk postal "station," one grocery store, no chain restaurants, one or two physicians and dentists, and a volunteer fire department. The Activity Center and the Swim Center did not exist, and "Lakeway" generally meant everything on *this side* of RR 620, which, incidentally, had minimal traffic.

We would hope that we have reached the geographical boundaries of our city without more expansion, but doesn't every generation want to "keep it like it is"? Expansion seems the norm these days. Regardless of growth and progress, we would hope that Lakeway never loses its small town spirit.

Fred Newton purchased a lot in Lakeway in 1986 and moved into a permanent home in 1995. In addition to numerous volunteer posts, he served as chairman of Lakeway's Board of Ethics, the Health Services Committee, and the Arts Committee. He and his family created the Lakeway Boulevard Sculpture Garden, featuring original bronze sculptures of children at play, in memory of his late wife, Florence:

Visiting Lakeway in 1986, my wife and I decided to invest in a Lakeway lot as a place to live after retirement. We were favorably impressed by the distinctive custom architecture and, after a meeting with volunteer City Manager Sam Huser, the extent of volunteerism in managing and maintaining the community. Retiring in 1994, we commissioned the building of the house we moved into in February 1995. We also both became volunteers.

The need for more medical services was apparent to many. In 1999, the City Council formed a volunteer Health Services Committee to research means of improving this condition. The committee joined with other organizations on the south shore of Lake Travis and, after significant research and meetings with Austin health service providers, distributed a report to all large health service providers in Texas. It described the sparse existing health services on the South Shore and included data regarding the then current population (about 25,000) and a five-year forecast of population (about 55,000). Medical services have increased dramatically, with prospects being very bright for providing not only excellent services but also professional employment for future residents.

Seeing a need to stimulate artistic endeavors, the City Council established an Arts Committee in 2000. This group of volunteers planned and produced opportunities for visual and performing arts that continue to enhance the quality of life in Lakeway. Attention is being drawn to Lakeway by professional productions such as the Brown Bag Luncheon Concerts and the TexArts musicals and the talent displayed in the amateur productions of the Sing-A-Longs and the Lakeway Players. This may influence some of the professional theater companies in Austin to look west for new venues. It also may influence an increase in live music and art galleries in the Lakeway area.

All Lakeway visionaries manifest a great admiration for the unique role volunteers have played in the community. Peggy Point, who received a Volunteer of the Year Award in 2006, became the first chair of the Heritage Commission in 2001 and also served as president of the Service League:

We came to Lakeway in 1992 when there were approximately 5,000 residents. Now we are at about 14,000. My hope is that the community spirit of caring and giving back can continue. The volunteer way has proven to be a godsend for us during this time of exceptional growth and with good leadership it will be able to continue with the growth that will come. We recently went to a program at the Lakeway Church which was given by three combined church choirs and was benefitting the Lake Travis Crisis Ministries. That is true Lakeway for me.

Charles Edwards and his wife, LaNell, have

been two of Lakeway's most committed volunteers. Charles served as mayor (1999–2003) and on the Zoning and Planning Commission and the Economic Development Committee. In 2011, he received the Lakeway Civic Corporation's Outstanding Citizen Award. LaNell was a councilmember (1995–1999) and received the LCC's Meritorious Service Award in 2004 and a special Lifetime Achievement Award in 2009:

> While Lakeway is not perfect in all aspects, it is by far the most dynamic place of twenty-four where we have lived. Our founders had a vision for Lakeway that has proven to be a tremendous foundation for what we have today. From a Community to a Village and now a Home Rule City, our solid growth in strength and stature provides a marvelous setting for all ages. A great revolving group of volunteers continues to step forward to work for the betterment of Lakeway. Our challenge for the future is to preserve the uniqueness of our City so our younger generations can enjoy living, working and volunteering in support of our Texas paradise!

Doris Besperka was an active member of both the Lakeway Historical Society and the Lakeway Heritage Commission. She also wrote a series of "Bedtime Stories" on important developments in Lakeway's past:

> The first twenty-five years gave Lakeway a firm foundation to build on. After the second twenty-five years with its incredible growth and problems, it remains a wonderful place to live. This is largely the result of the hard and time-consuming work of hundreds of volunteers. This gives Lakewayites a "Hands On" feeling, and this is the reason Lakeway is so very different from other communities.
>
> I predict that life in Lakeway will continue as it is as long as volunteerism exists. However, our young people are so involved with their personal lives and have so little appreciation of their Lakeway Heritage that volunteerism will slowly fade away. The City will continue to prosper, but it will lose its special spirit and be just like any other place.

As Lakeway city manager (1994–2004), Dave Benson played an active role in the expansion of Lakeway and its ETJ. In 1996, he predicted that Lakeway would become a city of 25,000 in the not too distant future:

> With its Hill Country and Lake Travis location, top notch schools, many recreational opportunities, upscale neighborhoods, and short commute to Austin, Lakeway could be the most desirable place to live in Texas. We have it all. My fondest hope for its future is that it remains residential in nature and that the current spirit of community volunteerism continues to flourish in all aspects of city life. Volunteerism made Lakeway what it is today and is what will always make it different from other Texas cities. My prediction for Lakeway in 25 years is that it will be a bigger version of what Lakeway is today—a super place to live.

P. A. Penley served on several important Lakeway entities, including the Administration, Personnel and Communications Committee and the Building Commission. He was on the Lakeway MUD's board of directors for eleven years and was also a reporter for the *Homeowners News*. In 2006, he received the Lakeway Civic Corporation's annual Outstanding Citizen Award:

> When we moved to Lakeway in late 1999, our impression was that it was a beautiful little village populated by friendly, mostly retired people, but a little hard to get to from Austin. Both RR 620 and Bee Caves Road were narrow two-lane roads, and driving over the top

of the dam was not for the faint hearted. When we visit Lakeway from our new home at Longhorn Village, it is still beautiful, but it has grown gracefully into a busy city with a much lower proportion of retired folks. Change is inevitable: if you build it, they will come—just like the Field of Dreams.

Good things come with growth, such as a convenient new hospital and a State Champion football team, but some of the closeness of the residents will continue to slip away. Our hope for the future is that involved men and women will continue the volunteer tradition that has served Lakeway so well in the past.

After an impressive career in journalism, Ernie Conine retired to Lakeway, where he served on the Historical Society Board. He warns that friends and neighbors rather than just developers must make the important decisions for the future.

Lakeway has greatly benefitted from an accident of history. A sizeable portion of the number of residents settling here in the last two decades were men and women of accomplishment in war and peace who wanted to do more than sail or play golf or tennis. They wanted to play an active role in their new community. The result was the system under which Lakeway was largely run by unpaid volunteers who built a tradition of hard work and friendly cooperation for the good of the city. The challenge now is to perpetuate that tradition in an era of a larger, younger population with more diverse views on what kind of Lakeway they want. The appropriate rate of population growth over the next 25 years, and the housing patterns best suited to accommodate it, will be difficult decisions. If Lakeway is to retain its unique character, they must be made not just by developers but by friends and neighbors working together to make their voices heard.

PART V

TIME LINES

A BRIEF TRAVIS COUNTY TIME LINE

250–100 million years B.C.

The area that would become Travis County sat atop the Llanorian Mountains. To the north and west were great plains and to the south and east a vast ocean. Evidence of an extinct volcano suggests a violent geological past. According to local naturalist and historian John Renford Taylor, "The residents then were a variety of creepy, crawly forms of life." Taylor concludes that approximately 100 million years ago, "the waters and plains reversed themselves and the Llanorian Mountains sank below thousands of feet of limestone." During this era, dinosaurs roamed the Lakeway area, evidence of which has been sighted at low water on the bottom of Lake Travis.

8000–10,000 B.C.

Hunting and gathering peoples, sometimes referred to as part of the Clovis migration or Paleo-Indians, roamed the area.

1300–1700

The Tonkawa and Lipan Apache Indians dominated much of the Hill Country.

1600s

Comanche and Kiowa Indian tribes moved into the area.

1629–1632

Traveling into Texas from what would become New Mexico, Father Juan de Salas reached the upper Colorado River, which the Spanish then called the Nueces. Later in the seventeenth century, Spanish and French explorers traveled up the lower Colorado, but most did not explore the area immediately above future Austin.

1691

Domingo Terán de los Rios became the first known European to cross what would become Travis County.

1721

The Spanish governor of Texas, the Marqués de San Miguel de Aguayo, led an expedition that passed through what would become Austin and up the Colorado River to what is now Burnet and beyond. This expedition strengthened Spain's claim to Central Texas, which it called Northern New Spain. The Marqués also described the Indians he called Apaches.

1730

The Spanish relocated their East Texas missions of San Francisco de los Neches, Nuestra Señora de la Purisma Concepción de los Hasinai, and San José de los Nazonis to an area near Barton Springs.

1800

By the end of the eighteenth century, there were well-worn trails and primitive roads that extended all the way up the Colorado River. Both the French and the Spanish attempted to make treaties with the Indians, many of whom traded up and down the Colorado. The Indians were particularly interested in Spanish horses, but they also traded for tobacco, liquor, and guns with the French. In the early 1800s, the Spanish had several outposts along the Colorado, but all disappeared because of Indian or political conflicts.

1821–1822

Stephen Fuller Austin, hoping to fulfill his late father Moses' dream of establishing a settlement in Texas, explored the Colorado for a suitable location. In 1822, he drew up a map of Texas to help guide those who wanted to establish settlements.

1827

After obtaining a land grant from the Mexican government, Stephen F. Austin established the Little Colony, near present-day Bastrop. One of the first men to settle in the Little Colony was William Barton, who later moved west to the springs that now bear his name.

1833

The notorious and legendary Indian scalping of Josiah Wilbarger occurred downstream from the Little Colony; Josiah miraculously survived and his brother John Wesley Wilbarger described the incident in vivid detail in his 1889 *Indian Depredations in Texas: Reliable Accounts of Battles, Wars, Adventures, Forays, Murders, Massacres, etc.*

1836

March 2 - Texans successfully declared their independence from Mexico and set up the Republic of Texas.

1837–1839

In October 1837, the first congress of the new Republic of Texas appointed a committee to find a suitable site for its capital. In 1838, Mirabeau B. Lamar, the newly elected president of the Republic, convinced the committee to select the tiny community of Waterloo, where four families had settled near the mouth of Shoal Creek. On April 13, 1839, Waterloo officially became Austin. On August 1, 1839, settlers and land speculators rushed in to purchase the newly platted lots. A newcomer named George W. Bonnell proudly proclaimed, "Like the ancient city of Rome, Austin is built upon seven hills, and it is impossible to conceive a more beautiful and lovely situation." One of those seven hills appropriately became Mount Bonnell.

Settlers also set their sights along the Colorado upstream from Austin, but the rugged terrain and Comanche Indians remained barriers. The new government launched several expeditions to wipe out the Indians as far as the confluence of the San Saba and Colorado Rivers. Sam Houston, however, as President of the Republic and a later U.S. Senator and Governor of Texas, preferred to make treaties with the Indians, as had the French, Spanish, and Germans. Houston had earlier been adopted by the Cherokee Nation and reportedly had a Cherokee wife.

1840

The new Texas government organized Travis County, which initially covered some 40,000 square miles. Today it is approximately 1,000 square miles. The population of Travis County in 1840 reportedly was 856. That same year Austin passed its first slave ordinance, which prohibited "any white or Mexican from making associates of slaves."

Anxious to encourage settlement, the new government offered generous land contracts, including agreements made with French, English, and, especially, German immigration societies. As a result, approximately 30,000 Germans arrived in the ports of Galveston and New Orleans between 1842 and 1845. Even greater numbers of settlers poured in from the Midwest and the South, lured not only by the promise of cheap land but also rumors of lost silver mines and a strong and abundant strain of wild cotton. Western Travis County, however, was still Indian country when the first white settlers arrived in the Bee Cave and Hudson Bend areas. Nevertheless, with abundant grass, bountiful springs, and a plethora of wild fruits, nuts, and game, these first settlers pronounced it paradise. Disillusionment soon followed.

1843

German immigrant Johann Heinrich Lohmann arrived in Galveston with his wife, Antoinette Sophia, and their four children. They traveled by oxcart to the Austin Colony, described at the time as "largely uninhabited with streets filled with grass and weeds . . . the abode of bats, lizards, and stray cattle." Somewhere along the line the final "n" was dropped from the Lohmann name. In addition, Johann's first and middle names were anglicized, so he became John Henry Lohman; nevertheless, his descendants, if not the city of Lakeway, have retained the double "n" at the end of the family name.

1845

December 29 - The Texas Constitutional Convention approved its annexation by the U.S. government. A myth later emerged that Texas retained its right to withdraw from the Union. What was allowed was the possibility of dividing Texas into five states.

John Henry Lohmann opened Austin's first dairy farm on a piece of land a couple miles north of the current University of Texas campus. Lohmann used an oxcart to deliver the milk of his eleven cows to the few dwellings that then made up Austin. He continued his dairy operation until the beginning of the Civil War when he moved west to what one day would become Lakeway.

1846

Austin became the permanent capital of Texas, although it had served as a temporary capital as early as 1839. It also had to win another election in 1872 before its status became accepted statewide.

1850

The Travis County census of 1850 showed a population of 3,138, of whom 2,336 were whites, 791 slaves, and 11 free blacks.

Wiley Hudson and his family settled on the bend of the Colorado River that now bears his name.

1854

Most Hispanic residents were expelled from Austin because "they associate too familiarly with slaves and instill false notions of freedom."

March - The Colorado River below Austin was open to navigation via steamboat, but the mouth at Matagorda Bay was often clogged with logs and debris. After the Civil War, newly built railroad lines ended commercial river navigation on the Colorado.

1860

The Travis County census listed a population of 8,080, of whom 4,931 were white, 3,136 slaves, and 13 free blacks. Of Austin's 3,500 residents, approximately 1,000 were slaves. The census recorded 470 farmers, three ranchers, forty-six stock raisers, four herders, and three shepherds living in the county. Corn was the primary field crop, followed by wheat.

1861

January - The Austin-based Secession Convention passed a resolution to secede from the Union. Voters statewide approved the resolution in February, although residents in Austin and Travis County turned down the resolution by a vote of 704 to 450. Nevertheless, by April 1862 the *State Gazette* could proudly state, "There are less than sixty 'Union shriekers' left in the Austin area."

According to Frank Brown's *Annals of Travis County and the City of Austin* (1901), a man named Butts twice attempted to lynch John Henry Lohmann at the beginning of the Civil War because he thought he was a Unionist. Shortly thereafter, Lohmann, his second wife, Rosine, and their children homesteaded on the Colorado River west of Austin on land that is now under Lake Travis.

1863

December - The labor of several hundred slaves helped construct fortifications to protect Austin.

1864

March - John Henry Lohmann's stepson, Charles Weber, was murdered near Hamilton Pool. One version has him scalped by Indians but another suggests the murderers were scallywags or bounty hunters looking for pro-Unionists.

1865

The Civil War exacted a horrific cost on Travis County that went beyond human casualties. Already by the end of 1864, the county's property tax receipts showed economic losses of up to 49 percent, much of it related to the loss of slaves.

August - Andrew Jackson Hamilton, who fled Austin during the Civil War and hid out in the Hamilton Pool area before becoming a Union general, became the first Reconstruction governor of Texas. Lakeway resident Tom Flinn, whose family helped settle the Austin area, suggested shortly before his death in 2008, "Real Texans should have shot that s.o.b Hamilton."

1866

Scholz Garden opened in downtown Austin, featuring the Austin *Saengerrunde* (German singing group). Both continue to thrive at 1607 San Jacinto Boulevard.

1870–1880

The population of Travis County more than doubled from 13,153 to 27,028. By the end of the decade there were more than 1,900 farms raising corn, cotton, wheat, oats, and livestock, and a number of these farms were in western Travis County.

September 29, 1875 - A U.S. post office was established at Flint Rock, with Paul Reinke as its postmaster. It was discontinued on October 6, 1882, shortly after Reinke was murdered.

A stagecoach line on the north side of the Colorado River passed through or near what would become Lakeway.

December 12, 1876 - The establishment of the Dripping Springs Community School District #10. As late as 1910, the district had only three teachers, but by 1935 it had added Dripping Springs Common School District #20. Future Lakeway residents would have to send their children to Dripping Springs schools until the Lake Travis Independent School District opened in 1981.

1882

January - The Austin and Northwestern Railroad opened an east–west route between Austin and Burnet, which facilitated the transportation of the special granite for the new capitol building. It also ended the need for stagecoaches in the area.

1889

Austin mayor-elect John P. McDonald called for a city-financed dam across the Colorado River. Work on this sixty-foot-high dam began in May 1891. The dam, which stretched for almost a quarter of a mile, generated its first electricity in 1895, but it collapsed during the floods of April 1900. It was partially rebuilt before being totally destroyed in September 1915. Not until 1940 was a new Austin Dam opened, later renamed the Tom Miller Dam. These early dams were primarily intended to prevent flooding, thereby safeguarding communities along the Colorado River.

1890

The Teck School consolidated two earlier schools at Hirsh [*sic.*] Creek and Hudson Bend.

Bee Cave residents Frederick and Ilsa Freitag donated land to western Travis County "in trust for public free school purposes." During these early years, pupils only went to school for a few months of the year because they had to help on the farms. They could also only go through eighth grade, after which they had to attend high school in Austin.

1900

The two main communities in the Lakeway area at the turn of the century were Bee Cave and Teck.

1934

The Texas legislature created the nonprofit Lower Colorado River Authority (LCRA) to provide reliable, low-cost utility and public services to Central Texas. These services would ultimately include electricity, flood management, water and wastewater utilities, and public parks. The LCRA eventually owned and operated the six hydroelectric dams along the Colorado River that created the Highland Lakes: Buchanan (Lake Buchanan), Inks (Inks Lake), Wirtz (Lake LBJ), Max Starcke (Lake Marble Falls), Mansfield (Lake Travis), and Tom Miller (Lake Austin).

1936

The U.S. Bureau of Reclamation began taking bids for a dam at Marshall Ford, the primary purpose of which would be to control floods and preserve the fertile soil along the banks of the lower Colorado River. The Brown and Root Construction Company of Texas began work on the dam in 1936, even though it had not yet been fully funded.

1937

U.S. Representative Lyndon Baines Johnson piloted the construction of the Buchanan and Inks Dams through Congress. One result was the formation of the Pedernales Electric Cooperative, which eventually would serve much of Lakeway. Johnson also procured final funding to complete the eighteen-story, 7,100-foot-long Marshall Ford Dam, which formed Lake Travis and was renamed the Mansfield Dam.

1941

January 27, 1941 - The Mansfield Dam began generating electricity.

1951

Lake Travis set a record low level of 614.2 feet.

1955

Max Schramm and his wife purchased approximately 700 acres of land, which became known as the Schramm Ranch. Brothers Nevis and Abe Hutto bought 2,600 acres along Flintrock Road. West and north of the Huttos was a large ranch owned by Gus B. Mauermann, which he sold to Jack Josey, who already owned several thousand acres in the county. Lakeway initially would be carved out of these parcels of land.

LAKEWAY TIME LINE

1962

October 24, 1962 - The incorporation of the Lakeway Land Company. John Crooker, Jr., G. Flint Sawtelle, and Lee Blocker, all with the Houston-based Gulfmont Hotel Company, had been looking for a site on Lake Travis to build a resort hotel. They later added investment partners George Sawtelle, Wayne Ankenman, Jack Josey, Ben Boshton, Andy Kivlin, Frank Denius, and W. A. "Tex" Moncrief. They eventually purchased 3,700 acres from Jack Josey for a planned resort community, anchored by the Lakeway Inn. As Sawtelle later told the story, "When we drove down toward the end of Lohman's Road and saw that expanse of water and the point of land just across the inlet, oh my, we were just about sold right then and there." At the time, Josey Tract I had no electrical power and the nearest phone was at Johnson's Trading Post on Highway 71. Nevertheless, after Sawtelle invited representatives of nearby electrical and telephone utilities to a gourmet lunch on the Lakeway Inn's recently poured deck, Lakeway got its first telephone, located at what is now Lohman's Crossing and Lakeway Boulevard, where a historical marker now stands. Electrical power soon followed.

1963

June 1 - The Lakeway Land Company opened a temporary sales office at 204 Lakeway Drive to sell lots in Sections 1 and 2. Kivlin, Blocker, and Sawtelle laid out the streets; the first to be paved was Lakeway Drive. Kivlin, who was the building contractor for the Lakeway Inn, also began building six spec homes. His wife, Sylvion, became Lakeway's first real estate agent.

June 6 - The Lakeway Yacht Club opened "to provide facilities for social intercourse among its members as well as providing facilities for swimming and other athletic activities." In actuality, there were no yachts, but as a private club it could sell alcohol. Prospective buyers were not allowed to buy homesites until approved for membership, although Civil Rights legislation in the 1980s ended this restriction. A 1973 amendment changed the name to the Lakeway Yacht and Country Club (LYCC). An additional amendment in December 1982 allowed anyone of legal age to gain membership if the individual rented a house or condominium or was a resident of the "Lakeway developed community," meaning areas subsequently developed by the Lakeway Land Company or its successors.

July 12 - The unofficial opening of the Lakeway Inn and Marina for local people.

July 13 - The official opening of the Lakeway Inn and Marina, which included tennis courts and a stable for riding horses. Among the early guests was a herd of goats that wandered in from a neighboring ranch to graze on the newly sodded grass near the swimming pool. The human guests included Lady Bird Johnson and Governor John Connally. The event received little coverage in Austin's media, which considered Lakeway too distant for a sensible commute.

July 14 - France's Bastille Day was also celebrated at the inn with the hiring of French-born Pierre Caselli as manager. Sharing equal time on July 14 was the birth of Pierre and wife Billy's son Christopher, who was the first child to be born in Lakeway.

Father Richard McCabe, who at the time headed Catholic Charities for the Diocese of Austin, held the first Catholic Mass in the Lakeway home of Walter Jenkins, who was then Lyndon Johnson's top administrative assistant. Soon needing more room, Father McCabe moved the service to the Lakeway Inn, where he occasionally held services in the Yacht Club bar.

The Lakeway Land Company established an Architectural Control Committee to enforce deed restrictions. Its objective was "to govern land use, type of structures, signs, nuisance factors, use of firearms, trash disposal, storage of boats and materials, pets, drainage, off-street parking, developments, easements, and types of building materials." It was reorganized in 1975 under the name Architectural Control Board and provided indemnification against lawsuits directed at its members.

The Lakeway Stables opened at the northeast end of the Airpark, where a historical marker now stands.

1964

Section 3 opened for land sales.

Al and Marge Saenger moved into Lakeway's first custom home at 104 Highlander.

Walter and "Sug" Graham purchased the first Lakeway Land Company spec home at 108 Comet. They also purchased one of the first lots on Comet Cove.

The Lakeway Land Company purchased Josey Tract II, bringing its total Josey acreage to more than 3,700 acres.

The Lakeway Land Company officially opened its Airpark with a 3,200-foot runway. Lee Blocker and his partners had originally purchased the land in 1962 "to have a place where people could live abutting the Airpark." Between 1929 and 1936, the Clifton George family had owned this property known locally as the Airfield Ranch, which included a grass landing strip.

1965

Section 4 opened for land sales.

Lee Blocker, Pierre Caselli, and the Lakeway Land Company began publishing the *Lakeway News*. Although including news about owners and visitors, its primary function was to promote the area. Its final edition was published in the fall of 1971. The following year Bob Alpert printed a similar broadsheet called *Lakewaves*.

The Lakeway Land Company opened its first permanent sales office at the corner of Lakeway Drive and Sailfish.

September 29 - The Lakeway Civic Corporation was established "to promote the special welfare of the community and of its property owners . . . and to acquire and maintain property and funds for charitable community services and recreational facilities." The LCC was originally administered by a five-person board of trustees (later expanded to seven). Three members were elected by the membership and two appointed by the Lakeway Land Company. The first board included Lee Blocker, Andy Kivlin, and Flint Sawtelle, all associated with the Lakeway Land Company, and residents Lloyd Jones (president) and H. A. West.

To fund its projects, the LCC took 10 percent of the purchase price of each lot sold or $200, whichever was less, and put it into the Lakeway Property Maintenance Trust Fund, which it established in 1966. The founding developers made an initial contribution of over $50,000 to cover lots sold before the establishment of the LCC. By the end of 1987, the trust had grown to almost $600,000 and by 2011 more than $1,000,000. Among LCC's earliest funded projects were a volunteer fire department, a community directory, police patrols, and obtaining and maintaining parks and greenbelt areas.

October 1 - The opening of the first nine holes of the Live Oak Golf Course. The second nine was finished in 1967. Along with a driving range and tennis courts, the founders of the Lakeway Inn and Resort had made good on their promised amenities.

October - The Lakeway Inn, addressing Lakeway's already problematic deer herd, offered a hunting package that included room, meals, and transportation to Lakeway shooting stands. Some twenty-three nimrods scored the first three days, including one who shot a ten-point buck.

December - The Lakeway Inn increased its capacity from 49 to 80 rooms.

1966

Sections 5 and 6 opened for land sales.

First home mail delivery in Lakeway.

June - Ann Gribble, Marie Garrison, and Sue Sterns opened a gift shop in the Lakeway Inn called The Ole Shop.

1967

Sections 7 and 8 opened for land sales.

Live Oak opened its second nine holes and its first permanent pro shop.

While building their home at 221 Corinthian, Bob and Betty Crocker discovered an interesting indentation along the shoreline of their property. Archeologists authenticated it as a dinosaur print, which is only visible when Lake Travis is at its lowest.

1968

Sections 9, 10, 11, and 14 opened for land sales.

Two tennis courts opened on Lakeway Drive.

The Lakeway Land Company founded Cablevision of Lake Travis as an amenity for its residents.

November - A headline in the *Lakeway News* stated, "Lakeway-Austin Commuters Find Drive Relaxing." The *Lakeway News* was, of course, a house organ of the Lakeway Land Company; nevertheless, at the time there were no traffic lights on RR 620 or Highway 71 to impede the flow of traffic.

December 16 - After a near-disastrous fire in August 1967, thirty-five homeowners unanimously approved the forming of a volunteer fire department. The Lakeway Civic Corporation funded normal operating expenses and the Lakeway Land Company deeded a suitable site and built a garage. Al Saenger served as the first volunteer fire chief.

December - The *Lake Travis News* published its first issue. Editor Harold H. Bredlow wrote, "You have my pledge that I will do all that is possible to make life in the Lake Travis-Mansfield Dam area richer and more meaningful." The paper also attempted to cover Cedar Park, Jonestown, Liberty Hill, Highland Lakes, and Lago Vista. It stopped publishing in 1973.

1969

Sections 12 and 13 opened for land sales.

Construction began on the Seawind Townhouses.

With funding from the Lakeway Civic Corporation, Lakeway hired its first security patrols.

The Lakeway Civic Corporation also provided financing for Henry and Kathy Goldsmith's mimeographed *Homeowners Bulletin*, meant to include news not published in the *Lakeway News*, which was a creation of the Lakeway Land Company. The *Homeowners Bulletin* continued publication until 1972.

January 26 - After turning over the government to President Richard M. Nixon, Lyndon Johnson and his family returned to the Hill Country and dined at the Lakeway Inn.

February - In a letter to the *Lake Travis News*, E. C. Stewart called for a bridge to be built connecting the south and north sides of Lake Travis. Before the Mansfield Dam formed Lake Travis, Lohman's Crossing Road used a low-water, pontoon bridge to cross the Colorado River to the north side. Stewart wanted Lakeway to connect with Leander, Eanes, and Dripping Springs to form a large enough school district to avoid being absorbed into the Austin School District.

June - Retired Air Force Colonel Jim Gribble opened the Country Store in his Tejas Building in what would become the Village Square on Lakeway Drive. By his own admission, Jim did not know a lot about construction. When he poured heavy rather than light concrete for the second floor, gravity took over and the first and second floors became one. Jim later recalled his longtime friend and banker telling him, "Jim, if you'd have known what you were doing you wouldn't have borrowed the money, and if I had known what I was doing, I wouldn't have loaned it to you." In addition to the Country Store, the Tejas Building included a Laundromat, a beauty shop, and an artist shop. Jim's wife, Ann, also moved her gift shop from the Lakeway Inn into the new building. After being repaired, the second floor contained several small apartments and individual rooms that the Lakeway Inn used for overflow guests. A historical marker commemorates the site.

December - By the end of 1969, there were 227 homes in Lakeway's 3,700 acres, ranging in value from $20,000 to $150,000. There were also approximately twenty miles of paved streets.

1970

Sections 16, 16a, 16b, and 17 opened for land sales.

Construction began on Andy Kivlin's Patio Homes on Lido Circle. On November 23, 1991, a historical marker commemorated Patio Homes as the first condominium development built in Texas.

The Lakeway Land Company purchased the Schramm Ranch.

May 28 - The incorporation of the Lakeway Ecumenical Church, although it did not yet have a building. Catholics and Protestants had held services in private homes before joining forces at the Lakeway Inn. As Father Richard McCabe enjoyed telling the story, the Baptists did not always appreciate attending services in the inn's bar.

November14 - The *Lakeway News* announced the opening of another deer season in Lakeway, with "hunting limited to mornings to calm the nerves of those who ride out on the horseback trails in the afternoon." The hunting fee was $10 per gun.

1971

Section 17a opened for land sales.

Thad Phillips opened his real estate business in the old Mauermann Bunkhouse on the two-acre plat that would later house the Lakeway Heritage Commission.

April - The short-lived Lohman's Ford Ferry began service between Point Venture on the north shore of Lake Travis and the Hurst Creek Road dock on the south side. At the time, it was the only inland ferry service in Texas. The one-way fare was one dollar for the two-mile crossing, and the ferry could carry eight cars. The twenty-minute trip saved drivers on the north side of Lake Travis twenty-five miles of congested road traffic.

April 26 - The original shareholders of the Lakeway Land Company, including Lee Blocker, who was then president, agreed to sell their stock to Bob Alpert, the president of the Dallas-based Alpert Investment Corporation, which had financial backing from the Connecticut Mutual Life Insurance Company. The reported price was $4.5 million, which included the Lakeway Inn. Alpert promised "to honor all previous commitments, both written and implied." He also changed the name to simply the Lakeway Company.

In the first of several expansions and renovations to the Lakeway Inn, Alpert added sixty guest rooms and additional meeting rooms. Lee Blocker agreed to stay on for several months, as did inn manager Pierre Caselli. Alpert brought in Ralph Hutchinson as chief executive officer. When Hutchinson left shortly thereafter, Alpert appointed Jim Gribble president. Unfortunately, this rapid turnover of executive officers continued for several years.

June - The newly reorganized Lakeway Company opened its sales and administration building at 1200 Lakeway Drive, next to the Tejas Building. The building also included a beauty shop, a design and construction company, and the cable TV operation. The old Lakeway Company sales office was sold to Byron and Bonnie Varner, who turned it into a private residence.

1972

Sections 7a, 16c, 16d, 18, 20, 22, and 22a opened for land sales.

The Lakeway Company began construction on its Yaupon Golf Course. Because of financial difficulties, the front nine was not finished until 1977 and the back nine in 1979.

Greenway Constructions began Stoney Creek Condominiums on Lido Circle, which opened in 1974.

The Lakeway Civic Corporation published the first Lakeway Residents Directory.

Construction began on the World of Tennis. World-ranked South African tennis pro Cliff Drysdale became "resident-touring pro" at Bob Alpert's multi-million-dollar project that included ambitious plans for townhouses and a tennis village. Lamar Hunt, who was also one of Alpert's financial backers, agreed to schedule several of his World Championship Tennis tournaments in Lakeway. Cliff Drysdale's wife, Jean, also a tennis professional, sent her impressions of her new home to the *Johannesburg Star:* "Texans are breezy, courteous, humorous, and overwhelmingly friendly. They also have a distinct language of their own. . . . Texans are immensely proud of their country. They love it and they want us to feel the same way. It is an infectious and heart-warming attitude."

February - The Texas Water Rights Commission approved a Lakeway Municipal Water District, which became the Lakeway MUD. In the early 1970s, the State of Texas had authorized municipal utility districts "to provide developers with a financing vehicle to pay for the installation of water and wastewater utilities where there were no municipal services." According to Byron Varner, "Texas laws governing MUDs in the 1970s were heavily weighted in favor of land developers. A MUD could issue bonds to finance construction of utilities and a developer could then use his own funds for other amenities." The developer could also control MUD policies by appointing his employees as directors, which Bob Alpert initially did. The Texas legislature later restricted such practices. Thus began an often acrimonious relationship between the Lakeway MUD and the Village of Lakeway and its residents, and especially with the so-called out-of-district customers.

February - Bob Alpert and his Lakeway Company published the first issue of *Lakewaves* under the editorship of Byron Varner, who also named the publication. Although it was meant to foster better relations among the developer, homeowners, and prospective buyers, Varner later admitted it was "too developer-oriented," leading Varner to help launch the *Homeowners News* in 1978.

September - The Lakeway MUD purchased the Lakeway Company's water system in September 1972 for $870,000 and took over its operation. When the MUD then extended its water services to newly developed areas, its costs were greater, in part because development was slower than anticipated. As a result, the out-of-district areas had to pay higher rates. This would lead to suits and countersuits over basically two questions: Were water rates reasonable for both Village of Lakeway out-of-district and in-district MUD customers and could the village directly or indirectly regulate rates for MUD's out-of-district customers?

November 20 - Lake Travis Elementary opened on RR 620, although it was then part of the Dripping Springs School District. Its 150 local children in grades 1 through 6 had previously been bused to Dripping Springs.

Renovations at the Lakeway Inn temporarily forced Catholics, Protestants, and Christian Scientists to move their services to Lake Travis Elementary.

1973

Sections 22b, 22c, 23, 26, 27, and 29 opened for land sales.

Construction began on Schooner Cove Villa.

Construction began on Casa Verde Condominiums.

The Lakeway Company sold 2.2 acres from its Sailfish Park site to the newly founded Lakeway MUD for its Water Treatment Plant #1. Over the next fifteen years, this sale led to acrimonious legal suits between nearby residents and the MUD over the latter's plan to expand this facility.

The Lakeway Inn expanded its number of rooms to 148, doubled the size of its kitchen and dining room, and added a second swimming pool.

Dr. Ben Houle opened Lakeway's first medical clinic in the Tejas Building.

January 7 - Former President Lyndon Johnson and Lady Bird hosted daughter Lucy Nugent, her husband, Patrick, and their two children at the Lakeway Inn. Two weeks later LBJ was dead.

January - Nude bathing in Hippie Hollow caught the attention of many western Travis County residents, especially after a graphic article appeared in the *Austin American-Statesman*. The Lake Travis Improvement Association and the Austin Baptist Association feared such "visible" activities might spread to other areas of the lake. State Senator Charles Herring introduced a bill making illegal "any obscene and indecent exhibition of his own person or the person of another in public." Several local authorities and a number of citizens agreed that the problem should be further studied.

May - Richard Seaman, the managing editor of the *Austin American-Statesman*, became vice president for public relations for the Lakeway Inn, marina, and golf course.

September 14 - The grand opening of the Lakeway World of Tennis featured a sixty-four-team mixed doubles tournament and a professional exhibition.

September 15 - News of the OPEC oil embargo wreaked havoc on the World of Tennis. Fifty prospective buyers had already put down payments on tennis townhouses. Within weeks all but eleven had backed out. The recession of 1975 also hurt sales, and only 105 of the planned 225 units were built.

October - The Lakeway Company commissioned a Master Development Plan for Lakeway's current 5,720 acres. In addition to the original land purchases from Josey, Schramm, Hutto, and Stewart were the new areas of Rough Hollow and Lakeway West.

December 17 - Groundbreaking for the Lakeway Ecumenical Church on 3.5 acres donated by the Lakeway Company. Growing numbers of Catholic and Protestant worshipers had encouraged Ralph Keller and Father Richard McCabe to seek funding for their own church building. They also formed a board of trustees consisting of four Catholics, four Protestants, and one Christian Scientist. The board then hired Austin's O'Connell & Probst architectural firm to build a church capable of holding 300 parishioners for an estimated cost of $200,000.

1974

Sections 28, 28a, 28b, and 28c opened for land sales.

Construction began on The Bluffs condominium project.

The Lakeway Company deeded five greenbelt areas to the Lakeway Civic Corporation, including Dragon Park, Lakeway Drive Parkway, Porpoise Park, Rebel Park, and Sailfish Park. In 1987, the LCC deeded these five parks to the Village of Lakeway.

Dr. Howard Bauer opened Lakeway's first dental practice in the Tejas Building.

The CBS Tennis Classic became the first of several professional tournaments hosted by the World of Tennis for both men and women. Despite this apparently promising beginning, Robert Alpert decided to sell all but 10 percent of his WOT interests to Lamar Hunt. In 1981, Alpert repurchased the WOT and made it part of the Hills of Lakeway. In 1987 the WOT was renamed the Hills Racquet Club.

January - After several years of deteriorating community relations, Bob Alpert agreed to meet with Lakeway Civic Corporation trustees to improve the situation. Alpert promised to "inform the community about practical decisions affecting the community" [and maintain] "a free flow of communications, and a new and improved package of recreational resources." In April, Alpert agreed to form the Lakeway Recreational Association (LRA) to administer recreational amenities for Lakeway residents. The LRA board consisted of eleven directors, six appointed by the Lakeway Company and five by members of the Lakeway Civic Corporation and the Lakeway Yacht and Country Club. Included also was a representative of the Lakeway Ladies Golf Association.

May 30 - The Austin City Council gave up its Extra Territorial Jurisdiction (ETJ) rights to the Village of Lakeway; however, Austin retained ETJ rights to lands adjacent to the village boundaries, such as The Hills of Lakeway and the World of Tennis. This decision freed Lakeway to become a general law village. Negotiations to do so had actually begun in 1971, when a group of concerned residents, fearing that Lakeway might be annexed by the City of Austin, asked the Lakeway Civic Corporation to help the community become a corporate village.

July 13 - By a margin of 243 to 85, voters approved the incorporation of Lakeway as a general law village, which resulted in taxing powers, along with the right to administer police and fire protection, street maintenance, building and zoning codes, and sundry other operations. Voters also voted in N. C. "Newt" Herndon as their first mayor and James T. Gribble, Jr. and Robert J. Derby as commissioners. Their initial term was for only eight months and all were non-salaried volunteers. The new Lakeway government operated in the Tejas Country Store Building. The Lakeway Civic Corporation requested a voluntary property tax consisting of 25 cents per $100 of the Travis County tax valuation to get the village started until a formal tax structure could be established.

July 19 - Byron Varner organized the Lakeway Men's Breakfast Club "to present information about local, state, and national events, and to promote good fellowship in the process." The Lakeway Inn hosted the initial meeting. The first speaker was Charles Herring, the general manager of the Lower Colorado River Authority. The Lakeway Yacht and Country Club took over the club's sponsorship in January 1978. Before moving to its permanent meeting place at the Lakeway Activity Center in 1999, the Men's Breakfast Club held its Wednesday morning meetings at the World of Tennis, the Alpenhof Restaurant, the Point Venture Ferry Boat, and the Live Oak Golf Clubhouse.

August - Mayor N. C. Herndon and Commissioners James Gribble and Robert J. Derby held their first public meeting in front of nearly 100 residents. They announced the appointment of several village officials and the creation of a Lakeway Police Department with Bearl Thomas Croft as its first chief. To finance the police department, each resident was assessed $7.50. Other officials appointed were Charles C. McDugald, municipal court judge; Dick Madison, village clerk, treasurer, and tax assessor-collector; Vincent S. Donoghue, attorney; Samuel C. Hamilton, engineer and building inspector; Alfred D. Powell, police commissioner; and A. T. "Cubby" Culbertson, street commissioner. Meetings of the commissioners were scheduled for the first Tuesday of each month at 9:30 a.m. in the Lakeway Inn. All served with no remuneration, thus further establishing Lakeway's unique program of volunteer governance.

December 1 - Opening of the Lakeway Ecumenical Church. There were three separate services that first morning for Protestants, Catholics, and Christian Scientists, respectively. The official dedication was held on June 9, 1975.

1975

Sections 30, 31, and 32 opened for land sales.

April - Voters elected James T. Gribble, Jr. as Lakeway's second mayor and O. I. "Tork" Torkelson and Manson G. Stell as commissioners. Gribble served as mayor until 1983; Torkelson and Stell stayed on as commissioners until 1981.

June - Byron and Bonnie Varner opened the Lakeway Branch Post Office on RR 620.

October - Lakeway mailed out its first tax notices.

1976

Lakeway commemorated its designation as a Bicentennial Community with a special Fourth of July celebration, setting a precedent for its impressive Fourth of July celebrations in the future.

The opening of World of Tennis Boulevard (later Lakeway Boulevard), north of Lohman's Crossing Road, gave Lakeway its second entrance off RR 620.

The Lakeway Recreational Association opened its clubroom.

Vernon S. Gunn became chief of police.

1977

The Lakeway Branch Post Office moved into the Lakeway Inn.

Opening of the first nine holes of the Yaupon Golf Course, with construction beginning on the second nine holes.

Construction began on Tres Vistas Townhouses.

April - Voters reelected Mayor James T. Gribble, Jr. and Commissioners O. I. Torkelson and Manson G. Stell.

April 15 - Gretchen Martin, who with her husband, Jack, purchased a Lakeway lot in 1965 and retired here in 1973, made her first Welcome Wagon call to new residents.

The creation of a Lakeway Fourth of July Committee to carry on the work begun by its predecessor, the Lakeway U.S. Bicentennial Committee of 1975–1976.

1978

Sections 24, 24b, 24d, and 26c opened for land sales.

The Lakeway Company opened its Equestrian Center on RR 620, replacing the earlier stables at the northeast end of the Airpark. The new center offered "miles of solitary trails" and an English-trained instructor in dressage, gymnastic jumping, and horse care. A historical marker inside Randalls Food and Pharmacy commemorates the Equestrian Center, which no longer exists.

April - In an effort to keep property owners informed, the village announced the periodic publication of a newsletter called *The Village Voice*. At the time of its first issue, there were 603 housing units in the village, of which 483 were single family homes. The rest were condominiums.

May 22 - Approximately sixty Lakeway residents met and organized the Homeowners Association of Lakeway, in part to challenge the Lakeway Company on homeowners' concerns such as changing policies, uncontrolled expansion, higher taxes, the MUD, and a continued lack of communication. All meetings were to be open, with no business conducted in closed sessions. Membership was open to all Lakeway homeowners and dues were initially set at $15. Elected officers were President Juanita Porter, Vice President Vic Dias, Secretary Kathy Goldsmith, and Treasurer Herb Walton. The Homeowners Association also planned a new publication for its members.

July 10 - Byron Varner edited and published the first issue of the *Homeowners News*. Its announced purpose was "to dispel rumors and to educate and better equip our residents to enjoy living, working, playing and progressing in our unique community." Initially a quarterly publication, it became monthly with its February 15, 1980, issue when Cubby Culbertson succeeded Varner as editor. Joe Burdick took over in 1981. Burt Folsom, Roy Jordan, Betty Herndon, and Roy Reed also served as early editors.

October - The Lakeway Company filed a $20 million suit against the Lakeway MUD and its five directors because they had "arbitrarily refused to extend requested services to new areas of development." The MUD had informed the Lakeway Company that any expansion would have to be at the company's expense, although if such an expansion were profitable, the MUD agreed to refund 70 percent of such costs and take over the system. Originally, MUD directors were officers in the Lakeway Company, but by this time a state law prohibited such an arrangement. This suit was settled early in 1979 in favor of the MUD.

1979

Sections 24c, 28II, 28III, 28IV, and 28V opened for land sales.

When fire destroyed the Lakeway Company's office building at 1200 Lakeway Drive, it moved its headquarters to the World of Tennis club building. Subsequently, the company built a new sales office at the intersection of Lohman's Crossing Road and World of Tennis Boulevard, which later became Lakeway Boulevard.

Completion of the second nine holes of the Yaupon Golf Course.

Establishment of the Hurst Creek Municipal Utilities District to serve The Hills of Lakeway.

Hurbert J. Tye became chief of police.

April - Voters reelected Mayor James T. Gribble, Jr. and Commissioners O. I. Torkelson and Manson G. Stell.

1980

A $250,000 renovation to the Lakeway Ecumenical Church more than doubled its seating and provided extra classrooms and a choir loft.

Construction began on the Cedar Glen Townhouses.

The City of Austin granted Lakeway expanded ETJ rights, which allowed it to annex Casa Verde and parts of Section 20.

February 29 - By a vote of 216 to 77, Lakeway voters passed a $350,000 bond issue to build a municipal building that would include a community meeting room, administrative offices, and facilities for police, fire, and emergency services. Lakeway resident Glen Davis volunteered to serve as general contractor. Groundbreaking ceremonies took place on January 2, 1981.

April 1 - In a series of confusing moves, the recently renamed Lakeway Land Corporation deeded its real estate to the Lakeway Development Company, 50 percent of which was owned by the Lakeway Land Corporation and 50 percent by the Connecticut Mutual Life Insurance Company. The Lakeway Development Company then changed its name back to the Lakeway Company.

April - Residents formed Citizens for Sailfish Park (CSP) to challenge the Lakeway MUD's plans to expand its Sailfish Park water treatment plant. This bitter dispute would last eight long years.

April - The Lakeway MUD and the Village of Lakeway continued their feuding over out-of-district customers having to pay higher bills. The village had mailed letters to its residents stating that the MUD's increases were illegal and not to pay them. The MUD responded that it would not accept partial payments and might disconnect service. Controversy over who had the right to set water rates would also continue for years.

June - Groundbreaking for the new Exxon gas station at the corner of Lohman's Crossing and World of Tennis Boulevard, which later became Lakeway Boulevard. The Exxon station would remain open until 2009.

November - The Circuit Court of Appeals denied Dripping Springs Independent School District's suit to stop Lake Travis Independent School District from breaking away and becoming its own district.

1981

The Hills of Lakeway publicly announced it was "a relatively wealthy retirement and second-home community designed to attract business executives and highly successful professionals basically from Houston and Dallas."

The Jack Nicklaus–designed Hills of Lakeway Golf Course opened, as did the Academy of Golf. Brochures advertising home sites along the fairways touted the "spectacular waterfall hole." Nicklaus had earlier remarked, "This is one of the finest pieces of natural land on which to build a golf course I have ever seen."

Thomas W. Evans became chief of police.

April - Mayor James Gribble began his fourth term. Newly elected commissioners were C. Ed Smith, Jr. and Leo C. Gravis.

April - After an announced increase in water rates for its out-of-district customers, the battle between the Village of Lakeway and the Lakeway MUD became so heated that the MUD announced a "District police officer" would accompany its employees if they had to disconnect water service for those refusing to pay the increase. The village sued the MUD for violating a village ordinance that called for negotiated rate increases. The MUD, however, refused to recognize the ordinance. On September 23, the MUD disconnected water to the Tejas Building, including its medical and dental offices, and to a residence on Porpoise Street. The village responded by arresting the MUD's general manager. The village eventually lost its suit when on May 30, 1984, the Texas Supreme Court ruled "No Reversible Error." The village then told its citizens to pay their full MUD bills, but only with a statement that they were doing so under duress.

August - Dr. Frank Jennings became superintendent of the newly established Lake Travis Independent School District (LTISD), which had broken away from the Dripping Springs School District. The new school district was a great relief for those parents whose children had been spending up to four hours a day on school buses. At the time of the break, the Dripping Springs School District covered 368 square miles, with the longest bus route covering 123 miles during its daily two round-trips. Lakeway area residents also insisted they were paying a disproportionate percentage of their tax base to the Dripping Springs School District.

A $7.3 million bond issue to finance a permanent LTISD junior and senior high school passed on August 15, 1981. In the meantime, some twenty-four portable buildings, plus a large gymnasium including ten classrooms, were erected on the grounds of Lake Travis Elementary to house the anticipated 225 junior and senior high school students.

1982

January 17 - Fire destroyed the Live Oak clubhouse, pro shop, and golf cart storage. All three facilities were rebuilt in 1983.

April 3 - The LTISD held its initial election for all seven members of its board of trustees. After the election, the new board members drew straws for staggered one-, two- or three-year terms.

April 12 - Dedication and grand opening of the new Village Municipal Building on Lohman's Crossing, which is commemorated by an on-site historical marker.

October 7 - A newly created "Play-Reading Group" held its first meeting.

November - The Lakeway Company donated fifty-five acres of the Schramm Ranch tract to the LTISD for construction of the Lake Travis Junior High and High School complex. The LTISD also purchased an additional fifteen acres.

1983

The Lakeway Ecumenical Church dedicated its new education building, which would be greatly expanded in 1987.

The Hudson Bend Volunteer Fire Department took over Lakeway's fire protection.

April 2 - After Lakeway voters approved moving to an aldermanic form of government, its governing body became the Village Council. C. Kenneth Shepherd was elected mayor, and C. Ed Smith, Jr. and Sam Huser were elected aldermen, all for two-year terms. James R. Hastings, J. Sloan "Tony" Leonard, and Kenneth W. Kennedy were also elected as aldermen but for one-year terms. Only 423 of the 803 registered voters cast their ballots.

June - The Connecticut Mutual Life Insurance Company sold its 50 percent partnership in the Lakeway Company to the Alpert Investment Corporation.

July - The Lakeway Civic Corporation granted Al Saenger its first Outstanding Citizen of the Year Award for his "willing, generous and dedicated contributions to the civic needs of the Lakeway community." This award would become a greatly respected annual event.

At the end of its first twenty years, Lakeway contained approximately 1,500 homes and 1,200 permanent residents.

1984

Opening of Lake Travis Middle School and the round gymnasium building.

A new bridge on Lohman's Crossing Road over Hurst Creek replaced its dangerous, low-water predecessor. The Lakeway Company and Travis County jointly financed the project.

Chaired by Roy Doran, the Lakeway Sesquicentennial Coordinating Committee organized Lakeway's celebration of the State of Texas's 150th birthday. In addition to collecting oral histories, committee members Jack Shepherd and Mike Kuhn began work on a time capsule to be opened in 2036.

During its two-year existence, the Lakeway Property Owners Association disseminated information on various issues. It also supported the Lakeway Unification Committee, which was formed in September 1984 to evaluate proposed properties to be annexed within Lakeway's expanding ETJ.

February - Travis Plaza was the first of several large, and sometimes controversial, commercial developments planned for the juncture of RR 620 and Lohman's Crossing. Travis Plaza's plans called for a premier, twenty-one-acre shopping center, with its individual buildings connected by covered walkways.

March - Formal establishment of the First Church of Christ, Scientist, Lakeway. Christian Scientists had been holding area services for fifteen years, but now received formal recognition from the First Church of Christ, Scientist, in Boston. The Christian Science Reading Room opened in Suite 2 of the Lakeway Village Square on Lakeway Drive.

May - Aldermen J. Sloan "Tony" Leonard, Kenneth W. Kennedy, and James R. Hastings were reelected for two-year terms.

October - The Lakeway MUD declared a moratorium on all in-district and out-of-district water hookups until the State Water Commission approved its plan to increase the district water supply. This decision reflected the MUD's ongoing dispute with Sailfish residents who opposed the MUD's plan to expand its Sailfish facility.

December - *Playboy* magazine did a photo shoot near Lohman's Crossing Estates, although the damsels were identified as some of Austin's finest.

1985

The Lakeway Company announced its intention to develop Rough Hollow.

David Lewis purchased the Village Square. At the time, this was the only land in Lakeway zoned commercial. Lewis planned to build an $11 to $12 million structure, which would include a financial center, a real estate company, and a medical center. Said Lewis of his investment, "A developer has three obligations: first to the bank, second to the community, and third to the land. . . . I want to minimize the sticks and bricks in relation to the dirt and still be economically feasible."

Construction began on Retama Gardens Condominiums.

Construction began on The Oaks Condominiums.

Dana Nunn opened her 620 Dance Center on RR 620. Over the next quarter century the Dance Center would grow into a 3,000-square-foot facility on Stroup Circle, with more than 400 class hours offered per week. Nunn said of her creation, "It's a place where young people can feel confident and let go, while doing something positive for themselves."

The Lake Travis Education Foundation was created as a nonprofit organization to raise funds for scholarships for students and grants for teachers in the LTISD. Over the next twenty-five years the foundation would raise more than $2.5 million for these worthy causes.

The Lakeway Civic Corporation selected A. T. "Cubby" Culbertson for its 1984 Outstanding Citizen Award. Culbertson had been Lakeway's first street commissioner and also an editor of the *Homeowners News*.

February 10 - The Lakeway Community Library opened, sharing space with the Lake Travis High School Library. Forty people immediately signed up for library cards.

February 11 - The LTISD hired Dr. Walter Marks as its new superintendent, giving him a three-year contract at an annual salary of $72,000. Dr. Marks planned to use a $19 million bond issue to build a separate high school building, which included an elaborate entrance and rotunda as well as a very expensive administration building. Unfortunately, many future voters cited this perceived excessive spending to discredit subsequent school bond campaigns. After leaving the LTISD in 1987, Dr. Marks became an even more controversial figure. In 1995, ABC's news magazine *Primetime* and CBS's *60 Minutes* featured stories on Marks for his extravagant and possibly illegal expenditures of public funds at two additional school districts. Unfortunately, these exposés once again reminded area residents of Marks's excessive spending while serving as superintendent of the LTISD.

April - The Committee for Lakeway Unity, composed of representatives of the Village of Lakeway, the Lakeway Civic Corporation, the Homeowners Association, the Lakeway Property Owners Association, and the Lakeway MUD, planned to conduct a joint study with the MUD as to whether the village should join the MUD or vice versa. The committee had collected more than $11,000 in pledges by April 15, 1985, a portion of which was to be spent on a professional firm to study the problem. The MUD, however, refused to spend any money on such a study. The controversial issue of annexation would continue to reappear in the future.

May - Voters approved a Travis County Rural Fire District and work began on a Lakeway fire station on Lohman's Crossing Road, which would be completed in 1987.

May - Mayor C. K. "Ken" Shepherd was reelected, as were Aldermen C. Ed Smith and Sam Huser.

May 14 - Lakeway passed an ordinance that dog and cat owners must register their pets with the village, along with proof of a rabies vaccination.

July 16 - The village adopted the Master Plan for Greater Lakeway covering population, land use, roads, utilities, police, fire, recreation, health care, organizations, education, and village management. Coleman Smith and Lester Weigle were chairman and vice chairman, respectively. Other members were Dick Graue, Harry Kolb, Raymond Norris, Dorothy Taylor, and O. I. Torkelson.

August 25 - The first meeting of the Greater Lakeway Women's Club. Formed by Donna McCarver, Ruby Saunders, and Carol Holt, it promised "to promote social, cultural and intellectual growth among Lakeway women." Its first meeting was attended by forty-five women. The club has grown to more than 450 members and twenty-two different interest groups, including book, investment, gardening, and antique clubs, as well as the Sing-A-Long Chorus, Dottie's Follies, and the Rhinestone Cowgirls Dancers. Additional groups focus on dining out, knitting and stitchery, poetry, crafts, and cancer support.

October 2 - The Austin Planning Commission approved a shopping center on the east side of RR 620 at Lohman's Crossing. Randall's would eventually relocate to this site.

1986

J. R. King Enterprises purchased Cablevision of Lake Travis and moved its corporate operation from Mississippi to Lakeway. It opened a new office at 919 South RR 620 in May 1990.

The branch post office moved from the Lakeway Inn back to RR 620.

The Equestrian Center closed. It was located on RR 620 where Randall's parking lot now exists.

Noon, March 2 - The bells of the Lakeway Ecumenical Church tolled 150 times in recognition of the 150th anniversary of Texas's Declaration of Independence from Mexico. The bells rang again on April 21, 1986, for San Jacinto Day, which marked Texas' final defeat of the Mexican army.

February - The Lakeway Civic Corporation named Roy Doran as its Outstanding Citizen for 1985. A retired World War II colonel who survived the Bataan Death March, Doran chaired Lakeway's Sesquicentennial Coordinating Committee.

March 5 - The *Lake Travis View*, "a new weekly designed to provide community news to residents within the Lake Travis Independent School District," published its first issue. An annual subscription cost $15. It continues to publish its weekly editions.

March - Plans announced to expand RR 620, which had first opened in 1935, to four lanes. This project would take more than ten years to complete.

April 12 - In its ongoing celebration of the State of Texas' 150th Anniversary, the Lakeway Sesquicentennial Coordinating Committee buried a time capsule in front of Village Hall to be opened in 2036. Among its contents were the Lakeway flag, miscellaneous golf memorabilia, a Bible from the Lakeway Ecumenical Church, a Mary Baker Eddy book, a copy of the Lake Travis High School literary magazine, programs from various local events, histories and membership lists of many business and recreational organizations, area photographs and maps, poetry and books by Lakeway residents, area fossils, telephone directories, LTISD information, Lakeway National Bank souvenirs, and articles about Lakeway and its residents. Also included were video cassettes of a Fourth of July celebration and various council meetings, winning essays in the Sesquicentennial Texas history contests, oral history cassettes, microfilmed memoirs of Lakeway residents, and a letter from former astronaut and Lakeway resident Alan B. Shepard, Jr.

May - Reelected were aldermen J. Sloan "Tony" Leonard and Kenneth W. Kennedy. Nat S. Kendall was elected for the first of his three terms as alderman.

June - The village of Lakeway refused to approve a zoning change and building permit for the MUD's planned expansion of its facility on Sailfish. In response, the MUD filed a lawsuit against the village for $1.8 million. The conflict intensified after the MUD threatened to sue the Lakeway Company for $700,000 if a court ruled in favor of the Citizens for Sailfish Park, an organization that insisted the MUD had promised the land in question would revert back to parkland after its new facility opened near the World of Tennis. Furthermore, early brochures of the Lakeway Company had seemingly designated this property as parkland. Another attack on the MUD came from a citizen's group called the Protect Lake Travis Association (PLTA), which demanded that the MUD exercise better control over wastewater effluent that was allegedly leaching into Lake Travis.

June - Featuring local talent, the newly established Theater on the Lake's first production was an Agatha Christie thriller.

September - The MUD's approval of a site for its nine-million-gallon effluent holding pond near Carefree Circle triggered another dispute with nearby residents.

September - Blaming high administrative costs, an organization calling itself the Coalition of Better Education for Lake Travis (COBELT) argued that the LTISD was spending too much money educating its students, especially given their low test results. COBELT discouraged teachers, dissenting parents, and administrators from attending its meetings. Despite COBELT's efforts, voters approved a $19 million school bond.

September 9 - Lakeway annexed the Airpark and its recently extended 4,100-foot runway.

October - Still hoping to improve the often acrimonious relationship between the village and the Lakeway MUD over water and wastewater rates, the Committee for Lakeway Unity scheduled a public meeting to work out final details for an annexation petition. MUD Board President Paul McDaniel agreed to a meeting, but only if the village pay $15,000 for the cost of a hearing and an election. When the village agreed to do so only if it received an itemized list of MUD's expenses, negotiations once again broke down.

November 11 - Alderman Sam Huser resigned to become a paid administrative assistant to the mayor. Richard Knowles was appointed to finish Sam Huser's term.

December 29 - Lakeway annexed the properties abutting the Yaupon Golf Course, plus the area connecting the village to its Lohman's Crossing entrance on RR 620.

December 30 - The American Retirement Corporation purchased a 36-acre tract on Lohman's Crossing from the Lakeway Company on which it planned to build "a luxurious retirement community."

1987

The average age of Lakeway residents dropped below sixty for the first time.

The Lakeway Company platted its planned Rough Hollow development.

Safeway opened Lakeway's first supermarket on what would become Lohman's Spur.

The LTISD opened its new administration building, dubbed the Taj Mahal by those who found it unnecessarily extravagant.

January - Bob Alpert's Lakeway Company sold the Lakeway Inn to the Dolce Group and Rothschild Property Investors of New York.

February - The Lakeway Civic Corporation recognized Manson Stell and Gene Vinyard (posthumously) for its 1986 Outstanding Citizen Award.

February - According to the *Lake Travis View* of February 18, the Lakeway Company turned down the village's offer to purchase the Live Oak and Yaupon Golf Courses for $5 million. The Lakeway Company had been trying to sell the two courses since 1986, although both were considered traditional amenities for Lakeway property owners and their guests.

February 12 - The village and the Lakeway MUD reached an agreement to drop all current lawsuits and to seek compromises on disputed decisions. The *Homeowners News* praised the agreement as "the final step in bringing complete unity to the Community." Unfortunately, the *Homeowners News* was overly optimistic.

February - The Lakeway Village Council voted four to one to allow the Lakeway MUD to build a 100,000-gallon elevated storage tank off Golfcrest Lane near the entrance of Lakeway that looked like a giant golf ball. The MUD also received a building permit for a 19-million-gallon effluent holding pond in Lakeway East, although Carefree Circle and Golfcrest Lane residents continued to oppose this plan.

March - The Lower Colorado River Authority (LCRA) granted the owners of Stewart's Landing a construction permit for a proposed marina at the end of Hurst Creek Road. The Hurst Creek Property Owners' Association (HCPOA) appealed the decision. Additional attempts to build a marina at the end of Hurst Creek would resurface in the future. The HCPOA also opposed the MUD's plan to build a water holding tank on a half-acre lot on Lohman's Crossing, just south of Hurst Creek Road.

May - C. Ed Smith was elected Lakeway's fourth mayor. Richard Knowles and Roger J. Schuler won seats as aldermen.

August - The Lakeway Company merged with the Alpert Investment Corporation.

August - Dr. Walter Howard replaced Dr. Walter Marks as superintendent of the LTISD, after Marks accepted a position as superintendent of the Richmond School District in California.

August - The village passed an ordinance forbidding the parking of trucks, mobile homes, RVs, and boats on the streets or in driveways for longer than seventy-two hours.

August - There were 2,426 dwellings in Lakeway, including 1,571 homes, 135 townhouses, 391 condominiums, and 329 duplexes. Of the 4,759 single-family lots, 33 percent of them now had houses. There were an estimated 3,000 permanent residents.

December - The new Hudson Bend Fire Station opened on Lohman's Crossing Road.

1988

The LTISD opened its Lake Travis High School, along with an athletic complex and expanded gymnasium.

January - Mayor C. Ed Smith proclaimed 1988 as Lakeway's Silver Anniversary Year. Byron Varner and Laurie Haberman co-chaired the Silver Anniversary Committee to plan Lakeway's twenty-fifth birthday celebration.

February 9 - The Lakeway Village Council changed the name of World of Tennis Boulevard to Lakeway Boulevard, which then ran from the north entrance of Lakeway to Lakeway Drive. Lakeway Boulevard would later be extended all the way to Flamingo.

February 13 - The Lakeway Civic Corporation chose Jim Gribble for its 1987 Outstanding Citizen Award. In addition to serving eight years as mayor and two years as village commissioner, Gribble had served as Lakeway Land Company president, MUD director, and on the boards of the Lakeway Civic Corporation, Yacht and Country Club, and the Architectural Control Committee. Meritorious Service Awards went to Jack Martin, Travis Porter, and Alf Powell.

March - In one of many such postings, the Texas Parks & Wildlife Department not surprisingly discovered that Lakeway had too many deer. Its recommendation was to cut the estimated herd of 1,000 in half and transport the surplus to East Texas in trucks. With the community split roughly down the middle on the value of these four-legged creatures, the surplus deer issue would continue to be a controversial challenge.

March - Lakeway had developed 3,300 of its acres, leaving 2,200 acres still undeveloped.

April - In a series of decisions, the village council ruled that utilities on new construction sites had to be underground, Open House signs were allowed but not For Sale signs, and single-family homes had to be at least 2,000 square feet, with duplexes and condos set at a minimum of 1,500 square feet. The council also passed a weed ordinance, with fines up to $1,000 and the right to mow weed-filled lawns and charge the owner.

May - In a change of policy, three slots on the MUD board were now to be filled by elected citizens.

May - Richard C. Knowles and Nat S. Kendall were reelected aldermen. William M. Evans was elected alderman for the first time.

June - Dr. George Cury resigned as principal of Lake Travis High School. He pointed out that during his three years student SAT scores had risen from two points below the national average to forty points above and that 77 percent of the graduates were now going to two- or four-year colleges.

June - The *Lake Travis View* published its first article on oak wilt. This disease, which brings slow and unsightly death to live oaks and red oaks, was first noticed in 1986 on Vanguard and Seawind. The village planned to dig a three-foot trench around the affected trees. Unfortunately, the disease has continued to spread to other parts of Lakeway.

June - The Trading Post on Highway 71 closed. Wiley and son Tom Johnson had first opened the Trading Post in 1937. It included a café, gas station, and small store. It would reopen in 1991 as Jim Bob's Barbeque.

June - A half-million Florida largemouth bass fingerlings were released into Lake Travis. They were supposed to grow faster than native Texas largemouth bass.

June - The Lakeway MUD's agreement to close down its Sailfish Park facility ended an eight-year dispute with the Citizens of Sailfish Park. The MUD also agreed to restore the park to its original condition by the end of 1992 and to pay CSP members for all legal expenses incurred since 1980.

June - The newly renovated Lakeway Inn changed its name to the Lakeway Resort and Conference Center. For the first time in its twenty-five-year history, the inn decided to restrict the use of its two swimming pools to members of either the LRA or the newly created Lakeview Club. The pools had been available to all Lakeway residents and property owners and had been noted as such in sales brochures.

July 22 - Mayor Ed Smith announced that 45 percent of Lakeway contained homes, with 1,800 lots remaining. The growth rate was approximately 10 percent annually.

August - Lakeway held a hearing on a $700,000 bond issue to purchase two tracts of land between the Exxon station and Cross Creek from the Lakeway Company. It was not made clear whether these fifteen acres were to be used for village facilities or parkland. Residents opposing the purchase argued that it was in the Hurst Creek floodplain, was too expensive, and would raise their taxes. On August 27, voters rejected the bond issue 442 to 287.

September - Inspired by Lakeway's twenty-fifth anniversary, the Lakeway Civic Corporation sponsored a committee to study the feasibility of creating a historical society. The result was a nonprofit organization that elected a board of trustees in January 1989. Coleman Smith served as president; Rella Giammalva, vice president; Travis Porter, second vice president; Kay Light, treasurer; and Byron Varner, secretary. Marian Fender and John Peet were also involved. Acquiring a building for an office, meetings, museum, and storage was its first objective. Its long-term intentions were to collect, preserve, catalog, store, and display Lakeway historical items; be a repository for records of Lakeway government and civic organizations; develop pride in Lakeway's heritage, growth, and development; educate community youth about the area's historical significance; promote Lakeway's historical sites and legends; and place significant historical markers throughout the community. It also hoped to raise funds to establish a museum. By 2001, there were 150 dues-paying members.

September - The village council appointed William A. Clifford to be presiding judge of the Village of Lakeway Municipal Court. Clifford had been serving as associate judge for the court since March 31, 1988.

September 20 - The objective of the newly created Lakeway Service League was "to facilitate neighbor-helping-neighbor in the Lakeway area." It would eventually use as many as 100 volunteers to perform its good deeds, especially the providing of transportation for those unable to do so themselves for doctors' appointments, shopping, and personal business.

December - Byron Varner published his *Lakeway: The First 25 Years*, which was funded by the Lakeway Civic Corporation.

December - The Lakeway Civic Corporation spent $17,000 on Dragon Park for swings, slides, climbers, bridges, nets, rings, basketball and volleyball courts, and soccer and baseball fields. The LCC also purchased a twelve-foot sequoia Christmas tree to plant in front of the Village Hall "as a symbol of the continuing life and spirit of the community."

December 13 - The Village Council agreed formally to take over the duties of the Lakeway Architectural Control Board in 1989, although for several years both had been responsible for enforcing architectural restrictions.

1989

February - Lakeway's first mayor, Newt Herndon, received the Lakeway Civic Corporation's 1988 Outstanding Citizen Award. Receiving the Meritorious Service Award were Herb Dyer, John Ford, Ralph Keller, and Tex Sodke.

April 2 - The LTISD dedicated its new high school, field house, and expanded elementary school.

April - Jack and Myrtle Hamilton donated $44,000 to the Lakeway Civic Corporation to purchase an 84-acre greenbelt along Hurst Creek downstream from Lohman's Crossing. This would eventually become the Hamilton Greenbelt. Several nearby homeowners objected, fearing such a park would mean noise, drugs, and crime. Others suggested a wildlife and nature preserve as an alternative. Compromises helped solve most of the objections, including an agreement to prohibit motorized vehicles and to locate the nature trails along the land's natural contours.

April - Lakeway's population exceeded the 5,000 inhabitants needed for home rule eligibility as mandated by the state legislature.

April - The MUD planned to fluoridate Lakeway's water at a monthly cost of $1.12 to customers' water bills. Several letters to the *Lake Travis View* objected to fluoridation.

April - The Lakeway Village Council requested that Austin extend the village's ETJ over 9,000 additional acres, including The Hills of Lakeway, Lakeway West, Brook Hollow, Rough Hollow, the Schramm Ranch, and additional footage along RR 620.

May - Richard McLaren defeated incumbent mayor C. Ed Smith. Alderman Roger J. Schuler was reelected and Veronica Bennett became the first alderwoman. During his campaign Mayor McLaren had promised to replace paid administrative assistant Sam Huser, but when the council moved Huser to a paid position as city administrator, McLaren resigned. Former mayor Ken Shepherd replaced McLaren as interim mayor in January 1990. Before his resignation, McLaren appointed Veronica Bennett as Neighborhood Advocate, to field and discount unfounded rumors. Current rumors had the City of Austin buying up Lakeway's golf courses for a new airport and Japanese nationals purchasing the Lakeway Company. Both rumors proved unfounded.

July - For the first time since the MUD's formation in 1972, consumers living outside its district would pay the same water rates as those living within its boundaries.

July - The Safeway store in the Lohman's Crossing Center became the AppleTree Market.

August - A new village leash law stated that dogs must be "restrained" at all times. Failure to do so could result in fines from $25 for a first offense to $2,000 for multiple offenses. In addition, all dogs and cats more than four months of age had to be registered.

1990

The official 1990 U.S. census reported 4,056 permanent residents in Lakeway, of whom 23 percent were nineteen or younger and 19.5 percent were over sixty-five. The median family income was $61,670, although for Travis County it was then only $35,931, and $31,553 for all of Texas.

January - The Lakeway Resort and Conference Center announced plans to open an 8,200-square-foot conference wing in the fall of 1990.

February 10 - Donald M. Oliver received the Lakeway Civic Corporation's 1989 Outstanding Citizen Award. Oliver had served on numerous committees and had been instrumental in bringing medical care to the community. He had also been a member of the original Zoning and Planning Commission in 1974 and again in 1979–1981, and he had served as trustee and president of the Lakeway Civic Corporation.

March - Lakeway launched a recycling program that included newsprint, flattened cardboard boxes, glass containers, and aluminum and tin cans.

April 20 - The Homeowners Association appointed Glenn Williams to head up a committee to investigate operating expenses at the Lake Travis Independent School District to ascertain if the district was spending more per child than comparable districts. The committee concluded, "Costs can be reduced by improvements in operating efficiency and productivity with no adverse impact on quality." Superintendent Walter Howard explained that LTISD's higher costs reflected the higher bond indebtedness of a new school district that went from 520 to 1,716 students in less than ten years. Howard also wanted to compare LTISD's spending to some of the state's top academic districts, such as San Antonio's Alamo Heights and Dallas's Highland Park rather than to nearby districts such as Burnet and Marble Falls.

April 21 - Official opening of Hamilton Greenbelt I.

May 5 - Lakeway voted 622 to 137 to become a Home Rule City, which, among other rights, allowed it to annex adjacent areas within its ETJ. Ken Shepherd was elected mayor and Ken Kennedy, Nat S. Kendall, Veronica Bennett, Roger J. Schuler, and Guy Brown, Jr. won city councilmember seats.

May - Lakeway's new status as a Home Rule City also renewed the debate over whether the MUD and the City of Lakeway should be consolidated. When the legislature approved the formation of MUDs, some lawmakers thought they could be dissolved when municipal governments were sufficiently developed to run their own utilities. Proponents of unification also thought the city might get better bond ratings than could the MUD.

May - The controversy over LTISD spending heated up. Superintendent Walter Howard wanted to hire twenty-three new teachers, but the board of trustees thought seven were sufficient. Resident Glen Davis suggested the district revert to county schoolhouses. As increasing numbers of families with school-age children moved into the district, tensions inevitably arose between older residents, who considered Lakeway primarily a retirement community, and younger families with school-age children.

May - Rumors surfaced that Bob Alpert was defaulting on a $57 million loan and was trying to sell his Lakeway Company. Alpert had already sold the Lakeway Inn and Resort in January 1987.

June - The golden-cheeked warbler and the black-capped vireo, both protected under the Federal Endangered Species Act, threatened to make properties in western Travis County more difficult and expensive to develop. Exacerbating the problem was the Balcones Canyonlands Habitat Conservation Plan, which called for setting aside thousands of acres as a preserve for endangered species.

June - The World of Tennis hosted the U.S. Tennis Association's Lakeway Pro Tennis Classic.

June - The local chapter of the Ladies of Charity, an international organization founded in the sixteenth century by St. Vincent de Paul, opened a Lake Travis Thrift Shop. Its motto was "to serve, rather than be served." The money it raised helped pay the expenses of the Crisis Ministries' Food Pantry. It soon had more than fifty volunteers. By the end of the year it had moved into the 620 Mall. On April 1, 2008, it moved again, this time to 1508 RR 620.

July - A petition containing 15,000 signatures requested that the Lower Colorado River Authority put limits on how far it could reduce Lake Travis water levels for the benefit of downstream rice farmers. The petition also asked that the standard level be raised from its current 660 feet to 667 feet above mean sea level.

July - A survey indicated that 92 percent of Lake Travis teachers believed they should have more input in decisions affecting curriculum and general school policies. A large majority also thought they should have better health benefits, and 67 percent said they had seriously considered leaving the teaching profession during the past three years.

July - A proposed school bond issue that would have resulted in an average $60 annual property tax increase resulted in several letters to the *Lake Travis View* offering money-saving suggestions, including the use of volunteers, especially for maintenance work, and not feeding students on field or athletic trips except for football. Several suggested cutting teachers, administrators, and electives; however, with one exception, there was no mention of the 12 percent increase in the athletic budget.

August - The LTISD's granting a 4.5 percent raise to school personnel resulted in another spate of negative letters, despite the fact that Lake Travis teachers' salaries were well below the national average. Particularly opposed to increased LTISD spending were Lakeway Homeowners Association spokesmen Glen Davis, Glen Williams, and Jim Finneran. Finneran, who was then president of the Homeowners Association, cited McDonald's as an example of free enterprise efficiency. Supporting the school board were Carl Russell and Debbie Wheeler, co-chairs of Citizens to Advance Responsible Education (CARE), who worked to pass the pending $8.5 million bond issue. CARE warned that "year-around, split-day schooling" would result from voting down the bonds. It also emphasized that Lake Travis students' SAT scores now surpassed the national average and that quality schools raised property values. Dissenters continued to claim that the LTISD was spending much more per pupil than comparable school districts. A specific anti-spending organization was Senior Citizens Against Runaway Expenditures (SCARE), although those over sixty-five did not have to pay any school tax increases. One very senior property owner, who disagreed with SCARE, wrote, "Well, someone had to pay for our children's education when we were young parents." An underlying issue for many seniors was their desire to keep Lakeway primarily a retirement community and their resentment of the areas outside of Lakeway that were sending their children to Lake Travis schools. At the time, the LTISD covered approximately 800 square miles. School board members who strongly supported the bond issue were Kevin Fleming, Pat Cristello, and Rick Wheeler.

August 14 - The city council approved the Master Plan for the Greater Lakeway Area, which promised "to manage growth by quality controls in keeping with city standards to maintain a residential-recreational community."

November - The LTISD's bond proposal was soundly defeated by a three to two margin, which resulted in personnel and educational cuts and the purchase of additional portable classrooms. Letter writer Carl Russell was so distraught that he urged, "Young people, take your kids and go away." Another letter writer insisted that the winners only defeated the children, not their adult proponents. Superintendent Walter Howard blamed the ghosts of the past, and particularly a former superintendent's alleged excessive spending. Howard then announced, "The bond election decision will have a very negative impact on the educational opportunities that we can offer the kids."

December 6 - At an LTISD board meeting, Reverend Bryce Sherwood of the Lake Travis Bible Fellowship hoped that evolution as fact would not be taught in the Lake Travis schools. He was invited to meet with the textbook committee to review possible texts.

December - The LTISD looked into year-round schooling to alleviate overcrowding. This discussion continued until finally rejected in 1991.

1991

The average Lakeway lot in 1991 sold for $13,500. The average condo went for $65,000 and single homes for $128,500.

January - Financial Resources Management hired the Buena Vista Hospitality Group to manage the properties formerly owned by the Lakeway Company, including the World of Tennis, the Lakeway Marina, the Lakeway golf courses, and several lakeside tracts.

January - The Lake Travis Chamber of Commerce opposed the Balcones Canyonlands Habitat Conservation Plan, which included a proposed 64,000-acre preserve to be partially paid for by fees from future developers. The Lakeway City Council agreed and sent a letter to the board of Balcones Canyonlands Habitat stating that such fees would restrict development and hurt tax revenues.

February - Coleman Smith was honored as the Lakeway Civic Corporation's 1990 Outstanding Citizen. He had been chairman of the Zoning and Planning Commission for five years and of the Master Planning Committee for three years. He had also served on the Committee to Develop a Community Center and on many of Lakeway's service clubs. In addition, he had been a strong advocate for unifying the village and the MUD, although he had served eight years as president of the Citizens of Sailfish Park in their quest to remove MUD's neighborhood water treatment plant and have the land restored as a park. Receiving Meritorious Service Awards were Petrea Sodke and the staff of the *Homeowners News*.

March - When the seven-mile Southwest Parkway finally opened on March 17, 1991, environmental protestors from Earth First sang AC/DC's 1979 hit, "Highway to Hell." Lakeway commuters, however, welcomed spending less time on the road. Developers Ben Barnes and John Connally had formed Southwest Travis County Road District No. 1 in 1985 to launch the Southwest Parkway project, but when collapsed real estate prices forced them to drop out, the county had to step in. Complicating matters was the discovery of several endangered species, most notably the golden-cheeked warbler, the black-capped vireo, and several cave-dwelling invertebrates. Environmentalists also feared the parkway would adversely affect the Edward Aquifer recharging zone. The eventual cost of Southwest Parkway was $243 million.

May - Hamilton Greenbelt II opened, adding an additional three-quarter-mile trail with access on Palos Verdes Drive.

May - Cole Rowland was elected mayor and Jim Finneran as a councilmember. In addition, Veronica Bennett was reelected as a councilmember. The number of volunteers doubled during Rowland's administration, which also increased public access to city business meetings, acquired the land for City Park, made plans for a Lakeway Community Center, and paid off the City Hall debt. Rowland also recommended the hiring of a city administrator.

May - The Lakeway City Council announced an election to approve the purchase of sixty-four acres of lakefront land for a park. The city planned to bid $375,000 for this plot of bank-repossessed land but needed voter approval. This triggered a long, heated campaign. Proponents argued the land was appraised at double its cost, Lakeway needed a large, family-oriented public park, and this was the last large piece of land with lake frontage. Opponents warned of unwanted users, increased crime, traffic problems, and police and administrative costs. Proponent Byron Varner wrote, "I believe that most of what made Lakeway great is more the product of the residents' efforts rather than the developers." Former mayor James Gribble opposed the park purchase, suggesting Lakeway already had sufficient public land. Above all, Gribble stressed keeping Lakeway private. Another former mayor, N. C. Herndon, worried that a public park "would be 'inviting' to people of all classes, some of whom might be very undesirable. Some may have unsanitary habits, be foul mouthed and dope users. . . . Would you want them to use the public restrooms or portable facilities?"

June 22 - The bond issue for the future City Park passed 753 to 734, a margin of nineteen votes.

June 25 - President Byron Varner and the Lakeway Historical Society placed their first seven historical markers:

- The Mauermann Ranch House (later the Josey Ranch), at Lohman's Crossing and Hurst Creek Road. Today it is the Heritage Center Building.
- Lakeway's First Telephone, located at Lohman's Crossing and Lakeway Boulevard.
- First Municipal Hall, 1204 Lakeway Drive
- Country Store Building, 1202 Lakeway Drive
- Lakeway Land Company's First Headquarters, 413 Lakeway Drive
- The Lakeway Inn, 102 Lakeway Drive
- The Lakeway Yacht Club

July 9 - The city council created an eleven-member Parks and Recreation Commission to assist and advise on the maintenance and operation of the city parks, greenbelts, and recreational facilities and to establish rules and regulations for the use of these amenities. John "Ken" Pettigrew was appointed its first chairman.

August 31 - The Lakeway Historical Society placed its eighth marker in front of the Alan Shepard home at 818 Mariner. In 1961, astronaut Shepard became the first American in space. Ten years later he landed on the moon, where he hit a couple of historic golf balls.

September - The city council accepted receivership of a tennis court on Ladin Lane donated by the Ladin and Yellen families of Houston in memory of the late Sidney S. Ladin, who had a second home in Lakeway.

October - The Lakeway Parks and Recreation Commission, which was responsible for planning the new City Park, circulated a questionnaire asking people what they wanted in their park. Of the 497 responses, only 37 were negative. The commission also held three open meetings to obtain further citizen input. Negative voices continued to worry about noise, congestion, crime, and falling property values.

Initial plans for City Park included two baseball diamonds, a multipurpose field, volleyball courts, a picnic area, amphitheater, community center, swimming pool, fishing pier, sand beach, hiking trails, and eighty parking places. George Blume, who had been instrumental in the city acquiring the park property, constructed a model of the proposed amphitheater, which he hoped would host a variety of music, dance, and theater productions. The plan also included a fine arts complex with practice facilities for music and theater camps and art classrooms. A master plan had to be submitted by January 22, 1992, to get State of Texas matching grants.

November - The Lake Travis Youth Association offered to spend $35,000 on a baseball park in the northwest corner of City Park. Jeff Sandefer, a Houston resident who owned a house on the north side of City Park, offered $375,000 to help build City Park but only if the city met his twenty-one conditions. His lawyer also threatened to sue the city if Sandefer's demands were not met. The city rejected his demands. In December, a Travis County district judge also turned down Sandefer's request for a restraining order to stop work on the ballfield.

December - The Christmas Flood, which began December 18, 1991, dumped eleven inches of rain in five days. Lake Travis rose to a record 710.41 feet, which was within three feet of the spillway and 29.3 feet above its normal level of 681.10 feet. The old record of 707.38 was set in 1957. Most affected in the Lakeway area was Graveyard Point at the end of Hurst Creek Road, where many homes were underwater. The estimated damage for Travis County was $29 million.

1992

January - Jeff Sandefer continued his attempt to block construction of the ballpark, this time claiming that the city was polluting the ground with sediment runoff and asbestos construction materials. When inspectors from the Texas Air Control Board disagreed, Sandefer hired an ecological consultant who announced that protected golden-cheeked warblers might use the area for nesting. This time it was Austin's Earth First and the Travis County Audubon Society that disagreed with Sandefer. The Lake Travis Youth Association did, however, agree to accept Sandefer's check for $100,000 in exchange for moving its ballpark outside of City Park. The ballpark eventually became part of the Field of Dreams Athletic Complex on Highway 71.

January 13 - Rick DeLong became Lakeway's chief of police, replacing Tom Evans. His salary was $29,160.

January 27 - Rotary International chartered the Rotary Club of Lakeway/Lake Travis as the 25,627th Rotary Club in the world. At the time, there were 1,132,600 Rotarians in 174 countries worldwide.

February - Ken Shepherd won the Lakeway Civic Corporation's Outstanding Citizen Award for 1991. He had served five years as mayor, as well as three years as a trustee and one year as president of the LCC. He was also a member of the Lakeway Charter Commission that led to the village becoming a Home Rule City. Meritorious Service Awards went to J. W. "Billy" Baldwin, William M. "Bill" Evans, and Howard Itten.

April - Former mayors Ed Smith and James Gribble, along with other members of the Keep Lakeway Private Committee, sued the city, demanding an election to determine whether the new park should be public or private. The city was forced to spend $15,000 in legal fees defending its actions. District Judge Scott McCowan denied the suit, stating, "You cannot buy land for a public park and make it a private park." The next issue was whether the city should keep or sell the parkland.

May - In a heated campaign, the Support Our Schools slate of Alan Thompson, Carl Russell, and Valerie Gore won LTISD seats over a slate of candidates that promised to sharply curtail school spending.

May - Burt Folsom, Ray Norris, and Elsa Hopkins won seats on the Lakeway City Council. Folsom and Norris wanted to sell the recently acquired parkland, and Hopkins wanted to keep it in its natural state. By a three to two margin they forced a public vote on whether Lakeway should sell the land or build its public park.

June - The Lakeway City Council mandated fences for all swimming pools. At the request of Rella Giammalva, the council also passed a resolution making Lakeway a bird sanctuary, wherein "it is unlawful to trap, hunt, shoot, or attempt to shoot or molest in any manner any bird or wild fowl or molest their nests."

June - The city council debated whether the city should purchase such Lakeway Company properties as the Live Oak and Yaupon Golf Courses, the Lakeway Marina, and perhaps even the World of Tennis. Two councilmembers suggested that money from the suggested sale of the parkland could go toward purchasing the two golf courses. Texas law, however, mandated that monies from the sale of the parkland could only go toward buying additional parkland.

July - The Springhill Catfish Restaurant opened on the corner of Highway 71 and RR 620. The building had formerly housed the Peking Palace.

July - A water taxi service at the Lakeway Marina transported Lakeway residents across Lake Travis to the newly opened Shades Restaurant, where one could dine on its floating deck while dropping french fries and other tasty morsels into the gaping jaws of giant catfish and carp.

July 4 - The Fourth of July Celebration featured cannons booming, a parachute drop, and a color guard marching smartly up the Live Oak fairway, with Mayor Cole Rowland leading the parade. The festivities included a special tribute to "Lakeway's Americans from Far and Near," with a special emphasis on foreign-born residents who had become American citizens. Included were naturalized citizens from Latvia, Germany, Holland, Norway, Lithuania, England, Canada, Columbia, and Peru.

August 8 - A record-setting 57 percent turned out to vote 1,286 to 736 to keep the park. Actively campaigning for retaining the park was the Lakeway Enrichment Organization, which constructed yard signs, did door-to-door and telephone canvassing, set up information stations, and wrote letters to the *Lake Travis View* and the *Homeowners News*.

August - The city council deemed political signs permissible on private property in Lakeway, but only one to a yard and not larger than six square feet. Signs were to be removed within seventy-two hours of the election.

August - When Michael Kuhn, who had been elected to the MUD board in 1986 and had served as board president since 1988, resigned on August 12, 1992, the *Homeowners News* applauded him for having improved relations between the city and the MUD.

September - The Texas Parks & Wildlife Department awarded Lakeway a $420,000 grant to aid in the development of its City Park.

September 9 - Mayor Cole Rowland appointed Bob Stover to head a Community Center Committee, which sent out questionnaires seeking input on two qualitatively different activity centers, one costing approximately twice as much as the other. Of the 664 respondents, 223 voted for the more expensive version, 170 for the cheaper version, and 252 wanted neither. The committee anticipated Lakeway reaching 10,000 residents by 2005 and in dire need of such a facility.

October 16 - At the dedication of seven new Lakeway historical markers, Charles H. McCoy surprised members and guests by donating two Lakeway lots to the Historical Society, saying, "I want to give back some of what I have received in the form of this land to a group who are 'givers' and not 'takers'." A historical marker was later placed in Heritage Park to honor his donation.

December - Hoping to pressure the Texas Water Commission to approve the expansion of its water treatment facilities, the Lakeway MUD sought a moratorium on any new water and sewer service connections in Lakeway.

December - The Buena Vista Hospitality Group announced that Anthony Montalbano, a Chicago developer, would officially take over the former holdings of the Lakeway Company, which it had purchased in 1991. Buena Vista also signed a five-year agreement to continue managing the Lakeway properties.

1993

January - The LTISD board forced Superintendent Walter R. Howard to resign, although he had eighteen months remaining on his contract. He received a payout of $80,000. The board appointed the director of Business and Finance, Bob Hart, to serve as acting superintendent.

January - The Lakeway MUD withdrew its threat of a moratorium on extending its services to new areas of Lakeway. The MUD was upset that it had been unable to expand its Palos Verde facility, in part because of a citizens' suit, but also because the Texas Water Commission had not approved its permit because of "fail-safe" issues.

February - The Lakeway Civic Corporation named Byron Varner Lakeway's Outstanding Citizen for 1992. Among Varner's many contributions were helping begin church services in 1971, creating and editing Lakeway Company's monthly newsletter, *Lakewaves*, in 1972 and organizing the Lakeway Men's Breakfast Club, serving as program chairman and emcee for its first four years, and again in 1987–1988. He also started the first Lakeway post office in 1975 and the *Homeowners News* in 1978, serving as editor for its first three years. He was also a driving force behind the creation of the Lakeway Historical Society. With Denys Cadman, Varner wrote *In the Beginning*, an expanded version of which came out in 1988 titled *Lakeway: The First 25 Years*. In addition, Varner served as president of the Lakeway Civic Corporation and was a board member of the MUD, where he worked to end the long-running controversy over differing rates. Meritorious Service Awards went to Paul Cook, Mike Kuhn, and Floyd Shelton.

March 1 - Richard Eason became Lakeway MUD's new general manager, replacing Roger Palmer who was retiring. At the time, approximately two-thirds of Lakeway had sewers, with the remaining one-third on individual septic systems. Most of the latter were in the older sections of Lakeway. For environmental and economic reasons (making it easier to sell houses and lots), the Lower Colorado River Authority canvassed septic owners about paying to be put on city sewers. Not enough responded positively to implement such a program.

March - After the defeat of two earlier bond issues, voters approved a new $11,150,000 LTISD bond issue by a margin of 882 to 659. The money was earmarked for additional classrooms, a gymnasium at the middle school, a new elementary school, and repairs and safety improvements on existing buildings.

March - After working with consultants and the Texas Parks & Wildlife Commission, the Lakeway City Council and Parks and Recreation Commission approved the layout for the new City Park.

April - The Eagle Development Company, in a joint venture with the General Electric Pension Trust and Ross Perot, Jr.'s Hillwood Development Company, proposed purchasing the holdings of the Lakeway Company. The result was a protracted legal suit that was not settled until February 1995.

April - The Texas Water Commission named Lake Travis the clearest reservoir in the state.

April 13 - The Lakeway City Council accepted and adopted the Community Center Committee's report for a planned activity center, agreeing that the two essentials were "it must serve the needs and interests of all segments of Lakeway, including youth, retired residents and all ages in between, and it must be designed to meet current and future requirements."

April 17 - Lakeway's first annual 5K race/walk was sponsored by Commonwealth Land and Title Company to raise money for the Lake Travis Parent/Teacher/Student Association and the Community in Action Organization.

May - Burton Barnes, who ran unopposed, was elected mayor. Barnes supported the City Park and the building of an activity center, as did newly elected Councilmember Jim Teddlie and reelected Jim Finneran. Outgoing mayor Cole Rowland had been a driving force for the acquisition and development of City Park. He had also doubled the number of Lakeway volunteers by mailing out questionnaires requesting volunteers for specific areas. Rowland asserted, "One of Lakeway's strengths has been the willingness of its citizens to take an active part in their municipal government."

May - There were scattered reports of a triangular, rainbow-colored UFO over Lago Vista, but it evidently steered clear of Lakeway.

May - A leak in the Lakeway MUD's Clubhouse Drive holding pond spilled thousands of gallons of treated effluent into Hurst Creek. Two months later the Texas Water Commission fined the MUD $26,100. The MUD explained that it had been blocked from expanding its facilities and that the release of effluent had done "no harm to the environment, public health, property owners, or water users." The fine was later reduced to $22,000, which MUD director Don Iburg called "distasteful." The leak would not be entirely stopped until January 1994.

June - The State of Texas included the Lake Travis Independent School District in its court-mandated "share-the-wealth" or "Robin Hood" school funding plan. The bill's announced intention was to identify large, under-taxed industrial or utility districts, but Lakeway was almost exclusively residential. In August, the LTISD put up two proposals for voter approval: Purchase attendance credits from the state with local tax revenues, at a cost of $930,000, or educate students from other school districts with local tax revenues. The LTISD eventually opted for the former rather than consolidating with one or more poorer districts.

June - Barbara Ellen's Hill County Restaurant opened on Highway 71 across from the Spring Hill Catfish House.

July - Formosan termites made their first appearance in Lakeway. They had originally appeared in Houston in 1965.

July - The World of Tennis hosted the Continental Airlines Pro Tennis Classic with a $12,500 purse.

July - Due to various problems caused primarily by unusually high rainfall over the past two years and deteriorating sewer lines, the Texas Water Commission cited the Lakeway MUD for major violations of its permit and the Texas Water Code.

July 1 - LTISD's hiring of Dr. Gloria Berry ended its five-month search for a superintendent to replace Dr. Walter R. Howard.

August - The Hudson Bend Volunteer Fire Department hired its first professional fire chief, Dwight Clark, who announced, "Volunteers do for nothing what I don't get paid enough to do."

August 19 - The city purchased a ten-acre site adjacent to the Village Square Shopping Center for a possible activity or community center.

September - After the Texas Parks and Wildlife Commission requested specific changes, the city approved a $399,800 contract with the Keystone Construction Company to build City Park.

September - A statewide survey discovered that a fear of crime was the number one concern of Texas residents.

October - Mayor Burton Barnes raised the issue of annexing The Hills of Lakeway, Rough Hollow, Lakeway West, and the World of Tennis. Barnes argued, "Our boundaries should include all of the Lakeway Municipal Utility District; then we could consider consolidation between the City and the MUD." Councilmember Jim Finneran, who also wanted to add a three-mile strip along RR 620, stated, "The added tax base would offset any added service costs and prevent further deterioration of a piece of land." Police Chief Rick DeLong suggested annexing the entire Lake Travis Independent School District. Representatives of The Hills and the World of Tennis responded that they did not want to be annexed, as did merchants on both sides of RR 620. In the face of this opposition, the city council temporarily dropped these annexation efforts.

October - Mayor Barnes announced his opposition to the Balcones Canyonlands Habitat Conservation Plan, which he called "possibly the most controversial program ever considered by Travis County since the argument years ago as to where the State Capital should be located." Travis County residents were to vote in November on a proposed $48.9 million land acquisition bond package to purchase 29,000 acres of undeveloped property in the western part of the county for the project.

October 17 - The 1,200 members of the Lakeway Church celebrated thirty years of ecumenical services with a picnic in Dragon Park. In addition, the Historical Society placed Historical Marker #19 on the church grounds to celebrate its founding.

November - Costs of the proposed two-story Activity Center were estimated at $3 million, to be raised by a bond issue that Lakeway taxpayers had to approve. Costs included roads, parking lot, furnishings, kitchen equipment, and an indoor swimming pool.

December - The LTISD purchased land for a new elementary school on the east side of Lohman's Crossing at a cost of $331,000.

December - The Texas Natural Resources Conservation Commission (formerly the Texas Water Commission) blocked the Lakeway MUD from spraying its effluent waste on its property near Lohman's Crossing Road.

December 31 - Lakeway set a record with 138 new home starts for the year. It also had reached 7,000 residents.

December - The Hudson Bend Fire Department's Ladies Auxiliary organized the Green Santa Program to collect and distribute food and toys to needy families in what would become an annual event. There is also a Brown Santa Program that collects food and toys for needy Travis County families. Headquartered in Austin, Brown Santa began in 1980.

1994

January - The City of Lakeway purchased ten acres of land on Lohman's Crossing behind the Village Square Shopping Center for future municipal use. A new City Hall building would open on this site in 2005.

January - The Lakeway City Council called for an all-or-nothing vote on May 7 on the proposed $3 million Activity Center, which included an indoor, heated swimming pool. Many pro and con letters appeared in the *Lake Travis View*. Letter writer Richard Hofner warned that Lakeway taxes would rise 40 percent if the Activity Center became a reality. Mike Bowens added, "The City Council needs to return to their basic charter of providing law enforcement, maintenance of infrastructure, and enforcement of regulations, and leave the empire building, monument production and misplaced social activism to our neighbors to the east." Councilmember Elsa Hopkins called the planned Activity Center "a tax-funded country club," and argued that the resultant tax rate would drive young families and those on fixed incomes out of Lakeway. Shelley Meyer countered, "We have the opportunity to create a place where we can all be together, young and old, enhancing our community's quality of life and pulling together towards a common goal." Mayor Burton Barnes estimated that the cost per family would be less than $250 per year.

January - Randall's replaced AppleTree in what is now called the Lohman's Crossing Shopping Center.

February - Longtime public servant Sam Huser resigned as city administrator. He had earlier been a city councilmember and an administrative assistant to the mayor. In April, retired Air Force officer David E. Benson replaced Huser, with the new title of city manager. In September, the city hired Terence Harkin as administrative assistant to the mayor and the city manager.

February - The Lakeway Civic Corporation donated $10,000 to the Lakeway Historical Society toward obtaining a permanent home. The Homeowners Association had earlier given $1,000 for the same purpose.

February 12 - The Lakeway Civic Corporation selected Henry D. Kolb as its Outstanding Citizen for 1993. He had served as president of the Lakeway Yacht and Country Club and of the Lakeway Ecumenical Church's board of trustees. He was also on the board of the Lakeway Recreation Association. He had been vice chairman of the Lakeway Master Planning Commission and as secretary of the LCC had worked on the development of the Hamilton Greenbelt. Receiving Meritorious Service Awards were Samuel C. Hamilton and O. I. "Tork" Torkelsen.

March - A portable post office opened in Lakeway.

April 9 - The gala opening of Lakeway City Park featured dignitaries, clowns, free hot dogs, chips, drinks, ice cream, and the Lake Travis High School Band.

April - Lakeway became one of 100 voting members of the Highland Lakes Group, which had been created at Shades Restaurant in September 1993 by Mayor Rusty Allen of Lago Vista, Bob Vann of the Protect Lake Travis Association, and Lakeway's former mayor Cole Rowland. The triggering mechanism was San Antonio's semi-secret plan to build a pipeline north on Interstate 35 to make Lake Travis part of its water system. The Highland Lakes Group began passing out buttons and bumper stickers, and Lakeway's Peg Hein composed song lyrics about the San Antonio Hose. A petition drive in Travis, Burnet, and Llano Counties requesting that the LCRA not allow San Antonio to obtain Lake Travis water garnered 26,000 signatures. To keep concerned residents, organizations, and businesses updated, the Highland Lakes Group also began sending out its *Water Matters* newsletter, which is still being published.

April - Lakeway MUD's President Don Iburg turned down the city's offer to become its water and waste department. Iburg stated that the MUD lacked sufficient facilities and that such a merger would be disadvantageous to its existing customers. He also suggested that residents in Sections 1–17 form their own MUD.

April 23 - The Lake Travis Parent/Teacher/Student Association sponsored the second 5K Travis Trot run, with proceeds helping fund college scholarships.

May 7 - The $3.5 million bond issue for the proposed Activity Center failed by a 3 to 1 margin. Fear of higher taxes and the expensive indoor swimming pool swayed many older voters.

May 7 - A proposal for a strong manager/council form of government passed, as did one permitting Lakeway to annex adjacent territory without the consent of the affected residents. Roy Hollowell and Richard Schultz became new councilmembers and Elsa Hopkins was reelected.

June - Sam Huser, his son Jeff Huser, and son-in-law Kevin Fleming opened their gated Estates of Lakeway Hills at the end of Lakeway Boulevard. The city council had unanimously approved the annexation of this fourteen-acre plat in the spring.

June - The Texas Natural Resources Conservation Commission (TNRCC) approved the Lakeway MUD spraying its treated effluent on the trees, shrubs, and grasses along Lohman's Crossing Road, which would cause future problems when Lakeway Elementary School opened in September 1995.

July - By a four to one margin, the Lakeway City Council voted to apply for federal money to build pedestrian and bike trails. The lone dissenter, Elsa Hopkins, suggested it was better for children to use their feet.

July 4 - For the first time, the annual Fourth of July festivities were held in the new Lakeway City Park.

August - The Lake Travis Republican Men's Club held its first meeting. The Lakeway/Hills Republican Women followed suit the following month.

September - After less than five months, there had been no reports of vandalism in City Park, and a survey counted more than 100 cars a day entering the park. Even many of those who had initially opposed its purchase were now supportive. The headline of the *Homeowners News* proudly proclaimed, "CITY PARK IS A REAL SUCCESS STORY."

October - The city council extended its RR 620 annexation plans 200 feet north of Lohman's Crossing so the county would have to pay for the road's widening. The 780 acres included the Round Mountain development and its plan for 120 homes.

October - The LTISD purchased five acres for a proposed elementary school on Hamilton Pool Road.

October - A new city council–appointed committee introduced a plan for a more modest Activity Center than the one defeated in the May bond election. Included were a great room, conference and meeting rooms, and kitchen facilities. Eliminated were the swimming pool and exercise facilities.

November - A Contract Post Office opened in Lakeway, which meant residents no longer had to travel to Oak Hill to pick up packages. The next step was to become a Classified Post Office, which would be completely run by postal employees.

November 6 - Mayor Barnes honored George Blume, Bill Dickson, Cole Rowland, Bob Stover, and Jim Vanderford as Lakeway's "Unsung Heroes" at the city's annual Volunteer Recognition Party.

November 13 - The Lohmann's Ford Chapter of the National Society of the Daughters of the American Revolution held its organizing meeting at the home of Lakeway's Jean O'Neill, with eighteen members present. The chapter installed Caroline Ryals as Organizing Regent. The chapter was confirmed December 12, 1994, and continues to be a strong leader in community affairs, including Veterans Day, Memorial Day, and Flag Day, and in the granting of awards to deserving local students.

December - James England became the new fire chief.

December - The Lakeway City Council voted to annex a 1,000-foot-wide strip along RR 620 from Vineyard Bay on the north to within a few hundred feet of Lohman's Crossing.

December - Byron Varner edited the first issue of *Historical Happenings*, which contained news and information about the Lakeway Historical Society. Unfortunately, only a few issues followed during the ensuing years.

December - The new $20,500,000 Mansfield Dam Bridge over the Colorado River opened on RR 620 just downstream from the dam. The previous narrow crossing road traversed the top of the dam.

December - The Homeowners Association hosted Breakfast with Santa for 240 adults and children.

1995

January - Controversies arose over the new Lakeway Elementary School scheduled to open on Lohman's Crossing Road. Parents living outside of Lakeway objected to restricting the school's pupils to Lakeway residents, insisting that doing so would be an economic and racial decision. They also feared that many of the system's best teachers would be transferred to the new school.

Quite a different controversy was the Lakeway MUD spraying its waste effluent on nearby trees. MUD general manager Richard Eason assured parents that there was no danger, but resident Fred Newton thought the whole deal "really stinks."

January - The Highland Lakes Group again urged area residents to sign a petition to the Texas legislature opposing a water pipeline from the Colorado River to San Antonio, Corpus Christi, and Houston. This long-standing controversy also affected water rights to Lake Travis. The petition sent to the LCRA contained 25,000 signatures.

January - The Lakeway City Council approved a $50,000 City Hall renovation to create additional office space.

January - Affected residents worried about the Pedernales Electric Cooperative's plan to double the voltage in its line crossing Lakeway. Fearing an increased rate of cancer, West Lake Hills residents had earlier blocked a similar increase in voltage in their lines.

February - The Lakeway Civic Corporation honored Sam Huser as its 1994 Outstanding Citizen. During his fifteen years of service to the community, Huser served on the Architectural Control Board, the Zoning and Planning Commission, as alderman (1983–1986), and as the city administrator (1986–1994). He also helped make City Park a reality, including procuring state funds for park improvements. Meritorious Service Awards went to Larry Folmer, Ray Norris, and the Lakeway Service League and two of its presidents, Peg Tolzman and Lee Warner.

February - After four years of litigation, the Eagle Development Corporation, a joint venture between the Hillwood Development Corporation and the GE Pension Trust, took over the assets of the bankrupt Lakeway Company. Ross Perot, Jr., the son of the Dallas billionaire, headed up Hillwood. Montalbano had been the original bidder for the assets, but had failed to close the deal on time. Included in the assets were the Live Oak, Yaupon, and Hills of Lakeway Golf Courses, the Lakeway Airpark, more than 300 platted lots and 23 acres in The Hills of Lakeway. In addition, there were 25 parcels in the City of Lakeway, platted over 183 acres, 1,265 acres of undeveloped land in Lakeway West, the 510-acre Schramm Ranch, 299 acres in Rough Hollow, the 384-slip Lakeway Marina, and the World of Tennis Racket Club. The Buena Vista Hospitality Group continued as local manager of these assets.

After the settlement, Hillwood began selling spec homes in The Hills. It also sold the World of Tennis, the Academy of Golf, and the Yaupon, Live Oak, and The Hills Golf Courses to the Cobblestone Golf Group of Del Mar, California.

March - Doris Besperka, a noted local photographer and historian, donated her large Lakeway photo collection to the Heritage Center.

April - An organization called the South Shore Group, later renamed Don't Bridge Lake Travis, objected to a proposed toll bridge across Lake Travis. The mayor of Lago Vista had instigated this $40 million project. Lakeway Mayor Burton Barnes referred to the bridge talk as "pie in the sky," pointing out that there had been similar proposals in 1969 and 1973.

April - Lake Travis High School received an "Exemplary" rating from the Texas Education Agency, a remarkable feat that less than 4 percent of the state's high schools achieved. Unfortunately, the high school would have difficulty maintaining this highest of the four possible ratings.

April - The so-called "Robin Hood" school financing reform cost the LTISD approximately $2.4 million for the 1995/1996 school year.

May - Jack O'Neill was elected mayor. Jon Champeny and LaNell Edwards won seats on the council. The new mayor promised not to approve excessive spending projects without first putting them to a vote.

May - The Lakeway City Council annexed the thirty-acre Coves of Lakeway, located near City Park at the junction of Brooks Hollow and Hurst Creek. It consisted of twenty-three single-family lots and one common area.

June - Byron Varner and the Lakeway Historical Society launched a campaign to raise at least $40,000 for a monument to honor current and former Lakeway wartime veterans.

June 21 - After twenty years, the Lakeway Ecumenical Church's board of trustees approved the separation of its two congregations. Although done at the instigation of Catholic parishioners, a spokesperson said, "It was a congenial separation forced by the need for more space." The Protestant congregation retained the Lakeway Church and compensated the Catholic congregation for its equity.

June - The Lake Pointe Development Company donated land for a new elementary school just off RR 2244.

July - Fourth of July celebrations are tremendous undertakings in Lakeway, and the 1995 version was no exception. Arts League President George Blume planned the $30,000 event, paid for by ticket sales. Its theme was "Victory–50 Years Later–Remembering the Price of Freedom." Included were a P-38 flyover, the music of the Austin Symphony Orchestra, fireworks, and lots of food and games for a crowd of 3,000.

July - More than 300 divers cleaned up Lake Travis, removing folding chairs, batteries, welding cables, and a dining room table.

July - The Lakeway Civic Corporation transferred ownership of Hamilton Greenbelts I and II to the city. Because it had no permanent employees, LCC could not maintain and police parklands.

September - Official opening of the new $4.7 million Lakeway Elementary School on Lohman's Crossing.

October - Grand opening of the public, nonprofit Lakeway Airpark under the new ownership of the Lakeway Pilots Association, which had purchased the Airpark from the Hillwood Company. The Lakeway Company had originally operated the Airpark.

October - By a four to three vote, the LTISD board stated it would emphasize "neighborhood schools" over racially or socio-economically balanced schools when drawing future school attendance zones.

November - The Lakeway Civic Corporation donated $30,000 to build a trail connecting Greenbelts I and II. This trail was completed in September 1996.

November - Behringer Partners of Dallas purchased the Lakeway Plaza and the Lakeway Marina from the Hillwood Development Company.

November 11 - The Lakeway Historical Society dedicated its Spirit of Freedom Monument, consisting of a five-sided granite obelisk with the names of 512 past and present Lakeway residents who had served in World War II. The guest speaker at this fiftieth anniversary of the ending of World War II was Brigadier General Ken Kennedy, a longtime Lakeway resident and former alderman and councilmember, who had served in World War II, Korea, and Vietnam. Private donations paid for the $50,000 memorial.

December - Lakeway again requested that the City of Austin release Rough Hollow, Lakeway West, and the Schramm Ranch to its ETJ. Doing so would expand Lakeway by more than 2,000 acres.

December - Jim Vanderford's selection as Lakeway's Volunteer of the Year recognized his technological skills in setting up the city's new computer system and expanded phone service. He had also advised the city council on the Lakeway MUD and on electrical power and cablevision issues.

1996

January - The estate of Jack Hamilton, who had died in December 1993, bequeathed $225,000 for the maintenance of the Hamilton Greenbelt. Jack and Myrtle Hamilton had earlier donated funds for the original purchase of the 84.5 acres.

January - More than 950 Lakeway residents signed a protest in an ongoing attempt to block the Pedernales Electric Cooperative's plan to double the voltage carried by its power line across Lakeway. Pedernales engineering manager Jim Allen responded that the PEC could do as it pleased because it had constructed the line in 1971 before the affected homes were built. This particular line served Cedar Valley but not Lakeway.

January - Lakeway and the LTISD agreed to share a police officer in hopes of curtailing drugs and alcohol on campus. The plan included drug-sniffing dogs patrolling the junior and senior high schools. Superintendent Gloria Berry defended the action, explaining that some parents ignored the problem while others were users themselves.

January - Pennsylvania-based Toll Brothers purchased 123 lots in The Hills of Lakeway for its planned construction of luxury homes.

February - Lakeway residents began using the new Lakeway zip code of 78734 for their mailing address.

February 5 - Mayor Jack O'Neill appointed Frank Black chairman of Lakeway's third and final Activity Center Committee. Black and his eleven volunteers recommended a scaled-down version from the one that voters had soundly rejected in 1994. The Lakeway City Council agreed to put a $1.6 million bond before the voters, pointing out that more than 1,300 meetings and social gatherings were being held annually in Lakeway.

February 6 - The Lakeway MUD petitioned the Lakeway Zoning and Planning Commission to re-zone 7.3 acres near the southeast end of the Airpark runway for the creation of an effluent pond and irrigation fields. Thirty-three residents signed a protest petition objecting to the project's proximity to nearby homes and the danger an increased bird population would have on planes landing and taking off. The city council turned down MUD's proposal.

February - The LCC's 1995 Outstanding Citizen Award went to Les Weigle for his many public service roles, including chairman of the first Lakeway Master Planning Committee and of the Amenities Acquisition Committee. In addition, he was a member of the initial Home Rule City Charter Commission, the Trust Committee for the LCC's Maintenance Trust Fund, and director, vice president, and secretary of the Lakeway Civic Corporation. He was also active in the Lakeway Ecumenical Church and served as director and secretary of the Lake Travis Education Foundation. Meritorious Awards went to Guy Brown, Jr. and Jim Finneran (posthumously).

April - Mayor Jack O'Neill promised The Hills of Lakeway that it would not be annexed without the approval of its residents.

April 13 - Lakeway held its first annual Art and Music Celebration on the Village Square. Featured were art exhibits, creative activities for children, and live music by local band PatKingCole.

May - Completion of City Hall renovations.

May - Vandals started a fire that did more than $200,000 damage to Barbara Ellen's Hill Country Restaurant, which was not rebuilt.

May 4 - Bonnie Grubbe and Jack Wright were newly elected councilmembers; Richard Schultz was reelected.

June - The Lakeway MUD opened a nineteen-acre, $2 million holding pond west of the World of Tennis, which doubled its capacity.

June - The Field of Dreams Athletic Complex opened on Highway 71.

June - The Lakeway Historical Society sold T-shirts to help pay the costs for landscaping and maintaining the Spirit of Freedom Monument. It also wanted to build a fund for doing oral histories with longtime Lakeway residents.

June 21 - The Lakeway Parks and Recreation Board approved the formation of Friends of the Parks, a volunteer group that would care for and improve parklands. Peg Hein, who with husband Marv would become co-president of FOP, announced, "The idea of Friends of the Parks is not so much to save money as it is to develop volunteer activities." Family memberships were available for $10.

August 5 - The Texas Education Agency gave the Lake Travis Independent School District an "Exemplary" rating, which was the highest of the four possible categories. Only 3 percent of the more than 1,000 districts received this rating. Unfortunately, the district's rating would often fall in subsequent years to "acceptable" or "recognized."

August - Although both the Lake Travis Republican Men and Women's organizations had long been active, there was no mention of the Lake Travis Democrats in the *Lake Travis View* until the August 15, 1996, issue announced a planning committee to discuss strategy. *Lake Travis View* reporter Cyndee DuHadaway wrote, "Yes, Virginia, there are Democrats in Western Travis County, and if you see it in the *View*, it is so." The Lake Travis Democrats had actually first organized in 1992.

August - The Yarmouth Group and Rothschild Property Investors of New York completed their purchase of the Lakeway Resort and Conference Center. Dolce International would continue to manage the property.

September - Corpus Christi released plans for a 104-mile pipeline to ship water from the Colorado River. The Garwood Irrigation Company, which owned senior water rights to draw water from the river, had long been selling water for irrigation purposes to downstream rice farmers. Because of a surplus, Garwood had already sold 35,000 of its allotted 168,000 acre-feet of water to Corpus Christi. The former Texas Water Commission, now the Texas Natural Resources Conservation Commission, had approved the transaction.

September - The LTISD announced a $44 million bond issue to build two new elementary schools, one middle school, and an expansion of the high school. The board also wanted to improve athletic facilities and build a new auditorium. The bond issue was voted down in October by a two to one margin. The rejection meant purchasing more portable classrooms and a higher student/teacher ratio.

September - The Lake Travis Library, located in Lake Travis High School, received a $6,600 grant from the Texas State Library and Archives Commission to help provide student and community access to the Internet.

October - Lakeway Partners, LLC purchased 1,276 acres in Lakeway West, 260 acres in Rough Hollow, and 700 acres from the Schramm Ranch that Ross Perot, Jr.'s Hillwood Group had bought less than two years before. The Lakeway Partners included local investors Rocky Piazza, Steve Dallas, and Jack Lieberman, as well as South Korean financier Danny Kim of the Dong Ah Company, which Kim said was the twentieth largest in the world. Piazza proudly announced, "For the first time in its history, the people who control the land in Lakeway will live in the area." City Manager Dave Benson stated that the annexation of these properties would not only allow Lakeway's ETJ to grow by approximately 40 percent, but it would also allow the city to expand to 25,000 inhabitants. The city council argued that Lakeway needed to annex this territory to bring it under Lakeway's zoning and building codes and to create additional tax revenues. Not all residents were enthusiastic about this large-scale expansion. Some feared losing the quality and ambiance of small-town life and becoming, as *Lake Travis View* letter writer Ernie Conine put it, "another overcrowded urban blob."

October - Byron and Bonnie Varner moved to St. Petersburg, Florida. No one had done more than Byron to research, record, and serve Lakeway and its people. In addition to *Lakeway: The First 25 Years* (1988, 2007), he authored, with A. Denys Cadman, *In the Beginning: A Brief History of Lakeway* (1981). He also edited and published several other publications, including *Historical Happenings, Homeowners News*, and *Lakewave*s, and was a driving force behind numerous organizations and committees. The Lakeway Civic Corporation had named him Lakeway's Outstanding Citizen for 1992.

October - The deer controversy continued to fester. One deer was heard to say, "We have to agree with the Indians. We should never have had such a lax immigration policy." The deer, however, were not invited to a Homeowners Association's Town Hall meeting on the subject, presided over by representatives of the Texas Parks & Wildlife Department. The extremes of opinion ranged from those who believed there should be no organized control to those advocating Lakeway deer hunts. The TP&W personnel insisted that the only foolproof control was to build a deer-resistant fence around the entire city. Tom Priddy, who headed Lakeway's Deer Committee, suggested that the city investigate sterilization procedures to control the herd. Another approach was to capture and relocate deer on an annual basis. The experts also recommended not feeding the deer, in part because corn has less food value than grass and often contains alpha-toxins that promote undersize deer.

October 20 - The newly formed Lakeway Band performed a free concert in City Park

November - The city council again voted to invite The Hills to become part of Lakeway's ETJ, pending Austin's approval. Residents of The Hills, however, voted to become their own municipality.

December - Mayor Jack O'Neill honored the city's more than 125 volunteers and their 30,000 hours of donated time. The mayor announced that their contributions equaled 14.4 full-time jobs, which, at a rate of $12 per hour, saved the city $360,000 annually.

December - Austin approved the transfer of Rough Hollow, Lakeway West, and the Schramm Ranch to Lakeway's ETJ.

1997

January - A number of Lakeway residents circulated a petition opposing the annexation of Rough Hollow, Lakeway West, and the Schramm Ranch, asking for a sixty-day extension before the city made its decision to approve or disapprove the Developer's Agreement, then in its fifteenth draft. Complicating the issue was a deadline of January 31, 1997, for annexation, after which the land reverted back to Austin's ETJ. Spence Warren, the author of the petition, wrote, "Most people moved here because we wanted a village and to build house for house. . . . The developers will sell the Lakeway ambiance in order to sell their apartment buildings and townhouses." The developers warned that they would build under Austin's ETJ if Lakeway turned down annexation. They also promised to build new roads in Rough Hollow, including one out of the canyon to Highway 71. City Manager Dave Benson rejected the petition, stating that only Austin could grant a delay. He also recommended not holding an election on the annexation of these lands. After Austin granted a brief delay, the Lakeway City Council voted unanimously for annexation on June 16, 1997.

January - The LTISD introduced a four-part $26 to $41 million bond issue for new buildings, improvements on existing facilities, including the football stadium, a new auditorium, and new technology. Opposition letters again reminded voters of what they considered excessive spending going all the way back to 1985. Such critics ignored the fact that the district had permanent classrooms for less than 75 percent of its students.

January 18 - By a margin of 868 to 507, Lakeway's voters approved the building of a downscaled, $1.6 million Activity Center.

January 21 - The State of Texas approved the incorporation of the Lakeway Community Foundation. Created by the Lakeway Civic Corporation as a tax-free legal entity, its purpose was "to foster improvements to the Lakeway community through the encouragement of tax deductible donations for various civic purposes." Serving as its original board of directors were Mary Louise Davis, Bill Dickson, John Brodnax, Roger Schuler, and Cole Rowland.

February - Retired U.S. Army Brigadier General Ken Kennedy was the recipient of the Lakeway Civic Corporation's Outstanding Citizen Award for 1996. Among his many volunteer assignments, Kennedy helped design the Yaupon water and sewer facilities, chaired the City Charter Review Committee, served five terms as a city council alderman and three years as a trustee of the Lakeway Civic Corporation, including one year as president of the board. Veronica D. Bennett, Nathaniel S. Kendall, and Burton C. Barnes (posthumously) received Meritorious Service Awards.

March - The city council approved zoning for a senior center, called The Towers of Lakeway, on thirteen acres in the 1900 block of Lohman's Crossing. The project had originally been planned for Lakeway Drive, but neighborhood homeowners objected to changing their residential zoning laws.

May - Mayor Jack O'Neill won reelection as did Councilmember LaNell Edwards. John Riley was also elected to the council. None supported the anti-annexation citizens.

May - Jim Gribble, who was president of the Tejas Corporation, sold the Country Store to Cutrer, Inc., which renamed it Cutrer's Country Market. The new owners promised to expand the store, hire friendly clerks, and feature quality products at cheaper prices.

May 27 - Several killer tornadoes swept down the Pedernales Valley, hitting hard in the Briarcliff and Hazy Hills areas. Tornadoes also touched down in Cedar Park and Anderson Mills. A Force Five tornado killed twenty-seven in the small Williamson County town of Jarrell. The recently opened Pao's Mandarin House donated all the proceeds from its June 6–8 food sales to victims of the tornadoes.

June - Lakeway Partners' preliminary plan for Rough Hollow called for single-dwelling homes on 57 of Rough Hollow's 330 acres. Ongoing issues included an access road, land put aside for public greenbelts and parks, school locations, and various types of housing. The developers strongly preferred a mixture of condos and single-family structures, but the city council and most Lakeway residents preferred only the latter. There were also questions about overweight developers' trucks driving on Lakeway streets.

June - Coleman and Mary Smith donated $125,000 to the recently created Lakeway Community Foundation for the acquisition and development of 4.6 acres along Hurst Creek between Lohman's Crossing and Lakeway Drive. The Smith Greenbelt was named in their honor.

June - Torrential rains pushed Lake Travis to 705 feet, which was only five feet below the record 710 feet set in December 1991.

July 4 - The Fourth of July Celebration's theme was "America's Future - Our Youth." Festivities included a parade, patriotic songs, flyovers by Lakeway pilots, the presentation of the flags of all fifty states, LTISD student essays, and even Bozo the Clown. The featured speaker was U.S. Congressman Ron Paul. The Tenth Annual "Under a Texas Sky" was held on July 5, once again featuring the Austin Symphony Orchestra.

August - The Village of The Hills elected its first officers, including a mayor, a marshal, and five aldermen.

August - The Lakeway City Council voted four to two to table both the unilateral annexation and the Developer's Agreement for Rough Hollow, the Highlands (formerly called Lakeway West), and Vista Royale (formerly the Schramm Ranch) for ninety days. In dispute was the amount of "green space and habitat" the developers were willing to set aside. Also of concern were minimum-size regulations for single-family homes and the proposed gating of parts of Rough Hollow that would block access to Lake Travis for other Lakeway residents.

September - Several critical letters appeared in the *Lake Travis View* objecting to turning Rough Hollow's Sections 37 and 38 into a gated community, including one from Mary Ellen and Kevin Roche suggesting that Section 38 be obtained by the city for a public park "with benches and walkways which would eventually be part of a six-mile network of trails from Hamilton Greenbelt to Rough Hollow."

In the meantime, Lakeway Partners had already begun offering lots in Rough Hollow starting at $80,000.

October - The Texas Education Agency rated the LTISD as "Recognized," as it did Lake Travis High School. Lake Travis Middle School and Lakeway Elementary received "Exemplary" ratings, which over the years they would continue to earn. Lake Travis Elementary was rated as "Acceptable."

October - During two public hearings to discuss the Rough Hollow Developer's Agreement, several Lakeway residents continued to argue for more public lands and trails, access to Lake Travis, and no gated sections.

October - A theater group of the Women's Club put on *Memories Are Made of This*. Sue Wright, who wrote a skit titled "A Question of Health," later became the driving force behind the Lakeway Players.

October 23 - Groundbreaking began on the new 24,000-square-foot, full-service Lakeway Branch Post Office on RR 620. When completed in July 1998, it served zip codes 78732, 78734, and 78738.

October - The Homeowners Association voted down a proposal to extend its membership beyond property owners and current and past residents of the Lakeway area.

November 17 - The Lakeway City Council unanimously approved the latest Rough Hollow Developer's Agreement. Sections 37 and 38 were to be gated, but no additional sections. The developers would construct 1.5 miles of greenbelt trails and put aside 3.5 acres per 1,000 residents for public parkland, on which they would spend $30,000 per acre for improvements. In addition, they were to set aside land for a new elementary school between the Highlands and Rough Hollow. Finally, they promised to build and open a road from the Highlands to Highway 71 before more than 50 percent of the subdivision was platted.

November 19 - Lakeway broke ground for its new $1.6 million Activity Center, culminating a ten-year struggle to build such a facility.

December - Lakeway recognized John Zuercher, Pat Vanderford, and George Blume as Volunteers of the Year.

1998

January - Lakeway launched its $100,000 "Let's Pave the Way Together" campaign to furnish the Activity Center. Donors' names were inscribed on varying-sized tiles to be placed in the courtyard and along the entryway. During the next six months, 423 individuals, 37 organizations, and 92 businesses contributed more than $116,000. Winston L. McGinnis, Jr. was selected director of the new Activity Center on August 17, 1998. Lakeway property owners paid a $12 annual fee to use the Activity Center. For nonresidents the fee was $85 per family.

February - By a margin of 1,939 to 1,305, LTISD voters passed a $41 million bond plan for a 650-student elementary school on Hamilton Pool Road, a 750-student middle school on RR 620 North, and a major expansion of the high school. Also included was a 1,500-seat auditorium, various athletic fields and improvements, and technological advances for classrooms and the administration.

February - The Lakeway City Council approved both a code and a board of ethics to cover all elected and salaried personnel, including volunteers serving on decision-making committees or commissions. Inserted also was a nepotism clause. The mayor and each councilmember were to appoint one member to the initial board and a seventh member was to be elected by a vote of the six appointed members. The code of ethics prohibited those affected from deriving material economic benefits from any transaction with the city or its vendors.

February - The Lakeway Civic Corporation granted its 1997 Outstanding Citizen Awards to Glenn Robert "Bob" Graham and Jack and Myrtle Hamilton (posthumously). While serving as LCC trustee for four years and president for two years, Graham played a key role in preserving its trust fund. He also served as village building inspector, a member of the Architectural Control Board, and assistant city engineer. Graham captured the essence of Lakeway when he said, "The city's volunteerism continues to be our community's strength and its defining character." The Hamiltons, in addition to serving Lakeway on many boards and commissions, were honored for providing the funds to purchase and maintain Hamilton Greenbelts I and II. LCC President John Brodnax said of the Hamiltons, "Jack and Myrtle lived so as to leave things better than they found them. Their love for Lakeway and their desire to improve it is an inspiration to all of us." Meritorious Service Awards went to Leon "Huck" Dorsey, Cynthia Evans, Kenneth Jackson, and Jack McClaran.

February - The Lower Colorado River Authority purchased the rights to 43 billion gallons of Colorado River from Garwood Irrigation, which, according to one source, "effectively tied a knot in the San Antonio Hose." Garwood, whose water rights dated back to 1900, had expressed a willingness to sell its surplus water to Corpus Christi and San Antonio.

April - According to the Texas Parks and Wildlife Department, a chemical discharge killed between 1,000 and 2,000 fish in a one-mile stretch of Hurst Creek. The source of the spill was not identified.

April - Lakeway annexed the World of Tennis and the St. Andrews district in separate actions.

May - Newly elected city councilmembers were Ann Gribble, Ray Norris, and Gerry Astorino.

May - Most Lakeway residents, objecting to excessive noise and crowds, supported the LCRA's ban on powerboat racing on Lake Travis. An exception was Emerald Point Marina owner Jack Carmody, who argued that 200,000 spectators would provide an economic windfall for the area.

May - The Lakeway Heritage Center's Spirit of Freedom Monument added the names of 318 Korean and Vietnam veterans to its 512 World War II names. In the ensuing years, the names of the Gulf War, Iraq, and Afghanistan veterans would also be added.

May - Parents of Lakeway Elementary children objected to the Lakeway MUD spraying its treated effluent on nearby cedar trees, especially after winds pushed the spray onto school grounds. MUD general manager Richard Eason responded, "The Lakeway MUD is operating in compliance and permit of the Texas Natural Resources Conservation Commission [and] reclaimed water is safe."

June - Dave's Dam Saloon, located on RR 620, just inside the Lakeway city limits, burned to the ground. Owner Dave Pardee had no insurance for the $300,000–$400,000 loss.

June - Sam Huser's The Towers of Lakeway broke ground. Initial plans also called for three condominium buildings.

June - The Lakeway MUD reduced its size by 40 percent when it de-annexed the Highlands and Rough Hollow.

July - A one-mile median trail on Lakeway Boulevard opened from Stoney Creek Cove to Scorpion Drive. A few months later it was extended another mile to Flamingo Boulevard. The Lakeway Civic Corporation donated $2,500 in a matching grant for the planting of trees along the median strip.

July - Texas A&M University's Target Cities Program chose Lakeway to conduct a yearlong study and to produce a comprehensive plan for its future. The plan, conducted by graduate students in urban and regional development studies, included its history, natural systems, demographics, economy, land use, housing, transportation systems, infrastructure, community facilities, urban images, and historic resources.

July - The Lakeway City Council approved $117,000 for furniture, a sound system, kitchen equipment, and incidentals for the new Activity Center. In addition, the Lakeway Civic Corporation donated $125,000 to help defray such expenses.

August - The crash of the South Korean stock market in January 1998 forced Lakeway Partners to search for new sources of financing after South Korean partner Dong Ah defaulted on his promised credit line. When they were unsuccessful, Lakeway Partners sold their Rough Hollow, Lakeway Highlands, and Vista Royale holdings to Credit First Suisse of Boston. Straus Properties was named the new development managers of these properties. However, it would be Las Ventanas and its local manager, Haythem Dawlett, who would eventually develop these properties, as well as Tuscan Village.

September - Fourteen Lake Travis parents volunteered to serve on the LTISD Attendance Committee to draw attendance lines for the various district schools. This had long been a controversial subject, particularly when a new school opened, and it continued to be an issue with the soon-to-open Bee Caves Elementary and Hudson Bend Middle School.

September - Copper, a drug-sniffing golden retriever, who had been working the high school and middle school for three years, twice found drugs during the past school year. Copper occasionally entered classrooms on his missions, although some parents strongly objected.

September - A group of parents of Lakeway Elementary students hired a lawyer to stop the Lakeway MUD from spraying trees next to school grounds with what they referred to as "chemically treated sewage." The LTISD had also requested that the MUD restrict its spraying to areas well away from school grounds. A Texas Natural Resources Conservation Commission official had determined there was no danger as long as the wind was not blowing too strongly or from the north and that as soon as the MUD could control its sprays there would be no danger to children. The MUD agreed not to spray on windy days. Angry letters from parents noted that because the MUD was already not allowed to release its treated waters directly into Lake Travis, it should not be allowed to do so near school grounds. Parents also wanted to run their own tests on possible dangers.

September 19 - The Lakeway Parks and Recreation Commission dedicated the new Children's Playground in City Park. The playground had been made possible by a gift from the Abigail Elaine Hendrix and Bernard M. Jacobsen Memorial Fund.

October 27 - Lakeway launched its new civic and emergency radio station at 1620 on the AM dial. It featured community announcements and weather alerts.

November - The new 80,300-square-foot HEB store opened in Bee Cave. An additional 27,000 square feet were planned for additional retail businesses.

November 11 - The Lakeway Historical Society and the Lohmann's Ford Chapter of the Daughters of the American Revolution sponsored a special Veterans Day ceremony to honor those veterans whose names were being added to the Spirit of Freedom Monument. More than 200 attended what has become an annual event.

December - Frank Black was honored as Lakeway's Volunteer of the Year, primarily for his tireless service as chairman of the Lakeway Activity Center Committee. He was also a former editor of the *Homeowners News*.

1999

February 14 - The Lakeway Church broke ground for its 18,000-square-feet Fellowship Center.

February 21 - The Lakeway Civic Corporation named Richard Shultz as its Outstanding Citizen for 1998. Shultz served two terms as president of the Homeowners Association and four years as a city councilmember. He had also been a director of the Lakeway Service League since its beginning in 1988. Meritorious Service Awards went to George Blume, Glen Davis, Tony Leonard, and Jim Teddlie.

April - Parker Kerby Development requested that Lakeway annex its planned 371-acre, 400-lot Flint Rock property. The developers also offered to donate $250,000 for the Lakeway Swim Park, which was then in its planning stage. In December, the Zoning and Planning Commission granted its approval.

April - Rocky Piazza's RCP & Associates announced a planned fifty-acre development just north of Lake Travis High School that was to include a Holiday Inn Suites, a movie theater, an office building with a medical facility, and several restaurants. The Lakeway Regional Medical Center was eventually built on this site instead.

April - Made possible by a donation from the Bernard M. Jacobsen Memorial Fund, the Butterfly Garden opened in City Park. Professional butterfly garden designers, who donated their time and expertise, selected the appropriate plants and trees.

May - Charles Edwards defeated Jack O'Neill for mayor. Hester Currens was elected and John Riley reelected to the Lakeway City Council. Riley would also serve as mayor pro tem.

May 12 - Thirty-six Lakeway "Pioneers" attended the first gathering of the Lakeway Quarter Century Club, appropriately held at the Spirit of Freedom Monument prior to the annual meeting of the Lakeway Historical Society. This has continued to be an annual event.

September - The Lakeway Historical Society hired University of Texas graduate Matthew Darby as its first professional archivist.

September - The Texas Natural Resources Conservation Commission refused to block the Lakeway MUD's spraying of treated wastewater on cedar trees adjacent to Lakeway Elementary School. The LTISD also stated it no longer objected to the spraying as long as it was closely monitored. A parents' group, however, headed by Chris Wilson, reported cases of mononucleosis, skin rashes, and respiratory problems. TNRCC's official report stated, "No process, certainly no water treatment process, can be proven to be absolutely safe for human health . . . so we must speak in terms of the probability or likelihood of the transmission of disease or injury from such an operation. For the Lakeway MUD cedar tract irrigation, we believe that the probability is extremely low." The angry mothers did not give up and eventually forced mediation. The issue was finally resolved when the MUD built a new filtration plant.

October - Glenda Foreman invited several friends to her home to sing some of her favorite songs. Out of this initial group of thirteen emerged the Lakeway Sing Alongs. Joann Anderson served as chair of the new group and Annette Tyson became director. One of their first public performances was the singing of Christmas carols in front of the Exxon station. They soon found a better venue at the new Activity Center, where their Green Santa Christmas Show became an annual hit. Currently, with more than eighty members, the Sing Alongs put on at least two major productions a year.

November 13 - After considerable controversy, many delays, and threatened legal actions, the Lakeway Activity Center hosted its grand opening. Former mayor Jack O'Neill thanked the many Lakeway officials, community volunteers, civic organizations, and local businesses that had made this day possible. The Homeowners Association, the Lakeway Yacht and Country Club, and the Lakeway Civic Corporation announced their plan to share office space in the new Activity Center.

December - Emmaus Catholic Church released its plans for its new edifice, capable of holding 2,000 parishioners.

December - The Lakeway Church began a large expansion, including adding an 18,000-square-foot, two-story building.

December 31 - City and MUD officials assured residents that they were ready for Y2K, despite the dire warnings that myriad catastrophes might immobilize the world at the stroke of midnight because computers were not ready for the twenty-first Century.

December - At its annual volunteer celebration, held for the first time in the new Activity Center, Mayor Charles Edwards announced that Lakeway's Volunteers of the Year were Jan and Ed Viska and Peg and Marv Hein. The Viskas were cited for planning and implementing Lakeway's Christmas decorations and the annual visit of Mr. and Mrs. Santa Claus. The Heins were feted for organizing Friends of the Parks and for their planting and landscaping efforts in Lakeway.

2000

February - The Lakeway City Council formally approved the creation of a Lakeway Arts Committee, the idea for which George Blume had introduced the previous fall. Its objective was "to encourage, develop, and promote the visual and performing arts in Lakeway." In addition to George Blume, its founding members were Fred Newton, Edith Knauer, Frances Nail, Mayo Davidson, Sherry Bird, Cathy Hendricks, Barbara Woodall, and Janet Wright. Among its subsequent achievements were the winter Brown Bag Lunch Concerts, which began in 2001, various evening concerts, an annual photo festival, public art projects and acquisitions, and a monthly arts calendar. Fred Newton and Janet Wright have each served as chair.

February - The newly opened Activity Center offered yoga, dance, bridge, and Spanish as the first of what would become a wide variety of classes.

February 23 - The Lakeway Civic Corporation presented its Outstanding Citizen Award for 1999 to Jim Vanderford. He had served as chairman of the Lakeway Capital Planning and Utility Development Committee since 1997 and had been a member of the Lakeway Land Use Committee since 1998. He also spearheaded the city's computer and telephone systems and installed computer systems for the LCC, Lakeway Yacht and Country Club, and the Homeowners Association. Frank Black and Marv and Peg Hein received LCC's Meritorious Service Awards.

March - The LTISD avoided a lawsuit by returning a parcel of land donated by Willie Nelson after failing to build a school within the stipulated five years. The site was near the corner of Highway 71 and Pace Bend Road, and would have served the families at the western end of the district who had long been clamoring for a school.

May - Richard Friedrich was elected and Ray Norris and Gerry Astorino reelected to the city council. Norris would also serve as mayor pro tem.

May - After Peg Hein successfully initiated a $6,000 grant from the National Tree Trust, Friends of the Parks planted more than 100 native trees in City Park.

May - After a long dispute over building and aircraft restrictions in the Lakeway Airpark, the city council voted to limit hanger size to 8,000 square feet and to prohibit gliders, ultra-lights, balloons, skydiving, and parachuting. The council also restricted takeoff weights to not more than 12,500 pounds.

July - The new Dog Park in City Park allowed Lakeway's canines to run free within a large fenced-in area.

July - After fourteen years of service, J. R. King Enterprises sold its Lakeway cable franchise to Time Warner.

August 19 - The Lakeway MUD opened its new $4 million wastewater treatment facility, located west of the World of Tennis. The cost was shared by the MUD and developers of recent properties. The new facility can treat 400,000 gallons per day, which then goes into a storage pond capable of holding 38 million gallons.

September - Lakeway's excessive deer population continued to be a problem. Possible solutions appeared on the November ballot, along with a $2.1 million bond issue to build a city pool. The council canceled the latter before election day because of higher than anticipated costs, but voters did approve lethal measures for thinning the deer herd by a margin of 1,614 to 1,573. The council then agreed to remove 600 deer a year by one means or another. The following February, the city council passed an ordinance forbidding the feeding of deer, with guilty parties subject to a fine of not less than $1.00 or more than $500.

October 1 - Dedication of the new Hudson Bend Middle School at 15600 Lariat Trail.

October 6 - Endeavor Real Estate broke ground on its Alta Vista Shopping Center on the east side of RR 620, featuring a new, 59,000-square-foot Randall's and an additional 40,000 square feet for other businesses.

December - San Antonio, at least temporarily, dropped its plans for a pipeline from Lake Travis to Bexar County.

December 2 - The city selected P. A. Penley and Deborah Davidson as its Volunteers of the Year.

2001

January - The 2000 census listed Lakeway as having 8,202 residents.

January - Viewpoints launched a series of fall and winter Sunday dinners featuring distinguished speakers. Programs were held on the third Sunday of the month.

March - The Lakeway Civic Corporation presented its Outstanding Citizen Award for 2000 to Cole Rowland. As mayor, Rowland's support had been critical to the purchase and development of the City Park land and the creation of the Parks and Recreation Commission. He also pushed through important amendments to the Lakeway City Charter. In addition, he was a past director and Citizen of the Year of the Lake Travis Chamber of Commerce and was Lakeway's leading spokesperson on water issues, having served as president of the Highland Lakes Group and editor of its newsletter, *Water Matters*. The LCC also granted Meritorious Service Awards to Patricia Jacobsen and A. P. Olbrich.

May - The Lakeway Players' initial production was the *Best L'il Courtroom in Texas*. In the fall it put on *The Elysian Fields*, which it followed with *The Scent of Lavender* in the spring. Sue Wright created original scripts for these first three plays, as she did for two later plays. Sue was also elected president of the Lakeway Players on February 11, 2002. Other officers were Pat Vanderford, vice president; Dan Kubala, treasurer; Angela Fleming, secretary; and Hank Nations, director-at-large.

May 5 - Charles Edwards was reelected mayor and George Blume and Ed Viska were elected councilmembers. By a margin of 1,210 to 1,122, voters also approved a $2 million bond issue to build a swim park.

May 15 - Located at 1602 Lohman's Crossing, Seton Lakeway expanded its health services to Lakeway.

June 28 - St. David's Healthcare Partnership opened a new rehabilitation clinic on Lohman's Crossing.

July - In a show of support for the proposed Swim Park, the Lakeway MUD deeded to the city twenty acres of canyonland west of its wastewater treatment plant.

July - Oak wilt continued to be a serious problem for Lakeway and surrounding areas. Since first identified in Texas in 1961, more than 100,000 live and red oaks have succumbed to this disease that attacks the trees' capillary system. It can spread underground through grafted or joined root systems, and aboveground insects can transport the oak wilt fungus. The Lakeway City Council appropriated $46,000 for additional trenches to curtail its spread. In part because of her oak wilt expertise, the city hired Carrie Burns as city forester in September 2001.

July 4 - Organized by Deborah Davidson, the Fourth of July festivities featured Lakeway's four retired generals, Tommy Thompson, George Edwards, Ken Kennedy, and Dick Drury. Parade Marshal Colonel Roy Doran (retired) had survived the World War II Bataan Death March. More than 3,000 attended the evening fireworks display in City Park.

July 16 - The city council passed a resolution changing the name of the Lakeway Historical Society to the Lakeway Heritage Commission. In addition, its funds and land were transferred to the City of Lakeway. In August, Peggy Point became the Heritage Commission's first chair.

Sept. 17 - The city council unanimously approved the annexation of the 229-acre Schramm Ranch, of which approximately 147 acres were zoned residential. It then annexed four acres on RR 620 across from the middle school, followed by 157 acres of school property, including the high school, middle school, and administration building. The annexations passed by a 3 to 2 vote, with Edwards, Blume, and Norris for and Astorino and Viska opposed.

November - LTISD Superintendent Gloria Berry announced she would retire on June 30, 2002.

December 17 - The city council unanimously voted to annex Cardinal Hills, located on the east side of RR 620 between Kollmeyer Drive and Stroup Circle. Cardinal Hills Investor, Ltd. planned to build 50 duplexes, 95 garden homes, and 150 single-family homes on its 100 acres, all to be served by Water District #17. Cardinal Hills could potentially add as many as 1,100 residents to Lakeway. Included also were thirteen acres of parkland.

December - Lakeway selected Bill Dickson as its 2001 Volunteer of the Year. Dickson was currently chair of the Lakeway Board of Adjustment. He had also served on the Land Use Committee, the Annexation Committee, the Activity Center Committee, and as assistant city treasurer. In addition, he had been the director and master of ceremonies for the city's Fourth of July festivities since 1993.

2002

January - Lakeway received a $500,000 Texas Parks and Wildlife grant for its Swim Center Park project. In addition, the Lower Colorado River Authority donated $100,000 to the project as part of its Partnerships in Parks Program. These grants, plus the $2 million bond issue, paid for the Swim Center Park, which included a six-lane heated lap pool and a 5,000-square-foot family recreation pool.

January - The Lakeway Civic Corporation funded a $12,000, 350-foot concrete walkway connecting the Hamilton and Smith Greenbelts. Lakeway now has five miles of trails and sidewalks that stretch from the far northeast end of Hamilton Greenbelt II to the Lakeway Boulevard intersection with Flamingo Boulevard.

February - The Lakeway Civic Corporation recognized John Brodnax as its Outstanding Citizen for 2001. He had also been named Citizen of the Year by the Lake Travis Chamber of Commerce in 1998. Brodnax, a former president of Lake Travis Rotary, had also served as president and trustee for the LCC and was on the board of the Lakeway MUD and the City Pool Steering Committee. LCC Meritorious Service Awards went to Bill Dickson, Ray Kilgore, DeWitt Smith, and Brian Hickey.

February 19 - The Lakeway Heritage Commission property was re-zoned from a private to a public park. In August, the city council officially named it Heritage Park, which included the Heritage Center and the Spirit of Freedom Monument.

February 19 - The Lakeway City Council designated the *Lake Travis View* as its official newspaper for legal postings.

March 10 - Dedication of the Smith Memorial Garden in memory of DeWitt Smith, who had long headed up the Parks and Recreation Commission. The garden was designed by Bob Schmeltzer and built by Friends of the Parks.

March 19 - The LTISD selected Dr. Donald Rockwell "Rocky" Kirk to replace Dr. Gloria Berry as superintendent. Kirk's official duties were to begin on July 1, 2002. The district was also expecting a shortfall of more than $3 million for the 2002–03 school year. To alleviate the situation, planned cuts included Spanish and physical education aides in the elementary schools and library aides at the elementary and middle schools. Included also were further reductions in staff and a realignment of programs.

April 20 - More than 150 dogs and humans participated in the Fourth Annual Friends of the Parks' 5K/10K Wilderness Run/Walk in the Hamilton Greenbelt, which for the first time included the primitive trail loop.

May 5 - Friends of the Parks introduced Family Parks Day, which included rides, games, and food for the entire family.

May 10 - Newly elected councilmembers were Karl Ansbach, Mike Doherty, and Glenda Foreman. George Blume was appointed mayor pro tem.

July 4 - In accordance with Mayor Charles Edwards proclaiming July 4, 2002, as "Celebrate Freedom Day," Lakeway's 26th Fourth of July Celebration honored World War II veterans, more than forty of whom rode in the morning parade. Featured also was the traditional vintage aircraft flyover. Unfortunately, the evening program had to be canceled because of rising waters in the park, although the fireworks went on as usual.

July 5 - Because of flooding, the LCRA closed Lake Travis to all recreational boating for five days. The lake crested at 693.3 feet on July 7.

November 11 - More than 500 people attended Lakeway's Veterans Day ceremony. Former CBS news anchor and current Lakeway resident Dan Rather gave the keynote address.

2003

January - The question of possible central sewers and wastewater services for Lakeway's Sections 1–17 again resurfaced. Because the cost might be as high as $10,000 per household, the Lower Colorado River Authority sent out 1,300 survey letters. At least 600 households needed to sign up, but when only 430 surveys were returned and less than half were positive, LCRA dropped the project.

January - In a move that triggered a series of forced and voluntary resignations, recently hired LTISD Superintendent Rocky Kirk terminated the positions of executive director of Special Programs and director of Transportation, Maintenance and Operations and replaced them with an executive director of Curriculum, Instruction, and System Accountability and a director of Budgeting and Accounting. He also asked the Lake Travis High School and Middle School principals to resign and moved or replaced three other principals. Kirk then appointed Bob Hart assistant superintendent and hired new athletic director Jack Moss, who announced, "I have high expectations. I expect every program to be successful, and the fact is that you measure that in wins and losses." Moss's first step was to fire football coach Charlie Sadler, whose team had gone 1-19 over the past two years.

January 23 - The City of Lakeway requested a "depredation permit" to trap and kill up to 500 deer. The meat would be donated to agencies that fed the homeless. The actual killing of the deer was to be done after they had left the premises.

January/February - The Rio Development Corporation announced its proposed 74-acre Avenue of the Lakes project to the north and west of the Lohman's Crossing entrance to Lakeway. The *Lake Travis View* called this "the biggest crisis ever to hit the City of Lakeway." The developers' plans included a Wal-Mart, a Lowe's, a high-end restaurant, two 24,000-square-foot office buildings, and several speciality shops. Rio also promised a greenbelt and park that would cover 30 percent of the area, featuring existing ponds and wildlife, and a site on which to build a city or regional library. The property, however, needed to be re-zoned commercial. News that a Wal-Mart might be going up at the entrance to Lakeway triggered a spate of letters to the *Lake Travis View,* most of them negative. Over the ensuing months, an intense debate boiled over among residents and city officials over the advantages and disadvantages of Big Box stores within Lakeway. Opponents cited Wal-Mart's track record of driving out small businesses, vacating its nonproductive older stores, increased noise and traffic, and negatively changing the atmosphere of Lakeway. Typical was Nellie Symm-Gruender, who wrote, "A Wal-Mart in the middle of Lakeway attacks every reason that I live in this area." She was writing as a citizen although she was also on the Lake Travis Chamber of Commerce board of directors, which worried about protecting Lakeway's small businesses. Letter writer Yvonne C. Connell asked, "Why does Lakeway have to follow the craze, which seems to be sweeping the nation, for megabox stores? Why can't Lakeway be a little unique and not follow the cookie cutter plan for Anytown, USA?" Among those supporting Big Box stores were letter writers Mike C. Ferrell and Rob and Toni West, who stressed increased tax revenues and the advantage of not having to drive to Austin to shop. RIO partners Robert Walker and Larry Stauffer estimated additional annual city revenues would be as high as $2 million from sales taxes and another $2 million from property taxes. In addition, they argued that because change was inevitable Lakeway was better off being involved in it. They also warned that other developers wanted to put government-sponsored, low-cost apartment housing on the property.

February 5 - At a Lakeway Zoning and Planning Commission hearing, Rio requested that its Avenue of the Lakes property be re-zoned from AG, Agriculture, to C-1, Office/Light Retail. Many in an audience estimated at 200 shouted their disapproval when Walker announced that he wanted "to preserve the integrity of the property." When resident Bill Schweitzer announced the forming of a grassroots organization to stop Wal-Mart, the audience cheered.

February 9 - The Lakeway Civic Corporation presented its 2002 Outstanding Citizen Award to Ray Norris, who was a member of Lakeway's first Master Planning Committee and a vice president of the Homeowners Association, for which he and his wife, Marge, compiled the initial Homeowners Association Handbook. Norris also had been a volunteer fireman and street director for Lakeway, chaired the Lakeway Building Commission for four years, and served six years as a city councilmember. Meritorious Service Awards went to Sue Potter, Joanna Gardner Wentz, and Hilary W. Amacker.

February 13 - John Hoopingarner, Bill Schwitzer, and several other opponents of Big Box development created the LakewayFirst organization "to help the citizens . . . preserve and enhance their quality of life." LakewayFirst cited Lakeway's 1998 Comprehensive Plan, which stated, "Aesthetic appearance greatly influences the perceptions both residents and visitors have about a community."

March 17 - More than 120 attended the city council meeting, most to voice their continued displeasure with Big Box development in Lakeway. Because the issue was not on the formal agenda, the council listened but chose not to discuss the matter. Many critics pointed out that Wal-Mart and Lowe's were definitely not "light retail." LakewayFirsters in the crowd argued that city staffers had referred to it as "a done deal," which Mayor Charles Edwards angrily denied. Edwards insisted that discussions to revise Lakeway's Comprehensive Plan had begun several months before Rio made public its plans for Lakeway. LakewayFirst member John Hoopingarner formally requested the city's records on the negotiations under the Texas Open Records Law.

March - The LTISD hired Jeff Dicus as football coach at a base salary of $61,250, plus $13,500 in stipends.

March - The city council authorized the mayor to hire a lobbyist to urge the legislature to make it easier to trap and then place deer on rural ranches. At the time, the Parks and Wildlife Department required ranchers to have a valid wildlife management plan approved by the department, which was an expensive undertaking. The Lakeway deer controversy inspired even more letters to the *Lake Travis View* than did the Big Box controversy.

April - The LTISD announced the closing of Lake Travis Elementary for the rest of the year because of mold problems. A month later the LTISD board stated that the closing would extend for at least two years. An estimated 850 students had to be relocated. After the input of a 45-member Relocation Advisory Committee, the kindergarten through fourth grade students were absorbed by Lakeway, Lake Pointe, and Bee Caves Elementary Schools. Fifth grade students were moved into the Hudson Bend Middle School. Lake Travis Elementary would eventually be torn down and replaced by a new building.

April 19 - Lakeway's Fifth Annual Wilderness Run/Walk in the Hamilton Greenbelt featured 160 runners, not including a sizeable number of four-footed participants.

April 21 - In a loud, boisterous meeting, the Lakeway City Council voted unanimously to re-zone the 42.9-acre Wunneburger tract and the 5.15-acre Witt tract on RR 620 from agriculture to office and light retail use. The city's Zoning and Planning Commission had previously recommended the council do so. This cleared the way for Rio Development to present its formal plan for a Wal-Mart Superstore, although Lowe's had already withdrawn from the project.

May - Gerry Astorino was elected mayor. George Blume was re-elected councilmember and Steve Swan was elected to his first term on the council. None had publicly opposed Rio's plan for Big Box development.

May 9 - The city council received a LakewayFirst-sponsored petition signed by at least 12 percent of the eligible voters requesting that voters be allowed to determine so-called Big Box commercial development. City Manager David Benson announced that if the petition were legal it would be placed on the agenda for the council's June 16 meeting. The City Charter called for an election to be held within 90 days of the certification of a petition calling for one.

May/June - There was also controversy over a 125-foot tower erected by four mobile phone companies. The tower was built in the form of a cross on the property of Emmaus Catholic Church, which received fees for its permission. One wag suggested changing the name of the street to Lohman's Cross. Another writer asked, "God, can you hear me now?" When some nearby residents, many of whom lived in the village of The Hills, objected to the giant cross blocking their view, Monsignor Richard McCabe responded, "It's legal, we have a 50-year contract; it stays—period!"

May 5–11 - The Kinko Golf Classic, played on the Jack Nicklaus–designed Hills Country Club, was the first major golf tournament held in the Austin area since 1994. More than 64,000 attended this senior circuit event, which was also covered live on the Golf Channel. Charities benefiting from the tournament included the First Tee of Greater Austin and the Austin Children's Hospital. Kinko continued to sponsor the tournament until 2009, when it became the Triton Financial Classic.

May 24 - Grand opening of the Lakeway Swim Center Park, to be administered by the Parks and Recreation Department. In addition to its two pools, the park included a bathhouse and picnic area. Families were encouraged to purchase hand-painted ceramic tiles as part of a "Splashdown" fund-raiser.

June 19 - Lakeway city attorney Tom Buckle declared it was illegal to put the Big Box petition to a vote, although a referendum might be legal. Councilmember Karl Ansbach successfully moved that ZAPCO consider a zoning ordinance to limit the size of commercial buildings.

July 4 - Marking the fiftieth anniversary of the Korean War Armistice, Lakeway's Fourth of July Celebration honored the war's 1.8 million veterans. Parade marshals were Lakeway founders Lee and Jean Blocker, Frank Denius, and John and Kay Crooker. The Austin Civic Wind Ensemble and the Mormon Choir from Austin provided appropriate music.

July - The city council approved city forester Carrie Burns' request for $115,000 to build a 4,630-foot-long, 48-inch-deep trench to contain the spread of oak wilt.

July - Mary Kay Davis filed a class-action lawsuit in district court against Lakeway officials, arguing that a Wal-Mart Supercenter would do irreparable harm to her home on Rolling Green Drive, that re-zoning of the involved property failed to comply with city ordinances, and that Office/Light Retail certainly did not apply to Wal-Mart.

August 18 - The Lakeway City Council unanimously passed a resolution to hold an election to create a library district for the residents of the LTISD, excluding Bee Cave. State law permitted library districts to be supported by a local sales tax of up to one-half of one percent.

September - The Texas Department of Criminal Justice blocked the trapping and shipping of Lakeway deer to Texas prisons where they were to be slaughtered to feed the inmates. The TDCJ explained that it had no holding pens and that the animals might be dangerous to those handling them. If Lakeway would agree to field dress the animals, the TDCJ would accept them. City Manager Dave Benson responded that Lakeway could not field dress deer or transport their carcasses in refrigerated trucks.

September - In what had become a semi-regular event, volunteer divers "fished" out six tons of trash from Lake Travis, including tires, cans, bottles, kitchen sinks, and a live, five-pound catfish trapped in a golf bag. Organizations such as the LCRA, Keep Austin Beautiful, the Colorado River Foundation, and Travis County Parks and Recreation sponsored the 750 volunteers who participated.

September 15 - Facing an overflow and agitated crowd in the Activity Center, the city council finally agreed to allow residents to vote on a non-binding referendum to allow commercial buildings that exceeded 100,000 feet. This decision also put Mary Kay Davis's lawsuit against the city on hold.

October 30 - In a letter to the *Lake Travis View,* Ted Stewart wrote that Gwendolyn and Joe Wunneberger, who had signed an earnest money contract to sell their land to Rio Development, were so upset over the resultant controversy over Wal-Mart that they were now willing to sell 30 of their 44.3 acres to the City of Lakeway for $3 million, although the property was currently listed at $4.9 million. They were also willing to take a note or accept certificates of obligation for 90 percent of the price at a competitive bond rate for a term of twenty years. Under this agreement, the city's down payment would only be $300,000. Stewart suggested that the front section along RR 620 could be zoned commercial, and the land behind could then be used for ballparks, a library, an art center, or green space. The Wunnebergers would also donate their historic log cabin to the city as a gesture of goodwill. Their cabin was the oldest structure in Lakeway.

November 4 - By a 1,880 (72 percent) to 749 (28 percent) margin, Lakeway voters rejected the non-binding referendum that would have allowed commercial buildings to exceed 100,000 square feet. The city council subsequently voted unanimously to reject the "C-4, Large Retail" zoning change, which effectively ended the Wal-Mart and Big Box controversy.

By a vote of 1,379 to 1,250, Lakeway residents did approve a $4.5 million bond issue to build a new City Hall at an estimated cost of $1,883,000, a new street department building costing $1,428,000, and to renovate the existing City Hall and street department building to create more offices for police and court personnel.

LTISD's $36.3 million bond issue passed by a vote of 2,662 to 1,383. Nearly one-third of this money was targeted for tearing down and rebuilding mold-infested Lake Travis Elementary.

November 11 - The annual Lakeway Veterans Day ceremony honored Korean War veterans. Monsignor Richard McCabe of Emmaus Catholic Church, who gave the invocation, speaker Jim Durham, pastor of the Lakeway Church, and Jim Henegar, who placed the memorial wreath, were all Korean War veterans.

December 18 - A group of citizens from Cherry Mountain requested annexation by Lakeway to head off Cherry Mountain Partners's planned 264-unit, low-income housing project in their subdivision.

December 24 - Zbranek Custom Homes, using materials and labor donated by more than sixty-five local businesses, built a house that sold for $575,000. The $100,000 profit from the sale went to the Lake Travis Education Foundation, a nonprofit organization that supports mini-grants and scholarships for LTISD teachers and students.

December - For the year, 265 deer had been trapped and taken to a meat processing facility in Johnson City, which donated the meat to the Capital Area Food Bank and other charitable agencies. Deer deaths from automobile accidents had been reduced from seventy-one in 1999 to only five in 2003.

December - Lakeway's crime rate dropped in 2003 despite an increase in population, including a 50 percent drop in burglaries, from forty-four in 2002 to twenty-two in 2003. There were also fewer cases of criminal trespassing, harassment, public intoxication, and excessive noise.

2004

January 4 - Water Control and Improvement District No. 17 (WCID17) broke ground on its $4 million Flintrock Wastewater Treatment Facility, which will serve the area's 2,000 homes. The treated water will be used to irrigate the Flintrock Golf Course.

February 12 - The Lakeway Civic Corporation honored former Lakeway mayor Jack O'Neill (posthumously) as its Outstanding Citizen for 2003. O'Neill had also served two years as president of the Homeowners Association and had been a board member of the Crisis Ministries, the Lake Travis Library, and the Lake Travis Improvement Association. In addition, he had organized Lakeway's initial Breakfast with Santa Program. Meritorious Service Awards went to LaNell Edwards and Peggy Point.

March - Mayor Gerry Astorino announced that the Lakeway City Council had begun planning for a one-story City Hall because it would be "more functional and allow our employees to interface more efficiently." He also said it would be easier to expand, although there should be no need to do so before 2015.

March - Many Bee Cave residents, as well as the Save Our Springs environmental organization, tried unsuccessfully to block Chris Milan's Shops of the Galleria, which was anchored by a 165,000-square-foot Lowe's. They considered the development an environmental threat to Little Barton Creek. Bee Cave mayor pro tem Zelda Auslander accused SOS of recruiting "soldiers within the community and infiltrating the system to spread its virus." Milan would also develop the Hill Country Galleria on the north side of Highway 71.

April - The Hamilton Pool Road Scenic Corridor Coalition tried to block the Lower Colorado River Authority's plan to construct a water pipe along Hamilton Pool Road. Its members opposed high-density development, growing congestion, and the despoiling of Little Barton Creek. Developers were planning to build 1,300 homes on a three-mile stretch of Hamilton Pool Road. According to *Lake Travis View* reporter Dot Fowler, "A plan to run a water line down the scenic corridor [of Hamilton Pool Road] has pitted neighbor against neighbor in a battle that could determine the future of development in the area." The pro-development Hamilton Pool Road Alliance had its own slogan: "Surface water now!"

April - California-based Las Ventanas Land Partners and its local manager, Haythem Dawlett, became the new developers of Rough Hollow and Lakeway West. Dawlett said the plans were for "2,000 homes, a little commercial development, parkland, a swim park with a public beach in the back of Rough Hollow Cove, and a marina."

April - After annexing 29-acre Rough Hollow Cove, the Lakeway City Council approved a zoning change to allow a marina with 280 covered slips, as well as a members-only yacht club and ship store. City Manager Dave Benson announced, "This isn't like Hurst Creek Marina or Lakeway Marina or any of the others we have in the area. You're not going to see any boats on trailers heading through Lakeway to this marina."

April - Toll Brothers announced plans for 271 homesites east of RR 620 on the Ridge at Alta Vista.

April - Twenty residents completed the Lakeway Police Department's second ten-week Citizens Police Academy. The program included forty hours of training, ranging from firearms safety to stopping traffic techniques.

May - A Lake Travis party boat capsized near Hippie Hollow when its passengers rushed to one side to catch a glimpse of nude sunbathers. No one was seriously hurt.

May 15 - Lakeway voters returned incumbent councilmembers Karl Ansbach, Glenda Foreman, and Mike Doherty. Voters also approved the creation of a full-service Lake Travis Library District to be funded by a quarter of a percent sales tax.

May 25 - Tom Rogers took over from the retiring Don Iburg as board president of Lakeway MUD. Tom Priddy, Allan Hitchcock, and Kay Andrews were elected board members.

June 7 - Lakeway hired Steve Jones for the newly created position of deputy city manager. Jones, who had been city manager of Pflugerville for seven years, would also serve as the city's Public Information and Training officer.

June - The Lakeway Airpark tore down its old operations building, popularly called "The Shack." Completion of a new building was expected to take two to three months.

July 4 - Ann Neighbors again chaired the Fourth of July Committee, which selected the theme "Freedom Is Not Free." Daytime music was provided by Capital City Highlanders Bagpipe Band. Serving as parade marshals were a Texas National Guard unit, the Lakeway Police Color Guard and Vietnam veterans. State Representative Terry Keel was the keynote speaker. Some 1,000 attended the day activities and 5,000 the evening's patriotic program featuring the Austin Civic Wind Ensemble and local church choirs.

August 3 - Lakeway Airpark suffered its first fatal airplane crash, when a small plane crashed into the upper level of Jackie and Larry Elliott's home in The Hills, killing all six passengers. An investigation reported the plane was overloaded and the pilot had been under investigation for earlier flying violations. The tragedy resulted in a tremendous outpouring of help from the Lakeway community. On September 13, the Elliotts hosted "an appreciation party" at the home of Jimmy and Joann Anderson to honor the professional and neighborhood "Heroes and Angels" who had assisted them after the crash destroyed the upper level of their home. Special recognition went to a repairman named Fernando, who had escorted Jackie Elliott out of the house after the crash.

August 31 - Because of budgetary problems, Seton Healthcare Network closed its Lakeway clinic at 1602 Lohman's Crossing.

September - Councilmember Glenda Foreman and resident Eric W. Winter wrote letters to the *Lake Travis View* urging passage of the November 4B sales tax referendum, whose revenues could be used for both civic and commercial projects. Winter stressed possible cultural projects, such as a bandshell in City Park, sports and recreational facilities, as well as property tax relief. Foreman argued that new businesses would allow residents to shop closer to home and provide entertainment possibilities such as a movie theater. Ernie Conine opposed, stating that the real objective of a 4B sales tax was to encourage more development. He did not oppose cultural amenities but suggested that Lakeway evaluate them on their own merits, rather than as a by-product of new businesses paying added sales taxes. Councilmember Steve Swan argued that if the referendum passed, the council would form a Lakeway Development Corporation, which would allow citizens "to have an early voice in determining what commercial enterprises come to Lakeway."

September 23 - Another plane crash killed two of its three passengers. A Cessna 421C Golden Eagle flying from New Mexico developed engine problems and tried to divert to the Lakeway Airpark. It did not make it, crashing into the Barton Creek Habitat Preserve near Bee Cave Road and Resaca Drive, perilously close to Lake Pointe Elementary, whose children had been dismissed an hour before the crash. Pilot Palmer Swift Haines and Margaret Ann Cardwell were killed, but Cardwell's son James was thrown clear of the crash and survived. A later National Transportation Safety Board report blamed pilot error for "improper positioning of the fuel selector valves . . . resulting in a loss of power to the left engine due to fuel exhaustion."

November 4 - Lakeway residents voted down the 4B sales tax referendum by a margin of 794 to 760. The city council would reintroduce the issue in 2007.

November - Another plane crash, this time in a field behind McDonald's on Highway 71 in Bee Cave. Fortunately, the lone occupant walked away from his plane, which had experienced engine problems.

November - Part-time Parks and Recreation employee Darby Grayson was appointed Lakeway's new recreation coordinator. The position called for her to develop programs and special events for all residents, but especially teens.

November 11 - Before more than 170 grateful citizens, Lakeway paid special tribute to Vietnam combatants at its annual Veterans Day ceremony in front of the Spirit of Freedom Monument in Heritage Park. The keynote speaker was Lakeway's Milton Kizer, who had served in World War II, Korea, and Vietnam.

December - The Lower Colorado River Authority's decision to begin negotiations with those seeking water service along Hamilton Pool Road intensified the ongoing conflict between developers and conservationists. In a public meeting, the LCRA argued that Lake Travis had sufficient water for the next 150 years of development, although it would back off this statement in 2008 when San Antonio again sought its water. Nonetheless, many residents objected to turning the Hill Country into high-density subdivisions. Gary Dinges editorialized in the December 16 *Lake Travis View* that Travis County needed to strengthen its development ordinances for unincorporated areas. Nevertheless, the LCRA gave final approval to the five-mile, sixteen-inch pipeline along Hamilton Pool Road.

December - Lakeway recognized former mayor Charles E. Edwards as its 2004 Volunteer of the Year.

2005

January - Todd Dellinger, a veteran of Broadway and former executive director of New York's Martha Graham Dance Company and School, opened the TexARTS Association, a nonprofit organization pledged "to serve youth and audiences with top quality training and performance." The TexARTS Academy, he said, "will allow all ages to study the performing and visual arts with top professional teachers from throughout the nation."

January - Friends of the Parks Trail Rangers worked more than 500 volunteer hours in the Canyonlands as part of Lakeway's matching contribution to a $600,000 Texas Parks & Wildlife grant given to the Swim Center Park project. In addition to building and improving trails in the Canyonlands, FOP workers hauled 4,000 pounds of concrete mix down steep trails to build a forty-foot bridge across a small stream at the bottom of the canyon.

February - The Lakeway Resort and Conference Center was sold to Behringer Harvard Investments, which planned a $15 million renovation of existing rooms and a new 5,000-square-foot ballroom. The Resort and Conference Center had been losing money because of a 17 percent occupancy rate. Behringer brought back Dolce International as manager, which had managed the property between 1987 and 2002.

March 10 - Lakeway signed a ten-year lease with CityCorp for the use of the Live Oak Tennis Courts.

April - The Lakeway Civic Corporation recognized Don Iburg as its Outstanding Citizen for 2004. Iburg had been president, vice president, and editor for the Homeowners Association from 1990 to 1992. He also served on a wide variety of community committees, but his most important contribution may well have been as president of the Lakeway MUD board, which he had headed since 1992. According to one admirer, he joined an organization that desperately needed modernizing: "Don developed a vision and plan to divest the district of underdeveloped and unneeded land. He sold bonds, developed innovative recycling methods, and expanded and upgraded facilities." LCC granted its Meritorious Service Awards to William V. Bergstrom, Ramzi Deeb, and Sue Wright.

April - LTISD's enrollment was slightly more than 5,000 students. It expected that figure to grow to more than 11,500 within ten years.

May - By a vote of 810 to 749, Steve Swan defeated Karl Ansbach for mayor. Julianne DeBower and Bob Neighbors were elected councilmembers.

June - A Texas Municipal Police Association report concluded that Lakeway police were "overworked, underpaid, ill-equipped, poorly trained, and had little faith in management." Twenty-seven officers had left the force over the past five years, a rate of 20 percent a year. The Lakeway City Council immediately authorized more than $43,000 for equipment and repairs on existing police vehicles. It also pledged to make salaries comparable to surrounding areas. On September 1, 2005, Lakeway hired a new police chief, Gordon Bowers, who had thirty-two years of law enforcement experience in Burbank, California.

June - Rocky Kirk was named Superintendent of the Year over forty-six other superintendents across fourteen Central Texas counties.

June 18 - Dedication of the new 10,000-square-foot Lakeway City Hall on Lohman's Crossing. The new building included city council chambers, as well as offices for administrators, the Parks and Recreation Department, and Planning and Development/Code Enforcement. After being renovated, the former City Hall building would become the new Justice Center. A new Public Works facility also opened at 3303 Serene Hills Drive.

July - Lower Colorado River Authority spokesman Robert Cullick announced that because the President George W. Bush administration was no longer enforcing federal guidelines limiting density of housing, roads, and other hard surfaces in the Hill Country, developers were free to follow state environmental requirements, which were more lenient.

July 4 - For the second year in a row, the Lohmann's Ford Chapter of the Daughters of the American Revolution won best parade entry at Lakeway's annual Fourth of July Celebration. This one featured a full-sized replica of a bald eagle carrying an American flag.

July 31 - Monsignor Richard McCabe, who had been a spiritual power on the Lakeway scene since its beginning in 1963 and a driving force behind the creation of the Lakeway Ecumenical Church, celebrated his final Mass at Emmaus Catholic Church.

August - Mike Boston replaced Matthew Darby as the part-time Heritage Commission archivist.

August 1 - Dedication of the new Lake Travis Elementary at 15303 Kollmeyer Drive. The old building had been closed and then razed after mold problems were discovered in May 2003.

September 10 - LTISD voters passed a $127 million bond issue by only 130 votes. The monies were to be used to expand the two middle schools and the high school, give a 3 percent raise to the teachers, break ground for a new elementary school at the intersection of Serene Hills and Trophy, and purchase land for seven new facilities. In addition, there were to be athletic upgrades and expansions. There had been considerable controversy over the location of the new Serene Hills Elementary because of the existence of a nearby elementary school and because residents in western Travis County continued their demand for an elementary school so their youngest children could avoid spending several hours daily on a school bus.

September 20 - The American Retirement Corporation broke ground on Lohman's Crossing for its new skilled nursing facility with rooms for up to 100 residents. ARC also announced plans for a five-story, 300-unit senior independent-living apartment building on the other side of Lohman's Crossing. This decision would result in considerable controversy with nearby homeowners because of its size.

September 23–24 - Some 400 evacuees from the Houston area, fleeing the ravages of Hurricane Rita, found temporary refuge in Lake Travis High School before being moved to Austin's Toney Burger Center. The victims received bedding, clothing, and hot meals. Advanced Spanish students served as translators when needed.

November 11 Sponsored by the Lakeway Heritage Commission and the Lohmann's Ford Chapter of the Daughters of the American Revolution, the Veterans Day ceremony featured Brigadier General Richard T. Drury's keynote address, "Tribute to our Active Duty Military and to the Veterans of Three World Wars." The Lake Travis High School Band and Choral Group provided patriotic music.

November 11 - The Veterans Day celebration also included the dedication of the new Lakeway Heritage Center building. In 1992, Charles and Jean McCoy had donated two lots on Lakeway Boulevard, one of which was sold in order to purchase a two-acre lot at the corner of Hurst Creek and Lohman's Crossing. At the time, there was a small, dilapidated building on the site that had formerly been a bunkhouse on the Mauerman Ranch before that property was sold to Jack Josey. The Heritage Commission stored its archives and artifacts in the bunkhouse, but when it was declared unsafe in 2004, the commission moved its materials into storage. It sold the second McCoy lot and began raising additional monies for a new building. The Lakeway Civic Corporation donated $20,000 for the restoration of the "Rock Room," which was all that remained of the original bunkhouse. Private sources provided additional funds, including $10,000 from developer Haythem Dawlett, who also did the landscaping. The City of Lakeway, which had taken over the ownership and administration of the newly named Heritage Commission in 2001, pledged the final $41,315. Lakeway architect Jim Little volunteered his time and expertise to the design of the new building.

December - The American Retirement Corporation requested re-zoning from Retirement (R-7) to Planned Unit Development (PUD) for its planned five-story, 700,000-square-foot building. Critics argued this would violate the 100,000-square-foot limitation. Mayor Steve Swan disagreed, stating that such a restriction applied only to commercial buildings. Letter writer Marc Burns countered, "As proposed, the project is too big, too high, and too close to neighboring homes." An ad hoc committee, calling itself the Independent Living Study Group, submitted a positive report on ARC plans on December 15, but with modifications. This dispute also resurrected bad feelings between Lakeway and The Hills, which bordered the proposed development.

December - Lakeway announced its plan to complete its annexation of the Clara Van area, which included Hurst Harbor Marina, the nine-acre development of Harbor Hills, Johnny Fin's floating restaurant, and a neighborhood of thirty or more homes. Older Clara Van residents, however, strongly objected. Some had settled in the area before Lakeway even existed, and several wrote letters or spoke out at subsequent city council meetings. As resident Colleen Bullard put it, "We were here long before the Lakeway City Council began to see only dollar signs." Those opposed to annexation feared additional taxes and Lakeway's stringent home and property codes. Mayor Steve Swan admitted the city had been approached by developers who had plans for those segments of Clara Van that had already been annexed, but he also promised residents they would be allowed to maintain their style of living, which often included fields instead of lawns, outbuildings, wildflowers, and chickens, all of which violated Lakeway codes.

December 3 - The city hosted its thirteenth annual Volunteer Appreciation Party to honor and thank Lakeway's hundreds of volunteers. Hester Currens and Jon Champeny were feted as Volunteers of the Year. Currens had served on the Zoning and Planning Commission, the Lakeway City Council, Friends of the Parks and the Parks and Recreation Commission. Champeny had been on the Homeowners Association's board and had negotiated the Developer's Agreement for the Lakeway Highlands. He had also chaired Lakeway's Comprehensive Plan Committee, its Annexation Committee, and the Lakeway Civic Corporation's Trust Committee.

2006

January - Lake Travis Library signed a three-year lease with Lohman's Crossing Partners. After twenty-one years of co-existing with the Lake Travis High School Library, this new lease allowed the library to move into the north corner of the Lohman's Crossing Shopping Center, where it celebrated its grand opening on June 2, 2006.

January 4 - The Lakeway Zoning and Planning Commission held a public meeting on American Retirement Corporation's planned multistory apartment building. Several of those opposed complained that ZAPCO restricted their speaking time although not that of ARC's supporters. ZAPCO then voted four to three to change its zoning ordinances in support of the ARC project, although the city council still had to grant its approval.

January 24 - Because of its desire "to reach out to new residents in our community," the Homeowners Association changed its name to the Homeowners Association of Greater Lakeway.

January 30 - The Lakeway City Council voted five to one to change the zoning codes from Residential to Planned Unit Development to facilitate ARC's now slightly smaller planned facility. The lone council dissenter was Mike Doherty, who still objected to its size. Among ARC's promised changes were three smaller buildings, 2.5 acres of land for a future Lake Travis Community Library District, and a park and a pond. ARC also planned a 150-foot setback from The Hills. Final architectural plans still had to be approved by the city council.

February - Toll Brothers Construction requested that Lakeway annex fifty acres on the east side of RR 620 and then re-zone it R-5 for condos instead of its present R-1, which allowed only single-family homes. Travis Oaks Trails residents were concerned about this planned high-density, 198-unit condominium project planned for twenty of the fifty acres in the Chandler Tract. Mayor Steve Swan confirmed the city was considering annexing and re-zoning the land to allow condos. Again, negative letters poured into the *Lake Travis View,* insisting that doing so violated Lakeway's mission statement that "all new development will complement our desired quality of life and will be an asset to the community." Toll Brothers temporarily withdrew its request after Mayor Swan announced, "The residents of Lakeway have made it clear they don't want this kind of development." However, the issue of developing the Chandler Tract would come up again in May.

February 8 - Sixth-generation Texan Charles McClure, who grew up on Lake Travis, was named editor of the *Lake Travis View.*

February 12 - The Lakeway Civic Corporation recognized P. A. Penley as its 2005 Outstanding Citizen of the Year. Penley had served on most of the city's major committees, as well as on the MUD, LCC, and Lakeway Church's boards of directors. The City of Lakeway had also recognized Penley as its Volunteer of the Year in 2000. Joann Anderson and Doris Besperka received Meritorious Awards.

February 22 - The Lakeway Heritage Commission hosted its first Veterans Forum. Guest speakers were Lakeway residents Richard Drury, Gerry Astorino, Charles Edwards, David Benson, and Don Karges, all of whom were retired commissioned officers.

February 23 - The Lake Travis Independent School District requested legal relief from what it considered the abuse of the Public Information Act. The district had received more than 1,000 requests, leading to some 63,000 pages of information over the past six months, more than 90 percent of which came from David and Melissa Lovelace, the parents of an LTISD student. Superintendent Rocky Kirk stated that the district had spent nearly $500,000 in the past seven months responding to these requests.

March 20 - Because Clara Van residents had unanimously opposed annexation, the city council granted their wish by a vote of four to two.

March 30 - Lakeway hired Chessalay "Chessie" Blanchard for the newly created position of deputy city manager.

May - There were no contested races in the Lakeway City Council election. Glenda Foreman was an incumbent and Dave DeOme and Bill Rhue ran unopposed, replacing Karl Ansbach and Mike Doherty. Voters also approved eleven proposed changes to the City Charter. Proposition one increased the number of councilmembers from six to seven, which included the mayor. The mayor and three council members were to be elected in even-numbered years. Proposition two limited office holders to no more than three consecutive terms.

June 22 - Despite the opposition of nearby residents and its own earlier reservations, the city council approved the Chandler Tract project on the east side of RR 620 on which Toll Brothers Construction was now planning to build 175 condos and eight single-family homes. The council explained that its lawyer had instructed them that Lakeway could be in violation of state law if it did not approve the development because until it officially annexed the area, existing city zoning ordinances did not apply. This was the ninth development that Toll Brothers had undertaken in Lakeway.

June - The widening of Highway 71 for the Galleria development caused enormous traffic jams and badly hurt businesses. Critics argued that the Bee Cave Parkway bypass should have been completed before tearing up Highway 71.

June - Owners Terry and Josephine Delooze and Brian and Miranda Valenta opened the Marketplace at Lakeway at the intersection of Lakeway Boulevard and Lohmans Crossing. The Deloozes had operated the Lakeway Country Market in the Village Square for the past six years, which they closed.

July - The grand opening of the 9,000-square-foot Skate Park, adjacent to the Swim Center Park.

July 20 - The American Retirement Corporation announced it would donate a park, worth approximately $250,000, to Lakeway in lieu of the city's required park fee for its new development. This was part of its restructured plan for its now 254-unit, five-story retirement housing facility on the south side of Lohman's Crossing, with another ninety villas and townhomes planned for the north side. ARC announced that the park would have a fish pond and walking and jogging trails. It also proposed donating land for a playground and the future home for the Lake Travis Community Library, although it had not yet signed a written agreement with the library board. Councilmember Bill Rhue suggested ARC present the council with a more detailed plan for these amenities.

August 10 - The Texas Education Agency dropped Lake Travis Independent School District from "Recognized" to "Acceptable." Lakeway Elementary, Lake Pointe Elementary, and Lake Travis Middle School retained their "Exemplary" ratings. Lake Travis High School dropped to "Acceptable" for just the second time in the past ten years. Assistant Superintendent Diane Frost blamed the reduced rating on low test scores of the "economically disadvantaged" and "Hispanics." Ratings were based on student performance on the previous year's Texas Assessment of Knowledge and Skills (TAKS) tests.

August 24 - By a vote of three to two, the Lakeway City Council voted to prohibit future gated communities. Mayor Steve Swan argued that open roads were important for emergencies and that there was more of a sense of community without gated communities. At the time, there were already fifteen gated communities in Lakeway, and several others were grandfathered in.

September - Concerned residents formed the Brooks Hollow Homeowners Association and the Save Lakeway Organization to oppose Harbor Ventures' plan to build its Crosswater Yacht Club Marina on Lake Travis at the end of Hurst Creek Road. Harbor Ventures had already petitioned the Lower Colorado River Authority for its approval. The initial plan called for 262 slips, two boat ramps, and a parking lot for 131 cars. Nearby residents feared noise, traffic, and possible spills from public toilets and floating septic tanks. At its September 18 meeting, the city council unanimously agreed to send a resolution to the LCRA opposing the marina, which would be inside Lakeway's ETJ but not within its city limits.

October - Travis District Court Judge Suzanne Covington dismissed LTISD's lawsuit against David and Melissa Lovelace. An editorial in the *Austin American-Statesman* supported the judge's decision, and pointed out that school systems often made it unnecessarily difficult for parents to get information. Nevertheless, on October 30, LTISD's trustees voted unanimously to appeal the judge's decision.

November 11 - The Heritage Commission and the Daughters of the American Revolution jointly hosted the annual Veterans Day Program at the Spirit of Freedom Monument in Heritage Park. The program dedicated a new wall commemorating veterans who had served in the Gulf and Iraq Wars. Lakeway's Jim Teddlie gave the keynote address.

November 16 - Byron Varner, who wrote *Lakeway: The First 25 Years*, and who so ably fulfilled countless volunteer positions in Lakeway, died in his St. Petersburg, Florida, home. Heritage Commission chair Peggy Point said of Varner, "He had a vision of preserving the history of Lakeway and he went about seeing that was done."

December 2 - Mayor Steve Swan honored Peggy Point and Don Karges as 2006 Volunteers of the Year. Point had served on the Service League and had been a driving force in developing the Historical Society and the Heritage Commission. Karges had served on several committees and had been chairman of the Zoning and Planning Commission.

December 3 - The Lakeway Sing Alongs presented two shows at the Lakeway Activity Center. Admission was an unwrapped child's gift to go in Green Santa's bag. Green Santa has been a longtime Christmas tradition in Lakeway.

December 9 - Breakfast with Santa was another long-cherished holiday tradition, featuring Mr. And Mrs. Claus, a passel of elves, Rudolph, and lots of kiddie photo-ops with Santa.

December - Lakeway is allowed to fine residents up to $1,000 for not properly removing trees with oak wilt if ordered to do so.

December - Hill Country Alliance director Christy Muse warned that unchecked development along Highway 71 would result in endless strip malls surrounded by sprawling subdivisions. As an example, she singled out Masonwood, a proposed subdivision recently annexed by Lakeway and located along the extended Serene Hills Drive and Highway 71. The preliminary plans called for 373 homes, a middle school campus, and retail businesses fronting Highway 71. Muse was especially critical of Lakeway officials who "don't hide the fact that they want as much commercial development as possible." Lakeway leaders responded that the city needed new sales tax revenues to lessen property taxes. Muse concluded, "Billboards and bright lights are converting this once scenic gateway to the Hill Country into another U.S. 183. Eventually, the solution for U.S. 183 was to build an elevated highway. Is this our vision for this region? If not, we've got to start planning."

2007

January - More than a million people are expected to move into Travis County in the next twenty years, with most of them taking up residence along the Highway 71 corridor.

January 1 - At 643 feet, Lake Travis was at its lowest level since 1964; however, by April 12, heavy rains had pushed the lake back up to 667 feet, a total of 24 feet in just over three months.

January - The requirements for Miss Lakeway to compete in the Miss Texas Pageant were "single, has never been married or given birth, and between the ages of 19 and 29."

January 12 - After numerous citizens objected, ZAPCO reconsidered a proposed zoning amendment that would have reopened the possibility of Big Box retail stores in Lakeway. The proposal would have allowed the Lakeway City Council to issue "special use permits" to circumvent the current restriction of 100,000 square feet. Those wanting to lift the restrictions were targeting possible businesses at the west end of Lakeway Highlands on Highway 71.

January - The American Retirement Corporation abandoned its five-story independent living project on Lohman's Crossing because of too few advance sales and residents' objections to the height and size of their planned buildings.

January - The LTISD clashed with the Richard Grumbles family over a planned court order to take over its land on Hamilton Pool for a school sportsplex and bus barn. Five generations of Grumbles had worked the 300-acre property for more than 100 years. Letter writer Nell Penridge suggested the LTISD exercise its power of eminent domain on land already owned by developers who were making huge profits. Ms. Penridge also presented the school board with a petition containing 215 signatures opposed to its action. Letter writer Elaine Johnston pointed out that Spicewood and Briarcliff, whose families had long pleaded for a school, would be a better site. After encountering such opposition, the LTISD board announced it would probably not take any further action.

February 1 - Grand opening of the 59,000-square-foot Summit Healthcare Skilled Nursing Center on Lohman's Crossing.

February 11 - The Lakeway Yacht and Country Club and the Homeowners Association merged and became the Greater Lakeway Residents Association (GLRA). New responsibilities included activity groups such as the Newcomers Alumni Club, language classes, bridge groups, the Greater Lakeway Play Group, the Travel Group, the Holiday Ball, and the Wine Club. The GLRA would also take care of the lending library in the Lakeway Activity Center, as well as sponsoring Town Hall meetings, Meet the Candidates Night, Info Fair, golf tournaments, Breakfast with Santa, and its annual meeting with the Lakeway Civic Corporation. Dues for the new GLRA were set at $30 per year.

February 11 - The Lakeway Civic Corporation granted its 2006 Outstanding Citizen of the Year Award to Marsha Bissett. She had served as a board member of the Lakeway Women's Club, the Garden Club, the Dinner Club, the Friends of the Library, and the LCC. She was also a board member of the Homeowners Association, editor of its *Homeowners News* in 1993 and 1994, and had assisted in publishing LCC's Residents Directory. Receiving Meritorious Service Awards were Fred Newton and Fred and Judy Hazen.

February 20 - The city council annexed 457 acres of the so-called Heard Tract, which was part of the Lakeway Highlands. Bee Cave annexed the other half of the tract. Doing so gave Lakeway frontage on Highway 71. Mayor Steve Swan spoke of "boundary protection," but he also made it clear the city was looking for revenue: "The city needs a better stream of revenue, and any retail development would help us create a better balance between property and sales taxes." Deputy City Manager Chessie Blanchard told residents, "The developer plans to construct 343 single-family homes, one 33-acre multi-family lot with a proposed density of 12-units per acre, and seven commercial tracts on 96 acres, yielding about 33 acres of developed commercial area." City Manager Steve Jones pointed out that the city's expenditures were increasing but revenues were falling; hence, there was a need for more revenue. The plan also called for a four-lane extension of Serene Hills Drive from Flint Rock Road to Highway 71.

March - Mayor Steve Swan and all but one member of the city council voted to put the 4B sales tax measure on the ballot again. The Lake Travis Chamber of Commerce also supported doing so. If passed, 4B would raise the Lakeway sales tax from 7.75 percent to 8.25 percent. Mayor Swan explained that 4B would be used to attract "desirable, citizen-supported development in Lakeway," including possibly a town square and certain cultural amenities. Dissenting councilmember Bill Rhue wanted specific projects to be spelled out. Letter writer Ernie Conine pointed out that 4B could also be used to lower property taxes, but the council chose not to offer that option.

April - Affected residents launched a "Make Flintrock Safe Alliance," warning that Flintrock Road could not handle the great increase in expected traffic with the development of Rough Hollow and the Lakeway Highlands. Mayor Swan acknowledged that Flintrock Road was unsafe, and hoped to get county help to improve it.

April 25 - Sue Collyer-Potter retired after twenty years of service. She was first hired as an assistant village secretary, then moved up to administrative assistant to the city manager, and finally became assistant city manager, with an emphasis on planning development and code enforcement.

May - A class action suit brought against the Pedernales Electric Cooperative, which served much of Lakeway, claimed that $164 million in excess revenues should be returned to its members. The suit also stated that PEC's board of directors were improperly paid thousands of dollars beyond their allowable per diem allowances and travel expenses. Additional suits would soon follow.

May 6 - The city took over the responsibility for Parks Day from Friends of the Parks and renamed it Lakeway Park Fest. It featured live bands, arts and crafts, food, and myriad amusements for children.

May 10 - All three passengers aboard a 1953 Cessna 180 survived a crash landing on the Flintrock Falls Golf Course. The plane had developed engine problems just short of the Lakeway Airpark.

May 12 - Steve Swan was reelected mayor. Bob Neighbors was reelected and Don Karges and Alan Tye were elected to the city council. The 4B sales tax referendum again went down to defeat, this time by a vote of 862 to 799. In 2004 it had lost 794 to 760.

May 28 - The Heritage Commission sponsored its first Memorial Day event. In addition to honoring all those who had served their country, the ceremony at the Heritage Park Spirit of Freedom Monument paid special tribute to deceased Lakeway veterans.

July - A group of Lakeway residents established the Patriot Fund as "a non-profit service to assist severely wounded and disabled service men and women by providing a conduit to promote independence, increase self-esteem and quality of life for these heroes." The Patriot Fund's initial goal was to raise $25,000 for a single Johnson and Johnson iBOT Mobility System, but by the end of November it had raised enough money to purchase six additional iBOT systems. By October 2009 the total had reached thirty. Chairman Mike Jackson pointed out that Lakeway's success in helping veterans had inspired other communities to follow suit.

July - The LCRA suspended Harbor Ventures' application to build its Crosswater Yacht Club Marina at Graveyard Point because of past violations at its Highland Lakes Marina, including docks and electrical wiring that did not meet standards. Planned floating septic tanks were also cited as a possible problem. Lakeway officials and most residents had opposed the marina because of noise and traffic problems, especially if it included a public boat launch.

July 4 - "Land of the Free and Home of the Brave" was the theme of Lakeway's annual Fourth of July Celebration. Rear Admiral and astronaut Stephen S. Oswald served as grand marshal and featured speaker. Evening festivities at the Emmaus Catholic Church featured the Austin Civic Wind Ensemble, several church choirs, and the usual fireworks. It was also the final time that Lakeway resident Zack Hager publicly sang his moving rendition of *Tattered Old Flag*. Susan Bowers, who coordinated the events, was also selected as Volunteer of the Month.

July 6 - Heavy rains, including nineteen inches in one day in Marble Falls, pushed Lake Travis to 701.6 feet, an increase of over 20 feet in one week. The LCRA closed down Lake Travis, forbidding all recreational activities. In the Lakeway area, Graveyard Point was hardest hit, with water reaching the second floor of some homes. This marked the highest lake level since 1991, when it had reached 710.4 feet.

August 7 - Haythem Dawlett, whose Las Ventanas Land Partners had replaced the American Retirement Corporation when the latter dropped its plans for a retirement community, presented a slide show of his planned Tuscan Village, featuring not more than 300 residential properties, including cottages, townhouses, and not more than 100 apartments. Also included were a central club facility, tennis courts, a swimming pool, walking trails, and a retail area. A majority of residents who spoke at the meeting approved of the project, stressing the need for relatively inexpensive housing for older residents who could no longer maintain large homes, but several residents from The Hills, whose homes backed up to the project, continued to have reservations.

September - Mayor Steve Swan announced that Lakeway had reached 14,000 residents, an increase of 75 percent in seven years, and had $2 billion in property values. The medium age was approximately forty, and 80 percent of the citizens were under fifty-five. Swan projected Lakeway's "built out" population to be approximately 25,000.

November 6 - Lakeway voters approved an additional half-cent sales tax to be applied to reducing property taxes. Also approved was another half cent to support the former Hudson Bend Fire Department, which had changed its name to the Lake Travis Fire Rescue-Emergency Services District #6, primarily because it now covered more than 200 square miles rather than the 25 square miles when it chose its original name. Its current stations are located in Hudson Bend, Lakeway, Bee Cave, Comanche Trail, and Steiner Ranch. At one time, it had been largely manned by volunteers; now most were professionals.

November 30 - Lakeway's fifteenth annual Volunteer Recognition Celebration honored Dorothy Chidsey, Pat Steele, and Gordon Hurd for organizing the thirty regular and more than twenty substitute volunteers who handle the reception desk at City Hall.

December 23 - Led by all-state quarterback Garrett Gilbert, the Lake Travis High School Cavaliers won its first Texas 4A Football Championship. The team would repeat in 2008, 2009, and 2010.

2008

January - Less than a month after winning the state 4A championship, Lake Travis High School coach Jeff Dicus informed his players that he had accepted a position at Duncanville. Forty-eight hours earlier Discus had said he was not leaving, but then announced he had changed his mind after a Sunday sermon about doing the big things in life. Stephenville's Chad Morris replaced Dicus and would win a state championship in his first year.

January - The Lake Travis Chamber of Commerce selected former mayor Charles Edwards as its 2007 Citizen of the Year, in part for his work as co-chairman of the Patriot Fund, which by this time had raised more than $200,000 to purchase additional iBOT Mobility System wheelchairs for injured war veterans.

February - After Pedernales Electric Cooperative refused to allow a state audit, state representative Valinda Bolton and others called for the resignation of PEC's board members. Board chairman W. W. "Bud" Burnett and general manager Bernie Fuelberg had resigned in late 2007, but now Bolton called for the resignation of the entire board, some of whom had been serving for more than forty years. Bolton insisted all had lost the trust of their member-owners. In addition to governing issues were the excessive salaries and financial perks board members had given themselves.

February - The Lakeway Civic Corporation selected Hester Currens as its 2007 Outstanding Citizen. Currens, who had been recognized in 2005 as Lakeway's Volunteer of the Year, served on the city council and as director and president of the LCC. She was also a member of the Zoning and Planning Committee and on the board of Friends of the Parks. Meritorious Service Awards went to Jean O'Neill, Janet Wright, and Bob Finken.

February - The Lakeway Service League celebrated its twenty-year commitment to helping neighbors in need. It held its first meeting in the Lakeway Village Hall in 1988. In addition to transporting residents to doctor appointments and clinics, the Service League has provided wheelchairs, walkers, and other types of medical equipment on a temporary basis, and without charge. Its financial support comes from civic groups and residents. According to Mayor Steve Swan, "Since 1988, this band of angels has transported more than 2,000 neighbors to appointments, delivered approximately 1,600 pieces of medical equipment, and spent over 10,000 hours staffing the office and responding to telephone calls."

February - After eleven fatal accidents over the past several months on Highway 71 west of Bee Cave, the Texas Department of Transportation announced $3 million in immediate modifications. An advocacy group formed in 2007, called Citizens for Change on 71, had petitioned the state to make Highway 71 safer. Parents living west of the most dangerous stretches had long requested that the LTISD build an elementary school closer to their homes. In May, the LTISD passed a resolution calling for the Texas legislature to rebuild Highway 71, noting that the district has lost two staff members and one student in the past three years.

March 26 - Richard Eason, general manager of Lakeway MUD, was the recipient of the Water Environment Association of Texas's 2008 Arthur Sidney Bedell Award for his administrative and leadership skills and for his expertise on water issues in the state of Texas.

March/April - TexArts's 6,000-square-foot Keller-Williams Studio opened in the Lohman's Crossing Plaza, and Ann Neighbors became president of the newly formed TexArts Lake Travis Guild. TexArts was founded in 2005 by Todd Dellinger and Robin Lewis "to educate our residents, young and old, in performance skills and producing quality shows for our entertainment." In its brief existence, it had established an academy for 160 young performers and produced five shows using professional and local performers.

April - *Newsweek* rated Lake Travis High School 503rd among the country's top 1,300 schools. The number of offered Advanced Placement courses was one of the determining factors.

April 21 - The Lakeway City Council unanimously re-zoned the future forty-one-acre Tuscan Village as a Planned Unit Development (PUD).

May - The city council canceled its election because Dee Ann Burns, Bruce Harris, and incumbent Dave DeOme were all running unopposed. Doing so saved the city $2,000. The council also approved extending Serene Hills Road to Highway 71, to be financed by the developer.

June 5 - At age ninety-five, former Lakeway mayor and top Conoco Oil executive Ken Shepherd received his college diploma. He had begun his studies in the depths of the Depression, but tough economic times, World War II, and a compulsory speech course that he had failed three times left him three credits short of his degree. After the intervention of his daughter Sue Alborn, the University of Missouri granted him his engineering diploma.

June - The city council unanimously approved the developer's plan for a 100-bed, 270,000-square-foot Lakeway Regional Medical Center, which was to include a hospital, medical office buildings, retail space, a daycare center, a hotel, and restaurant space. The council also approved Tuscan Village's General Development Plan.

July 4 - Lakeway's annual Fourth of July Celebration featured former Navy SEAL and Medal of Honor winner Lieutenant Commander Michael Thorton and four of the recipients of the Lakeway Patriot Fund's iBOT motorized wheelchairs for men and women injured in Iraq and Afghanistan.

July 21 - The Lakeway City Council voted six to one to reduce its extra-territorial jurisdiction (ETJ). Some of the land in question was on the north side of Lake Travis in Point Venture, and another piece was on the south side of Highway 71.

July - As part of his planned Tuscan Village retirement community, developer Haythem Dawlett pledged land valued at $1 million for a permanent home for the Lake Travis Community Library.

August - A Bee Cave institution, Jim Bob's Barbeque closed after seventeen years. The original structure was built in 1935 and housed Johnson's General Store and Trading Post. It later became a convenience store, a dry cleaners, a feed store, and a bait shop. Proprietor Bob Sanson announced that although he wanted more time for his family and other interests, it was the two malls and the reconstructed Highway 71 fronting his place that made him decide to close. The well-known, red-painted building was briefly reopened under new ownership, with its original Trading Post name.

August 13 - Lee Blocker, a founding father of Lakeway, died. The *Lake Travis View* stated, "He saw the potential of the Lake Travis area from the very first time he laid eyes on it. And he stayed. He made Lakeway his home for more than forty years." Fellow Rotarian Rodney Reynolds said of him, "He was the most kind and gentle man I have ever known." Mary Reynolds echoed her husband's words: "When God made Lee Blocker, he broke the mold because there is only one Lee Blocker. . . . He never got involved in anything that he didn't give his heart and soul to. He was a real inspiration to everyone he met."

August 25 - Opening day for Serene Hills Elementary. The 94,000-square-foot structure, built at a cost of $14 million, included forty-two classrooms, two computer labs, a science lab, two art labs, a library, a gymnasium, and a cafeteria.

September 8 - The Lohmann's Ford Chapter of the Daughters of the American Revolution placed a historical marker in front of the Heritage Center honoring John Henry Lohmann, one of the earliest settlers in the Lakeway area. The land he homesteaded is now at the bottom of Lake Travis.

September 20 - At a cost of $6,000, the LTISD produced two thirty-second spots that aired on Fox Sports regional telecast of the Texas-Rice football game. The ads highlighted the district's academic and athletic achievements. Fox did not charge for the actual air time as part of a deal to televise an earlier football game between Lake Travis and Westlake.

October - Mrs. Joyce Champeny donated $50,000 toward the construction of the future Lake Travis Community Library. Mrs. Champeny was a past president of the Lake Travis Republican Women's Club and the Greater Lakeway Women's Club. Her love of literature was summed up in her declaration, "I never met a book I did not like."

October 20 - The LTISD announced that the $127,000,000 bond issue, passed in 2005, made possible a $55 million expansion of the high school, to house up to 2,500 students (current enrollment is at 1,857). New classrooms were also added, as well as a career center, a multipurpose building, and agriculture facilities. Athletic improvements included the tennis courts, running track, and strength training center. Renovations were also made to the science and fine arts facilities, the cafeteria, and the gymnasiums.

October 21 - Jack Wright collected, resized, and arranged the framing of the photographs of the eleven men who had served as Lakeway mayors. These portraits are now displayed in the City Hall auditorium: H. C. Herndon, 1974–1975; James Gribble, Jr., 1975–1983; C. Kenneth Shepherd, 1983–1987 and 1990–1991; C. Ed Smith, Jr., 1987–1989; Richard McLaren, 1989–1990; Cole Rowland, 1991–1993; Burton C. Barnes, 1993–1995; Jack O'Neill, Sr., 1995–1999; Charles Edwards, 1999–2003; Gerry Astorino, 2003–2005; Steve Swan, 2005–2009; Dave DeOme, 2009–? At the ceremony, former mayor Gerry Astorino explained how to be a successful mayor: "You just surround yourself with the most talented people that you can find and get out of their way. Let them do their jobs." In Lakeway this has primarily meant fellow volunteers.

October 26 - At the groundbreaking ceremony for the new Lakeway Regional Medical Center complex on RR 620, Mayor Swan said, "This may be the most exciting day in the history of Lakeway." Actual construction was scheduled to begin in March 2009, with completion set for early in 2011. The plans now included a full-service, 100-bed hospital, daycare and rehabilitation facilities, and medical offices, as well as a hotel, retail shops, and a restaurant.

November - The Lake Travis Specialty Hospital, which expected to open by the end of 2009, remained under construction behind the Lakeway Post Office. It was initially licensed for forty medical-surgical and six intensive-care beds.

November - State senator Kirk Watson introduced a bill to designate Highway 71 as a scenic highway, which would ban future billboards. The senate had voted down a similar bill introduced by Watson in 2007.

November - The LTISD received its annual Texas Education Agency ratings: Lake Travis High School, "Academically Acceptable"; Lake Travis Middle School, "Exemplary"; Lake Travis Elementary School, "Recognized"; Lake Pointe Elementary School, "Exemplary"; Lakeway Elementary School, "Exemplary"; Bee Cave Elementary, "Recognized."

November 15 - Friends of the Park paid tribute to George Blume, Cole Rowland, Donna Schmidt, Carolyn Huser, and Peg Hein for their roles in making City Park a reality. In May 1991, Mayor Cole Rowland and the Lakeway City Council had called for an election to approve the purchase of the sixty-four-acre lakefront property for a city park. The proposal passed by only nineteen votes.

November 27 - The city council voted five to two to re-zone 1.04 acres on Lohman's Crossing from Planned Unit Development (PUD) to Government, Utility, and Industrial (GUI) to allow the Lakeway MUD to build a two-million-gallon storage tank. The city and the MUD, however, disagreed on the placing of the tank. The city wanted it moved at least 200 feet from the road for aesthetic reasons related to the planned Tuscan Village. MUD general manager Richard Eason argued that to do so would cost $750,000. When both Tuscan Village developer Haythem Dawlett and the city refused to pay this cost, the tank was constructed where MUD had originally planned. Janet Wright and the Lakeway Arts Committee promised to make the controversial tank an objet d'art.

December 5 - Bill Chandler and Glenda Foreman were honored as Volunteers of the Year at Lakeway's annual appreciation dinner. Chandler had served as Lakeway's treasurer for ten years. He had also served on the Heritage Commission, the Service League of Greater Lakeway, Friends of the Parks, the Fourth of July Committee, Homeowners Association, the Lakeway Civic Corporation, and the Newcomers Club. Foreman had been a city councilmember (2002–2007) and was also a member of the Greater Lakeway Residents Association, Seton Associates, Hudson Bend Auxiliary, Friends of the Parks, the Heritage Commission, and the Women's Club, where she served as both vice president and president.

December - Haythem Dawlett's planned Tuscan Village for seniors fifty-five and older began signing up buyers for its Founders Club. Applicants paid a $1,000 priority deposit, after which they could secure their selection. Dawlett's plan called for 280 residences, including villas, town houses, and condominiums ranging from 1,200 to 2,300 square feet, with prices beginning at $250,000. Also in the plans were walking trails, a clubhouse and fitness center, a spa, indoor and outdoor dining, an outside covered pool, retail shopping businesses, and the Lake Travis Community Library, for which Dawlett promised to donate the land.

December - CityCorp, which owned four golf courses in the Lakeway area, turned Yaupon and Live Oak into private courses that could also be accessed by members of the Hills Country Club, Flint Rock Falls Club, the World of Tennis, and guests of the Lakeway Resort and Conference Center.

December - The Lakeway Boulevard Sculpture Garden, featuring original bronze sculptures of children at play, was created in memory of Florence Newton and funded by her family and friends.

December - The controversy continued over the mismanagement of the Pedernales Electric Cooperative. After an eight-month investigation, Navigant Consulting issued a 391-page report that described secret bank accounts, spending irregularities, inflated executive salaries, conflicts of interest, shredding of documents, erased data from computers, manipulation of the elective process to its board, and the funneling of large sums of money through an outside law firm.

December - Lake Travis High School won the Texas 4A state championship for the second successive year. Quarterback Garrett Gilbert was selected from more than one million high school football players as Gatorade/ESPN's Football Player of the Year. The award reflected not only his record-breaking achievements on the gridiron, but also his leadership qualities and exemplary work in the classroom, where he earned a 3.78 GPA.

December 29 - Competing against 3,000 participants representing seventeen states, the Lake Travis High School cheerleaders won a national championship, just days after the football team won its state championship.

2009

January - The Lakeway Civic Corporation selected Frank Black as its Outstanding Citizen for 2008. Black had been president of the Homeowners Association and editor of the *Homeowners News*. In addition, he had been a board member and president of the LCC, and had been especially active in the campaign for the Lakeway Activity Center. Bill Schulte, Carol Black, and Bill Chandler received Meritorious Service Awards.

January - The Texas Education Agency 2007–08 Academic Excellence Indicator System Report classified the LTISD as a "Recognized" district, which was the second best of the four possible classifications. Lakeway Elementary, Lake Travis Middle School, and Lake Pointe Elementary received the top rating of "Exemplary." Lake Travis High School and Hudson Bend Middle School were graded as "Academically Acceptable." LTISD's new director of communications, Marco Alvarado, praised the district, attributing its success "to various strategies that were implemented during the 2007–08 school year."

January - Bee Cave re-zoned forty-four acres between Highway 71 and the newly completed Bee Cave Parkway for the new Bee Cave Backyard musical venue. The original Backyard, which opened in 1993 on Highway 71, was torn down to make room for the Shops of the Galleria mall.

February - Travis County Water Control and Improvement District No. 17 celebrated fifty years of service to the Lake Travis area. WCID 17 began in 1959 with meetings in the La Hacienda Café at the corner of RR 620 and Hudson Bend Road. Its first water treatment plant, constructed in 1960, was meant to serve 400 customers via a small six-inch water main. It had a single operator and one pickup truck. In 1961 it built a small cement-block office building at 3900 Eck Lane. In 1984 it constructed a new twenty-four-inch main that extended south along RR 620 all the way to the new high school. WCID 17 has since expanded its services in Hudson Bend and added Lakewind, Comanche Trail, and the 4,500-acre Steiner Ranch. As of 2009, it had more than 4,000 customers and could daily treat twelve million gallons of water in its three wastewater plants. Its service areas now extend all the way to properties near Highway 71. It has received the highest rating of "Superior Public Water System" from the Texas Commission on Environmental Quality.

February 11 - The Lakeway MUD's board of directors passed a non-binding policy asking its board members to speak with "one voice" when members disagreed. Opponents argued that this was a free speech violation.

February 17 - The Lakeway City Council voted unanimously to take possible legal action to annex the Lakeway MUD. The issues, as defined by the city, centered on MUD governance and its out-of-district customers who received water but not sewage service and were not allowed by state law to vote in MUD elections or have representation. To further complicate the annexation question, state law permitted Texas cities to annex MUDs that were completely within their city limits; however, the Lakeway MUD serviced additional areas outside of Lakeway. As a result, the city council asked state senator Kirk Watson for special legislation that would allow it to annex the MUD.

March - In a letter to the *Lake Travis View*, Lakeway MUD treasurer Alan Hitchcock accused the city of bullying tactics and wanting "to feed at MUD's financial trough." The MUD's directors then voted three to two to oppose the city's attempt at annexation and to form an ad hoc committee to spend up to $200,000 on a legal and public relations campaign to retain its independence.

March - At the instigation of Senator Kirk Watson, the City of Lakeway stated it would drop its plan to annex the Lakeway MUD but wanted the right to appoint two additional members to the MUD's board of directors, bringing the total number to seven. Mayor Steve Swan insisted that the city was not seeking to acquire land or assets but to ensure transparency and representation for out-of-district customers. Citing two surveys, the city also argued that customers would pay less if it actually annexed the MUD. MUD officials countered with their own survey, which concluded that a large majority of its customers wanted the MUD to remain independent.

April 8 - Mayor Steve Swan announced, "I am hopeful the addition of two board members will lead to greater transparency in the operations of the Lakeway MUD, and will facilitate cooperation between the City of Lakeway and the MUD." MUD board president Tom Rogers responded that he had no objections to two additional board members as long as they were elected rather than appointed.

April - The Lakeway Sing Alongs celebrated its tenth anniversary with a spring show, "A Decade of Sing Along." The group began in 1999, with eight men and women singing "the old songs" in Glenda Foreman's living room. There are currently more than eighty members putting on several shows a year.

April - The LTISD reported on the use of its $163 million bond issue monies. Specifically mentioned were improvements to various elementary schools, the construction of the new Serene Hills Elementary, and district-wide technology and utility upgrades. The report also listed monies spent on land acquisitions for anticipated "future growth and facilities." There was no specific mention of the Cavaliers' state-of-the-art weight room or indoor practice facility, which had opened in 2007 and 2008. On December 17, 2008, the *Austin American-Statesman* reported that the cost of these two facilities was $5.6 million.

April 14 - The Hill Country Galleria was hit with a foreclosure notice. If the developers did not find new sources for financing a $191 million construction loan by May 5, 2009, the Hill Country Galleria could be sold at auction. In the meantime, all its stores remain open for business.

April - Plans for a Crosswater Marina at the end of Hurst Creek Road resurfaced. Lakeway officials and residents had opposed the original permit the Lower Colorado River Authority granted to Harbor Ventures in 2006, which had also been suspended because of Harbor Ventures' code and environmental violations at its Highland Lakes Marina. Kemp Properties had now taken over the project.

April 23 - LTISD's trustees unanimously nominated Superintendent Rocky Kirk for Texas Association of School Boards' Superintendent of the Year.

April 27 - The ongoing battle between the city council and the Lakeway MUD escalated when the city sought a court restraining order to stop the MUD's Ad Hoc Committee from meeting until it posted public meeting times and brought all financial matters before its board. City Manager Steve Jones also cited the MUD's willingness to spend $200,000 to fight the city's annexation plan "without oversight or public knowledge."

April - The Texas Section of the American Water Works Association recognized Lakeway MUD for having the "Best-Tasting Drinking Water in Texas."

May 8 - Dave DeOme was elected mayor and Alan Tye, Joe Bain, and Dennis Wallace won city council seats.

May - Federal judge Craig Gargotta ruled that the Hill Country Galleria would be able to continue operating during its bankruptcy proceedings.

May - The City of Lakeway and the Lakeway Municipal District agreed to end their protracted battle over the city's attempted annexation of the MUD and its demand for more transparency in MUD governance. To implement this compromise, Senator Kirk Watson filed a bill calling for two additional elected positions on the MUD board and allowing out-of-district customers to vote in board elections, although not on district bond or tax proposals. During the three-month controversy, the city and the MUD spent more than $200,000 of taxpayers' money on legal and assorted other fees. Unfortunately, Senator Watson's bill, which passed the Senate, was allowed to die in the House with the end of the session.

May - Lakeway dedicated its "Gateway Sculpture" on RR 620 at the southern end of the city limits. Lakeway Arts Committee chair Janet Wright designed the sculpture.

May 14 - Groundbreaking ceremony for Tuscan Village, whose history goes back to the American Retirement Corporation's original 2003 plan for a retirement community. After ARC dropped the project in 2007, developer Haythem Dawlett stepped in.

June 1 - Selected as the new director of the Lake Travis Community Library was Morgan McMillian. Although she had worked with library patrons of all ages, one of her special strengths was children's literature.

June 16 - Following its recognition for being the Best-Tasting Drinking Water in Texas at Texas Water 2009, Lakeway MUD's drinking water was judged third best tasting in North America by the American Water Works Association.

June 30 - After temperatures reached record highs for sixteen out of seventeen days, a new high of 110 was set on June 30. To make matters worse, Central Texas was suffering severe drought conditions.

July 4 - The Fourth of July theme of "Flying High - The Red, White and Blue" featured a 1,000-foot flyover by four U.S. Air Force F-16 fighter jets, as well as 118 parade entries. Parade marshall and keynote speaker was U.S. Navy Captain Greg Wooldridge, retired.

August 11 - Because Lake Travis had dropped to its third lowest level in history, Travis County closed the last of the twelve public boat ramps on the lake. The drought, which had started in 2007 and was made worse by record low precipitation and high temperatures in 2009, resulted in stringent water restrictions on Lakeway residents.

August 16 - The city council unanimously voted down Crosswater Yacht Club's appeal to build a marina at Graveyard Point. Going back several years, Crosswater, formerly known as Harbor Ventures, had been involved in a series of controversial designs and resultant lawsuits over its planned marina at the end of Hurst Creek Road. When Crosswater ignored the council's decision and began construction on August 25, Lakeway code enforcement officials ordered a stop because Crosswater had no Lakeway Site Development Permit.

September 12 - The death of Lakeway's Monsignor Richard McCabe. The monsignor helped start the Lakeway Ecumenical Church and was the founder of Lakeway's Church of the Resurrection of the Lord, Emmaus. Never shy about voicing his opinions, he was a strong social activist, who stated his motto on his business card: "To comfort the disturbed and to disturb the comfortable."

September 14 - The Lakeway City Council unanimously accepted the findings of a legal investigation by a third party that the council had justifiably lost confidence in the ability of Police Chief Gordon Bowers to administer his department effectively. Cited were hiring and budgetary practices and a high turnover rate. Bowers claimed he was being attacked because the Lakeway Police Officers' Association endorsed specific candidates for mayor and the city council. On October 5, Bowers and the city council reached a severance agreement that included six months pay, with full employee benefits, and $8,154 for unused vacation time.

September 27 - Opening of Weed-Corley-Fish Funeral Homes & Cremation Services at 411 RR 620 South. Weed-Corley-Fish had operated in Austin for four generations, but it was Lakeway's first funeral home.

October 23–26 - After experiencing the hottest summer in more than 100 years and the worst drought in the Hill Country since the 1950s, several days of rain raised hopes that the drought might finally be ending. Lake Travis was at 632 feet on October 21. Five days later it had risen to 643 feet, but authorities warned that the drought would not be officially over until Lake Travis reached its full level of 681 feet.

November - LTISD announced that three high school seniors were National Merit Semifinalists and eleven were Commended Students.

November 3 - Voters turned down LTISD's request for a two-cent property tax increase that would not be subject to the state's recapture laws, popularly known as the Robin Hood assessment. LTISD also lost its appeal to the Texas commissioner of education to have the district's "Academically Acceptable" rating upgraded.

November 16 - The city council hired Todd Radford at its new police chief. Radford had twenty-one years of law enforcement experience and held a B.A. in criminal justice administration and an M.A. in strategic leadership. He had also served two years as a lieutenant with the Lakeway Police Department.

November 18 - The Texas Commission on Environmental Quality (TCEQ) turned down a request by Leander and Granite Shoals to lift a ban on effluent discharges into the Highland Lakes, a ban that has been in effect for more than twenty years. Lakeway, Austin, and several other regional governmental entities applauded TCEQ's decision.

December - In response to an anticipated decrease in its sales tax and building permit revenues, the city reduced its budget and froze several unfilled staff positions.

December - The Lakeway MUD's board of directors created a Community Advisory Committee, including members from both inside and outside the district. Former mayor Cole Rowland was named out-of-district co-chair and Keith Williams became the in-district co-chair. Other members were Tom Brewer (appointed by the city) and Nathan Miller and Chad Pearce (appointed by the MUD board).

December 4 - Before more than 200 fellow volunteers, Janet Wright was awarded Lakeway's Volunteer of the Year for 2009, while LaNell Edwards earned a Lifetime Achievement Award.

December 12 - Close to 400 guests attended Lakeway's annual Breakfast with Santa. The Lakeway Sing Alongs provided musical accompaniment for Santa, Mrs. Claus, and a couple of elves.

December 19 - Lake Travis High School won its third consecutive 4A state football title and its forty-sixth victory in a row when it defeated Longview 24-17.

2010

January 2 - Brigadier General James Vande Hey, who was one of Lakeway's most illustrious residents, died. He was a Pearl Harbor survivor who flew more than 200 combat missions, including leading the first long-range fighter sweep over Tokyo. He and his wife, Jean, had lived in Lakeway since 1971.

January 10 - The Lakeway Church opened its two-story, 14,000-square-foot, $4 million Student and Children's Center.

February - Lake Travis exceeded 670 feet, which was a 40-foot increase since October 2009, when Travis County was suffering its worst drought since the 1950s.

February 6 - Official opening of the two-mile Highlands Boulevard connecting Rough Hollow to Highway 71 at Bee Creek Road.

February 16 - The annual Lakeway Civic Corporation meeting and awards ceremony recognized Bill Dickson and Veryl Johnson (posthumously) as its Outstanding Citizens for 2009. Meritorious Service Awards went to Jim Bissett and Fred Roth. The LCC announced that since its beginning it has contributed more than $1,200,000 to worthy community projects.

March 31 - The U.S. Department of Housing and Urban Development insured a $166.9 million mortgage loan for the planned privately owned Lakeway Regional Medical Center. The project, which was being built on RR 620 just north of the Lake Travis High School, had been stalled for the past year. Its planned services will include cardiology/cardiothoracic, women's health, physical therapy/sports medicine, gastrointestinal, respiratory, and speech-language pathology. The eight-story, 230,000-square-foot facility is scheduled for completion in 2012. Also planned for the site is a parking garage, a daycare center, medical office buildings, a hotel, and retail businesses.

April 21 - The Lakeway MUD's newly formed Community Advisory Committee, while finding no fault with water quality, wastewater service, or day-to-day operations, nevertheless recommended that the MUD improve its financial transparency, conduct its meetings with civility and decorum, and allow "its individual Board members to speak publicly on subjects about which they differ from the majority."

May - Lake Travis High School's Elyse Cunningham, Lauren Gilbert, and Ian Steigmeyer were selected as National Merit Scholars.

May 12–17 - Organized by Lakeway archivist Mike Boston and a host of Lakeway volunteers and financed in part by the Lakeway Civic Corporation, the American Veterans Traveling Tribute and the Price of Freedom Tribute were put on display at Lake Travis High School. The exhibits include a replica of the National Vietnam Veterans Memorial Wall, as well as World War II, Korean War, and Vietnam War time lines, first responder tributes, and a remembrance of 9/11.

May 19 - The newly elected Lakeway MUD board selected Karl Ansbach as its president, replacing Tom Rogers, who decided not to run again. Rogers said he was particularly proud of the MUD's success in maintaining low water and wastewater rates during his twelve-year tenure. He also cited comparatively low taxes and the winning of several national awards. President Ansbach promised a board that would present a unified position once its votes had been taken on an issue. The board also voted in Jerry Hietpas as vice president and Kay Andrews as secretary and treasurer.

June - In a *Newsweek* rating of the top 1,600 high schools in the country, Lake Travis High School came in at 862. For sake of comparison, Austin's Liberal Arts and Science Academy rated 52; Westlake, 58; Westwood, 90; Anderson, 321; McNeil, 565; New Braunfels, 672; Cedar Park, 780; and Dripping Springs, 829. *Newsweek* based its ratings on "how hard school staffs work to challenge students," measured by taking the number of advanced tests given at a school and dividing it by the number of graduating seniors. In 2008, *Newsweek* had rated Lake Travis High School 503rd among the country's top 1,300 schools.

July - Citing the fact that the contract sale of the original Stewart Tract in 1944 contained a restrictive covenant barring any commercial businesses, Judge Lora Livingston of the 261st Civil District Court decided in favor of Graveyard Point residents in their ongoing legal battle to prevent Harbor Ventures, Inc. from building its marina.

July 4 - "Military Service - A Family Affair" was the theme of Lakeway's annual Fourth of July Celebration, featuring grand marshals Rosie Babin and her son, Corporal Alan "Doc" Babin, Jr., a combat medic who was badly wounded in Iraq. There were also patriotic speeches and music, a parade, and the usual elaborate fireworks. A few miles to the south, Willie Nelson hosted his own Fourth of July festival at the Backyard in its new location on Bee Cave Parkway.

September - The LTISD received an "Exemplary" rating from the Texas Education Agency for the past school year. It marked the first time since 1997 that it had received this highest of ratings.

September 7 - The Abercom International School opened its doors in Lakeway at 601 Ranch Road 620 South. It offered children two and a half years old and older an International Baccalaureate Primary Years Program, whose stated mission was "to serve families in search of an education system that combines a highly-portable, inquiry based global education philosophy with the acclaimed content and rigor of the English National curriculum."

September 10 - Lake Travis High School's forty-eight-game winning streak in football ended with a 14-10 loss to Aledo. The streak was the third longest in Texas high school history.

September 12 - More than 1,000 divers and shoreline volunteers picked up 1.14 tons of trash during the sixteenth annual Lake Travis Underwater Cleanup.

September 20 - The Lakeway MUD hired Earl Foster as its new general manager, replacing Richard Eason, who had served in that capacity since 1993. Foster had previously worked as MUD's wastewater supervisor between 2000 and 2004.

November 2 - Dallas's international real estate firm of Behringer Harvard announced that Houston-based Redstone Companies Hospitality will replace Dolce Hotels and Resorts as manager of the Lakeway Resort and Spa. Behringer Harvard had purchased the inn in 2005. New general manager Troy Matthews, who is the resort's tenth general manager in the past five years, promised to rebuild long-strained relationships with Lakeway residents.

November 15 - The Lakeway City Council announced at a public hearing that it planned to approve a development agreement with Crosswater Yacht Club to build its long-planned marina at Graveyard Point. Going back to the 1980s, Crosswater, formerly known as Harbor Ventures, had been involved in a series of controversial designs and resultant lawsuits over its planned marina at the end of Hurst Creek Road. When Crosswater began construction on August 25, 2009, Lakeway code enforcement officials ordered a stop because the work was being done without a City of Lakeway Site Development Permit. After Kemp Properties purchased the property, the city reconsidered its building permit. Because the proposed marina falls within Lakeway's ETJ but is not within its city limits, the city can only enforce building code standards. Crosswater plans 249 boat slips, 125 parking spaces, a fueling station, and a ship's store with limited hours of operation. Area residents argued that the initial sale of this property, which was then known as the Stewart Tract, prohibited commercial development and that one resident had recently won a court decision upholding this legal precedent and additional residents had pending legal suits against Crosswater.

Despite residents' opposition and the fact that in the past it had opposed such a plan, on December 20, 2010, the Lakeway City Council unanimously approved a development agreement with the Crosswater Yacht Club.

November 15 - The city council held the first of three scheduled public hearings on its plan to annex the Villas of the Hills; the residents, however, objected to being annexed. The Lakeway MUD, which services the area, also opposed annexation. Nevertheless, on December 20, 2010, the city council unanimously voted to annex the Villas of the Hills.

December - The Green Santa Program, which distributes nonperishable food items and new, unwrapped toys to needy area families, celebrated its eighteenth year. When the program began in 1993, it served seven families. By 2009, that number had risen to 168. Green Santa coordinates its efforts with local churches and with the Lakeway Police Department's Blue Santa and Travis County Sheriff's Brown Santa programs. The presents are distributed by the Ladies Auxiliary of the Hudson Bend Fire Department.

December - Lake Travis High School qualified three National Merit semifinalists, eight National Merit Commended Students, and two National Hispanic Recognition Scholars. The following February, Amanda Sawyer, Kyle Connell, and William Hoenig were named National Merit finalists.

December 2 - Lakeway selected Nancy Clayton and Larry Elliott as Co-Volunteers of the Year for 2010. Both had been active in the planning and coordination of several Fourth of July celebrations. Mayor Dave DeOme estimated that over the past year Lakeway's 185 volunteers had saved the city $225,000.

2011

February 15 - The Lakeway Civic Corporation selected former Lakeway mayor Charles Edwards as its Outstanding Citizen of the Year for 2010. Edwards had served on the Zoning and Planning Commission and the Economic Development Committee. He was a board member of Friends of the Parks and an enthusiastic supporter of building the Lakeway Swim Center. He was also a past chairman of Lakeway's Deer Committee and is currently co-chairman of the Lakeway Patriot Fund, which raises money for iBOT motorized wheelchairs for men and women injured in Iraq and Afghanistan. Glenda Foreman, Jim Hord, and the Lakeway Sing Alongs received Meritorious Service Awards.

March - Lakeway and seven other communities in Central Texas could lose 9-1-1 emergency support if cuts proposed by Capital Area Council of Governments are approved. CACOG is funded by the Commission on State Emergency Communications, which is facing cuts of at least 25 percent of its previous budget.

March - The Lakeway MUD's new W-3 Operations Office on Nautilus received a Gold Leadership in Energy and Environmental Design from the U.S. Green Building Council. Its efficient use of lighting, water, materials, and heating and cooling will result in an estimated 34 percent in energy savings.

March 3 - Haythem Dawlett and his Legend Communities officially deeded 1.7 acres from its Tuscan Village property on Lohman's Crossing to the Lake Travis Community Library District. The library hopes to begin its 10,862-square-foot building in the summer of 2011, with a planned opening approximately a year later. After its founding in 1985, the Lake Travis Community Library shared space with Lake Travis High School until 2006, when it leased space in the Lohman's Crossing Shopping Center. The Dawlett-donated property is valued at approximately $1 million. In addition, Friends of the Library have donated $80,000 towards the cost of the new building. Additional fund-raising is ongoing.

March - Because no candidates filed by the March 14 deadline to run against the incumbents, Mayor Dave DeOme and Councilmembers Joe Bain, Alan Tye, and Dennis Wallace, Lakeway's annual May election was canceled, thus saving the city approximately $5,000.

March - The Serene Hills Drive extension opened between Flint Rock Road and Highway 71.

March–May - Plans to put a Planet K store in the old Trading Post building on Highway 71 stirred up considerable controversy among Bee Cave residents and their governing officials. One of the oldest buildings in Bee Cave, the Johnson Store opened in the 1930s. More recently, it had been Jim Bob's Barbeque. Planet K is an adult novelty store, which, according to one of its advertisement, "sells imported cigarettes, pipes, vaporizers, incense, underground books, erotica, and more." Bee Cave initially argued that the Planet K owners did not have the necessary building permits. When Planet K then announced it was planning to paint a mural on the front of its building, Bee Cave took the owners to court, but lost its case in the 261st District Court. Additional litigation seems sure to follow.

May 16 - Residents from Brook Hollow requested that the Lakeway City Council not annex their properties at the end of Brook Hollow Road. Although only eighteen residents are involved, they objected to losing their "less-than-structured lifestyle" if they were to come under Lakeway's more rigid housing codes. Some of the affected families could trace their ownership to before there was a Lakeway.

May 17 - By a three to one margin, Lakeway voters approved the sale of up to $1.25 million in bonds to help fund the new Lake Travis Community Library.

APPENDIX

LAKEWAY ANNEXATION HISTORY
ParcelBase_Lakeway_City_Limits selection 4
ORIGINAL VILLAGE OF LAKEWAY
1977 - 1989
1990 - 1999
2000 - 2010
Village of The Hills
Every effort has been made to ensure the accuracy and completeness of the data. The City of Lakeway assumes no liability for any errors or omissions either assumed or implied.
October 19, 2010
1 inch = 1,100 feet
City of Lakeway
N
E
S
W

LAKEWAY'S VISION AND MISSION STATEMENTS, 2002

VISION STATEMENT

The City of Lakeway will continue to be a unique, prestigious, growth-managed community that will meet the needs of its citizens through the efforts of its local government and civic-minded volunteers, who will ensure a continued high quality of life by providing safe, secure neighborhoods, cost-effective, efficient government services and by managed growth.

MISSION STATEMENT

* We will use our resources in a cost-effective manner to provide quality streets, parks and greenbelts, recreational activities, and professional government services.

* We will maintain a secure environment for all citizens by carefully planning ingress and egress to the city and by providing a well-trained police force.

* We will continue to encourage, foster, develop, and utilize a strong volunteer corps in many facets of city government.

* We will ensure that all new development will complement our desired quality of life and will be an asset to the community.

* We will work with local merchants to ensure that business development is mutually beneficial to the business interests and the quality of life in Lakeway.

* We will work with our neighboring municipalities to ensure local area growth is compatible with our objectives.

* We will attempt, where possible, to maintain natural physical buffers on our borders, such as Lake Travis and the Texas Hill Country, to ensure the separate identity and character of Lakeway.

* We will strive to ensure that RR 620 and other commercial corridors are developed in a manner that reflects the uniqueness, special character, and quality of life in the City of Lakeway.

LAKEWAY GOVERNANCE: MAYORS, COMMISSIONERS, ALDERMEN, AND COUNCILMEMBERS

N. C. Herndon	Mayor	1974–1975
James T. Gribble	Commissioner Mayor	1974–1975 1975–1983
Robert J. Derby	Commissioner	1974–1975
O. I. Torkelson	Commissioner	1975–1981
Manson G. Stell	Commissioner	1975–1981
Leo C. Gravis	Commissioner	1981–1983
C. Ed Smith, Jr.	Commissioner Alderman Mayor	1981–1983 1983–1987 1987–1989

(Note: Commissioners became aldermen in 1983.)

C. Kenneth Shepherd	Mayor	1983–1987 1990–1991
J. Sloan Leonard	Alderman	1983–1988
Sam Huser	Alderman	1983–1986
James R. Hastings	Alderman	1983–1986

(Note: Aldermen became councilmembers in 1990.)

Kenneth W. Kennedy	Alderman Councilmember	1983–1990 1990–1992
Richard C. Knowles	Alderman	1986–1989
Nat. S. Kendall	Alderman Councilmember	1986–1990 1990–1992
Roger J. Schuler	Alderman Councilmember	1987–1990 1990–1991
William M. Evans	Alderman	1988–1990
Veronica Bennett	Alderwoman Councilmember	1989–1990 1990–1993
Richard McLaren	Mayor	1989–1990
Guy Brown, Jr.	Councilmember	1990–1992
Cole Rowland	Mayor	1991–1993
Jim Finneran	Councilmember	1991–1995
Burt Folsom	Councilmember	1992–1994
Elsa Hopkins	Councilmember	1992–1996
Ray Norris	Councilmember	1992–1994 1998–2002
Burton Barnes	Mayor	1993–1995
Jim Teddlie	Councilmember	1993–1995
Roy Hollowell	Councilmember	1994–1996
Jack O'Neill, Sr.	Mayor	1995–1999
LaNell Edwards	Councilmember	1995–1999
Jon Champeny	Councilmember	1995–1997
Bonnie Grubbe	Councilmember	1996–1998
Jack Wright	Council Member	1996–1998
Richard Schultz	Councilmember	1994–1998
John Riley	Councilmember	1997–2001
Ann Gribble	Councilmember	1998–2000
Charles Edwards	Mayor	1999–2003
Gerry Astorino	Councilmember Mayor	1998–2002 2003–2005
Hester Currens	Councilmember	1999–2001
Richard Friedrich	Councilmember	2000–2002
George Blume	Councilmember	2001–2005
Ed Viska	Councilmember	2001–2003
Karl Ansbach	Councilmember	2002–2006
Mike Doherty	Councilmember	2002–2006
Glenda Foreman	Councilmember	2002–2009
Steve Swan	Councilmember Mayor	2003–2005 2005–2009
Julianne DeBower	Councilmember	2005–2009
Bob Neighbors	Councilmember	2005–2009
Dave DeOme	Councilmember Mayor	2006–2009 2009–
Bill Rhue	Councilmember	2007–2009
Dee Ann Burns-Farrell	Councilmember	2008–
Bruce Harris	Councilmember	2008–
Joe Bain	Councilmember	2009–
Alan Tye	Councilmember	2009–
Dennis Wallace	Councilmember	2009–

LAKEWAY CIVIC CORPORATION'S OUTSTANDING CITIZEN OF THE YEAR AWARD WINNERS

1983	Al Saenger (first recipient)
1984	General "Cubby" Culbertson
1985	Roy Doran
1986	Manson Stell and Gene Vinyard (posthumously)
1987	Jim Gribble
1988	Newt Herndon
1989	Don Oliver
1990	Coleman Smith
1991	Ken Shepherd
1992	Byron Varner
1993	Henry D. Kolb
1994	Sam Huser
1995	Les Weigle
1996	Ken Kennedy
1997	Bob Graham and Jack & Myrtle Hamilton (posthumously)
1998	Richard Schultz
1999	Jim Vanderford
2000	Cole Rowland
2001	John Brodnax
2002	Ray Norris
2003	Jack B. O'Neill (posthumously)
2004	Don Iburg
2005	P. A. Penley
2006	Marsha Bissett
2007	Hester Currens
2008	Frank Black
2009	Bill Dickson and Veryl Johnson (posthumously)
2010	Charles Edwards

LAKEWAY CIVIC CORPORATION'S ANNUAL MERITORIOUS SERVICE AWARD WINNERS

1988	Jack Martin, Travis Porter, and Alf Powell
1989	Herb Dyer, John Ford, Ralph Keller, and Tex Sodke
1990	None
1991	Staff, *Homeowners News*, and Petrea "Tiny" Sodke
1992	Billy Baldwin, Bill Evans, and Howard Itten
1993	Paul Cook, Mike Kuhn, and Floyd Shelton
1994	Sam Hamilton and O. I. "Tork" Torkelson
1995	Ray Norris, Larry Folmer, and the Lakeway Service League
1996	Guy Brown and Jim Finneran (posthumously)
1997	Burton Barnes (posthumously), Veronica Bennett, and Nathaniel Kendall (posthumously)
1998	Leon "Huck" Dorsey, Cynthia Evans, Kenneth Jackson, and Jack McClaran
1999	George Blume, Glen Davis, Tony Leonard, and Jim Teddlie
2000	Frank Black and Marv & Peg Hein
2001	Pat Jacobson and A. P. "Block" Olbrich
2002	Bill Dickson, Ray Kilgore, DeWitt Smith, and Brian Hickey
2003	Sue Potter, Joanna Gardner Wentz, and Hilary W. Amacker
2004	Peggy Point and LaNell Edwards
2005	Sue Wright, Ramzi Deeb, and William V. Bergstrom
2006	Doris Besperka and Joann Anderson
2007	Fred & Judy Hazen and Fred Newton
2008	Jean O'Neill, Janet Wright, and Bob Finken
2009	Carol Black, Bill Chandler, and Bill Schulte
2010	Jim Bissett and Fred Roth
2011	Glenda Foreman, Jim Hord, and the Lakeway Sing Alongs

PHOTO CREDITS

p. vi	Photo courtesy of Wendy Severance
p. 3	Painting courtesy of Sandi Boston
p. 4	Painting courtesy of Sandi Boston
p. 5	Photo by Lew Carlson
p. 7	Photos courtesy of the Dolph Briscoe Center for American History, University of Texas at Austin
p. 8	Photo courtesy of Jessie Griffith
p. 9	Photo courtesy of the Dolph Briscoe Center for American History, University of Texas at Austin
p. 11	Photos by Lew Carlson
p. 15	Photo courtesy of Peg Hein
p. 16	Photo courtesy of Lakeway Heritage Center Collection
p. 18	Photos courtesy of Lakeway Heritage Center Collection
p. 19	Photos courtesy of Lakeway Heritage Center Collection
p. 20	Photo courtesy of Western Hill Country Historical Society Collection
p. 21	Photo courtesy of Western Hill Country Historical Society Collection
p. 24	Photos courtesy of Western Hill Country Historical Society Collection
p. 25	Photo courtesy of Western Hill Country Historical Society Collection
p. 26	Photo courtesy of Western Hill Country Historical Society Collection (top)
p. 26	Photo courtesy of Austin History Center (bottom)
p. 27	Photo by Lew Carlson
p. 28	Photos by Lew Carlson
p. 29	Photo courtesy of Lakeway Heritage Center Collection
p. 30	Photo courtesy of Lakeway Heritage Center Collection (top)
p. 30	Photo courtesy of Jack Wright (bottom)
p. 31	Photo courtesy of Fred Hazen
p. 32	Photo courtesy of Jeanne Hutto (top)
p. 32	Photo by Lew Carlson (bottom)
p. 33	Photo by Lew Carlson
p. 36	Photo by Lew Carlson
p. 37	Photo courtesy of Lakeway Heritage Center Collection
p. 38	Photo courtesy of Lakeway Heritage Center Collection
p. 39	Photo courtesy of Lakeway Heritage Center Collection
p. 40	Photo by Lew Carlson (top)
p. 40	Photo courtesy of Lakeway Heritage Center Collection (bottom left)
p. 40	Photo courtesy of Mary Stewart Hicks (bottom right)
p. 41	Photo courtesy of Peggy Maul Smithers
p. 42	Photo courtesy of Peggy Maul Smithers (top)
p. 42	Photo courtesy of Lakeway Heritage Center Collection (bottom)
p. 43	Photos courtesy of Mary Stewart Hicks
p. 44	Photos by Lew Carlson (top)
p. 44	Photo courtesy of Lakeway Heritage Center Collection (bottom)
p. 45	Photo courtesy of Lakeway Heritage Center Collection
p. 46	Photo courtesy of Lakeway Heritage Center Collection (top)
p. 46	Photos by Lew Carlson (bottom)
p. 47	Photo courtesy of Western Hill Country Historical Collection
p. 49	Photo courtesy of the Lower Colorado River Authority Corporate Archives
p. 51	Photo courtesy of Lakeway Heritage Center Collection

p. 53 Photos courtesy of Lakeway Heritage Center Collection
p. 55 Photo courtesy of the Lower Colorado River Authority Corporate Archives
p. 56 Photos courtesy of Lower Colorado River Authority Corporate Archives
p. 57 Photo courtesy of Lower Colorado River Authority Corporate Archives
p. 59 Photo courtesy of Lakeway Heritage Center Collection
p. 61 Photo courtesy of Lakeway Heritage Center Collection
p. 62 Photos courtesy of Lakeway Heritage Center Collection
p. 63 Photos courtesy of Lakeway Heritage Center Collection
p. 64 Photo courtesy of Lakeway Heritage Center Collection
p. 65 Photos courtesy of Lakeway Heritage Center Collection
p. 66 Photos courtesy of Lakeway Heritage Center Collection
p. 67 Photos courtesy of Lakeway Heritage Center Collection
p. 68 Photo courtesy of Lakeway Heritage Center Collection (top)
p. 68 Photo courtesy of Fred Hazen (bottom)
p. 69 Photo courtesy of Lakeway Heritage Center Collection
p. 70 Photos courtesy of Lakeway Heritage Center Collection
p. 72 Photo courtesy of Lakeway Heritage Center Collection
p. 75 Photo courtesy of Lakeway Heritage Center Collection
p. 76 Photo courtesy of Lakeway Heritage Center Collection
p. 78 Photo courtesy of Bill Hawkins Photography
p. 82 Photo courtesy of Lakeway's *Homeowners News,* October 1993
p. 83 Photo by Lew Carlson
p. 84 Photo courtesy of Lakeway Heritage Center Collection
p. 85 Painting courtesy of Johnnie Fields
p. 87 Photo courtesy of Lakeway Heritage Center Collection
p. 91 Photo courtesy of Bill Hawkins Photography
p. 93 Photo courtesy of Dallas Gorman
p. 94 Painting courtesy of Johnnie Fields
p. 95 Paintings courtesy of Johnnie Fields
p. 96 Painting courtesy of Janet Campbell
p. 97 Painting courtesy of Janet Campbell (top)
p. 97 Painting courtesy of Linda Wells (bottom)
p. 98 Painting courtesy of Linda Wells
p. 99 Painting courtesy of Linda Wells
p. 100 Painting courtesy of Judy Hazen (top)
p. 100 Painting courtesy of Cole Rowland (bottom)
p. 101 Photos courtesy of Dallas Gorman
p. 102 Photos courtesy of Bill Hawkins Photography
p. 103 Photo courtesy of Cal Rice
p. 104 Photo courtesy of Bill Hawkins Photography
p. 107 Photo by Lew Carlson
p. 108 Photo by Lew Carlson
p. 109 Photo courtesy of Mary Montgomery
p. 110 Photo courtesy of Bill Hawkins Photography
p. 111 Photo by Lew Carlson
p. 112 Photo courtesy of Lakeway's Friends of the Parks
p. 113 Photo courtesy of Cal Rice (top)
p. 113 Photo courtesy of Lakeway's Friends of the Parks (bottom)
p. 114 Photos courtesy of Bill Hawkins Photography (top)
p. 114 Map courtesy of Lakeway's Friends of the Parks and George Blume
p. 115 Logo created by Janet Wright for Lakeway's Friends of the Parks
p. 116 Photo by Lew Carlson (top left)
p. 116 Photo courtesy of Lakeway's Friends of the Parks (top right)
p. 116 Photo courtesy of Bill Hawkins Photography (bottom)
p. 117 Photo courtesy of Lakeway's Friends of the Parks
p. 118 Photos by Lew Carlson
p. 119 Photos courtesy of Lakeway's Friends of the Parks
p. 120 Map courtesy of Lakeway's Friends of the Parks and George Blume
p. 121 Photo by Lew Carlson
p. 122 Photo courtesy of Lakeway Heritage Center Collection
p. 123 Photo courtesy of Lakeway Heritage Center Collection
p. 126 Photo courtesy of Lakeway Heritage Center Collection
p. 127 Photo by Lew Carlson
p. 128 Photo courtesy of Linda Levine (top)
p. 128 Photos by Lew Carlson (bottom)
p. 129 Photo courtesy of Lakeway's Friends of the Parks
p. 130 Photos courtesy of Lakeway's Friends of the Parks
p. 131 Photo courtesy of Dallas Gorman (top)
p. 131 Map courtesy of Lakeway's Friends of the Parks and George Blume
p. 133 Photo courtesy of Bill Hawkins Photography
p. 136 Photo courtesy of Dallas Gorman
p. 137 Painting courtesy of Linda Wells
p. 138 Photos courtesy of Lakeway Heritage Center Collection
p. 139 Photos courtesy of Lakeway Heritage Center Collection
p. 140 Photo courtesy of Lakeway Heritage Center Collection
p. 141 Photos courtesy of Lakeway Heritage Center Collection
p. 142 Photo courtesy of Bill Hawkins Photography
p. 143 Photo courtesy of Dallas Gorman
p. 144 Photo courtesy of Lakeway Heritage Center Collection
p. 145 Photo courtesy of Lakeway Heritage Center Collection
p. 146 Photo courtesy of Lakeway Heritage Center Collection
p. 147 Photo by Lew Carlson
p. 148 Photo courtesy of Lakeway Heritage Center Collection
p. 149 Map courtesy of the Lakeway Parks and Recreation Commission
p. 150 Courtesy of the Lakeway Parks and Recreation Commission
p. 151 Photos by Lew Carlson
p. 152 Photo by Lew Carlson
p. 153 *Lake Travis View,* July 9, 1986
p. 155 Photos courtesy of Dallas Gorman
p. 156 Photo courtesy of Dallas Gorman (top)
p. 156 Photo courtesy of the Lakeway Parks and Recreation Commission (bottom)
p. 157 Photo courtesy of Bill Hawkins Photography
p. 159 Photo courtesy of Jack Wright
P. 160 Photo by Lew Carlson
p. 165 Photo courtesy of Bill Hawkins Photography
p. 207 Map courtesy of the City of Lakeway
Back flap of dust cover Photo by A. G. Thomas
Back of dust cover Photo courtesy of Bill Hawkins Photography
Front of dust cover Painting courtesy of Johnnie Fields